EVALUATING SEX OFFENDERS

To The Wiz, Blackbelt Gurl, Mom, Bro, and Indoor from
Skippy, Him, Dennis, Schmotz, and Hey Guy

EVALUATING SEX OFFENDERS

A Manual for Civil Commitments and Beyond

DENNIS M. DOREN

Sand Ridge Secure Treatment Center

SAGE Publications
International Educational and Professional Publisher
Thousand Oaks ▪ London ▪ New Delhi

For information:

Sage Publications, Inc.
2455 Teller Road
Thousand Oaks, California 91320
E-mail: order@sagepub.com

Sage Publications Ltd.
6 Bonhill Street
London EC2A 4PU
United Kingdom

Sage Publications India Pvt. Ltd.
M-32 Market
Greater Kailash I
New Delhi 110 048 India

Printed in the United States of America

Library of Congress Cataloging-in-Publication Data

Doren, Dennis M.
  Evaluating sex offenders: a manual for civil commitments and beyond /
Dennis M. Doren.
      p. cm.
Includes bibliographical references and index.
  ISBN 0-7619-2113-3 (c) -- ISBN 0-7619-2114-1 (p)
  1. Sex offenders--United States. 2. Insane--Commitment and
detention--United States. I. Title.
  KF9325 .D67 2002
  364.15′3--dc21

                                                    2002000199

            05 10 9 8 7 6 5 4 3

Acquiring Editors:	Nancy Hale and Margaret H. Seawell
Editorial Assistants:	Vonessa Vondera and Alicia Carter
Production Editor:	Claudia A. Hoffman
Copy Editor:	Kate Peterson
Indexer:	Molly Hall
Cover Designer:	Janet Foulger

Contents

Introduction

Risk. We learn from an early age that it is an integral part of life, although attitudes toward it vary widely. Many people avoid or insure against any risk they can, focusing on its potential relationship to tragedy. Others seek it out, relishing in its sweet precariousness.

No matter what approach you take, life does not let us avoid all risk, not even that which we abhor and fear most. Instead, we try to manage and reduce risk. We reinforce riverbanks to avoid flooding into our homes. We vaccinate our babies against diseases that kill and maim. We buy insurance against financial ruin. These efforts do not control all of the risk, however. They simply lower its likelihood.

One view of why governments exist is for the purpose of diminishing life risks in people's everyday lives. Military forces are maintained for safety from external attack. Traffic lights are installed to lower commuter danger. Consumer laws are passed to limit the effects of unscrupulous entrepreneurs. Official currency is designed with sophistication to minimize the risk of our being duped by counterfeiters.

In each case, the government's hand reaches out ostensibly to protect people while simultaneously causing everyone's life to be that much more controlled. Traffic lights interrupt our ability just to continue traveling as we have desire. Consumer laws mean greater degrees of bureaucracy for even the most ethical in business. Although it may be reasonable to say that few of us really like being controlled by governmental imposition, we also understand that this is the price we pay for lowering the overall risk we face. At times, this seems worth it to us. Presumably, at times, this trade-off seems quite out of balance.

This view of government suggests there is often some degree of struggle between the process of protecting people from unwanted risk and unreasonably taking away those same people's ability to live their lives (i.e., infringing on individual rights). Such appears to be the basis underlying the controversy concerning the sex offender civil commitment laws in the United States.

Virtually no one disputes that these statutes, typically described under the rubric "sexual predator" laws, have been implemented for the protection of potential victims. Likewise, there does not seem to be any real dispute that some degree of risk for sexual victimization to the general populace exists from a subset of the sex offender population. The controversy seems to stem from varying degrees of concern that these laws represent a significant imbalance between (1) how these laws protect against that general public risk and (2) individuals' rights to live their lives without improper government interference and control. The typical concern is that individual rights are being too sacrificed for the protection against the risk.

As will be described in Chapter 1, one of the mandates of all current sex offender civil commitment laws is that, for someone to be committed, prosecutors need to present evidence concerning the mental condition of individuals and the concomitant risk for enacting certain criminal sexual behaviors in the future. Such evidence virtually always can only be presented to a court through expert witnesses, mental health clinicians with certain training background. These laws cannot effectively be implemented without the cooperation of some mental health professionals.

If you, as a potential expert examiner, have concerns about the appropriateness of these laws, it may be that you will choose not to participate in the implementation of them. This book will not take issue with that ethical stance. In fact, to be clear, I very much respect the process of professionals limiting their practice to areas that do not compromise their values and ethics. Nothing in this book will state differently.

Among people who also feel concerns about the appropriateness of these laws, however, there is a second perspective taken on proper and ethical professional conduct. From this viewpoint, the acknowledgment is made that prosecutors will find people to do the necessary work, such that a personal avoidance of participating simply means that the commitment process will proceed around you and without you, but proceed rather unimpeded nevertheless. With that acknowledgment comes a different ethical responsibility: It may be better to participate in the commitment process to ensure that only the most clear cases meeting criteria are committed instead of the broader group that would likely be committed without your helping to ensure that proper evaluation procedures are used. In other words, this stance assumes that the process of prosecutors using only evaluators in favor of these laws could lead either to an inflated frequency of assessment findings that subjects meet commitment criteria or to the wrong cases being identified due to poor evaluator training.

With this view in mind, participation in the commitment process is felt ethical even for people who otherwise do not think these laws represent the proper balance between societal protection and individuals' rights. Despite concerns about the laws themselves, this stance suggests that these people should work to ensure their evaluation procedures and court presentation involve the smallest degree of error possible, based on the best science has to offer.

Of course, there are likely many people who do not have significant ethical concerns about the current set of sex offender civil commitment laws. For them, the process of participating in the laws' implementation does not represent an ethical quandary.

This book is intended to offer detailed descriptions to mental health professionals regarding the most current sex offender civil commitment evaluation procedures. The assumption is made, regardless of evaluators' personal feelings regarding the laws, that if they are doing this type of work, the most accurate and up-to-date information will be useful. In keeping with this purpose, this book contains summaries of various research findings that support the recommended assessment methodology.

The chapters herein are generally in the same order as an evaluator considers issues during an examination. Initially, in Chapter 1, there is a description of the evaluation issues within the current set of sex offender civil commitment laws. This is to facilitate examiners' understanding of the task they face and the issues that must be addressed in any evaluation useful to the courts. In effect, this chapter describes the context, purpose, and issues to be addressed within sex offender civil commitment evaluations, what is more typically described as the referral questions.

Chapter 2 presents the essential procedures for the assessment. Issues of what information is necessary, how to obtain it, how to organize it, the role of the interview, and so on are addressed. This chapter is meant as a practical guide for getting started in the assessment.

Chapters 3 and 4 take a very detailed look at relevant diagnostic issues. Although most clinicians who come into the civil commitment world feel familiar with standard psychiatric diagnoses, there are many diagnostic pitfalls into which civil commitment evaluators have tumbled on the witness stand. The information in these chapters should help ensure that the reader does not share that plight.

The next three chapters (5, 6, and 7) delineate different aspects of the risk assessment portion of the evaluations. These sections involve the greatest reliance among the chapters in this book on research results. Significant strides in empirical findings have pushed risk assessments in recent years beyond the days of unaided clinical judgment, with the current relevant research being described and summarized herein. These chapters are designed to serve as a detailed explication of current risk assessment procedures. Because the risk assessment is often highly contested by individuals undergoing sex offender civil commitments, it is expected that these chapters will also serve as a resource for evaluators looking to find research direction and references pertaining to some aspect of such procedures.

How to communicate the assessment findings is the topic of Chapter 8. The contents of the evaluation report and issues related to court testimony are described here. This section ends the chapters logically ordered for evaluators.

Finally, the last chapter delves into a topic that some people may have thought should have come first: ethical issues. Obviously, this introduction started with a discussion of one such issue, the very fundamental one of whether or not one should participate in conducting sex offender civil commitment evaluations. A wide variety of other ethical issues arise once that question is answered (for whatever reason) in the affirmative. The reason this chapter was left to the end was not at all reflective of a paucity of ethical issues to discuss, or because the delineation of ethical issues was in any way considered of minor importance. Instead, I believed that the most fruitful discussion of ethical issues would occur only after issues of diagnoses, methodological concerns, and evaluation reporting were completely explicated. Ethics may best be delineated in a context. By saving this chapter to the end of the book, each ethical concern is portrayed within a very clearly defined context. The hoped-for result is that the reader can see most unmistakably what the issues are and different conceptualizations for how those issues might be resolved.

Overall, this book is a composite of information from a variety of sources. Research results from around the world play an important part in what is presented, but not everything known and relevant comes from research. My experiences in performing evaluations; in supervising others' work; in serving as a consultant; in acting as a peer reviewer; in the role of organizer and conduit for an interstate consultation network; in receiving training; and in doing training for evaluators, attorneys, judges, victim assistants, and general mental health clinicians all serve as a basis for the information contained in this book.

The number of people to whom I could, and possibly should, express appreciation is too great to write here. I would like to make special mention of the people who assisted me the most. Dr. Anna Salter, the person who first developed the idea for this book, has contributed greatly to the information herein. She reviewed the contents of this book with scores of substantive suggestions, ultimately resulting in a manual that is far more informative, user friendly, and, frankly, more readable. Her extensive and generous assistance with the development of this book is matched only by how much she has taught me ove the years about working with sex offenders. She has been a great editor, consultant, teacher, and friend.

A special team of colleagues also should be mentioned: Drs. Patricia Coffey, Carole DeMarco, Sheila Fields, James Harasymiw, Craig Monroe, Caton Roberts, Susan Sachsenmaier, and Lawrence Stava. Working with them has been instructive, insightful, frustrating, rewarding, invigorating, amusing, and, possibly most important for this book, a major reason why I had to keep working hard to remain knowledgeable about current research results. Their failure to accept the things I said at face value, without empirical demonstration, served us all well.

Most of all, I wish to thank Pattie, my wife, for understanding my need to hide away to write this book, for being supportive during my times of anxiety, and for giving me the emotional world in which we both knew it would all turn out fine. It is having someone like her in one's life that makes working hard both worthwhile and still second on one's life priority list.

CHAPTER 1

Relevant Components of Sex Offender Civil Commitment Laws

The Evaluation "Referral Questions"

Laws are like sausages. It's better not to see them being made.

— Otto von Bismarck

nless you do not care where you end up, you need to have some idea about where you want to go and how to get there before you start traveling. Likewise, to accomplish a task, one needs to know what constitutes the task's necessary components. Such is obviously true in conducting sex offender civil commitment assessments.

This chapter describes aspects of sex offender civil commitment laws from the 15 states where such laws existed at the time this book was written. The purpose for this chapter is to present two items to evaluators: (a) the statutory issues that examiners need to address and (b) some of the most common debates that exist concerning the interpretation of statutory terms. All 15 current statutes are reviewed, though the selection of concepts and terms is restricted to those of direct relevance to evaluators. The pertinent issues included here are

1. the different types of assessments,

2. who is allowed to do these evaluations,

3. the criteria for commitment (in detail), and

4. the issue of lesser restrictive alternatives.

Although many other aspects of sex offender civil commitment laws may be of high significance to attorneys, judges, treatment personnel, and the like (such as legal procedures, time frames, and definitions of certain terms), those other components were considered beyond the scope of this book.

In the summaries below, descriptive statements are made that were accurate at the time this book was written, but may no longer be true by the time it is being read. Hence, the summations and examples offered below should likely be read as illustrative rather than as giving an evaluator the complete knowledge necessary to proceed in an assessment. Implemented sex offender civil commitment laws have already been substantively changed in the short time they have existed by the time this book was written. Assuming that the content of these laws will remain static is probably faulty.

The Relevant Statutes

There are 15 states with actively implemented sex offender civil commitment laws, with a 16th such law on the books but not yet implemented (Virginia's). For reference, these statutes are listed below. The names from each statute are enumerated as well to show the degree of variability and overlap in nomenclature.

1. Arizona: Sexually Violent Persons, 37 Arizona Revised Statutes, Section 36-3701-16

2. California: Sexually Violent Predators, California Welfare and Justice Code, Article 4, Section 6600 et seq.

3. Florida: Jimmy Ryce Involuntary Civil Commitment for Sexually Violent Predators' Treatment and Care Act, Chapter 394, Part V

4. Illinois: Sexually Violent Persons Commitment Act, 725 I.L.C.S. Section 207/1 et seq.; Sexually Dangerous Persons Act, 725 I.L.C.S. Section 205/0.01 et seq.

5. Iowa: Commitment of Sexually Violent Predators, Iowa Code Section 229A.1-4

6. Kansas: Commitment of Sexually Violent Predators, Kansas Statutes Annotated 59-29(a); SB 671, 1998; HB 2102, 1999

7. Massachusetts: An Act Improving the Sex Offender Registry and Establishing Civil Commitment and Community Parole Supervision for Life for Sex Offenders [Note: the phrase "Sexually Violent Predator" is used in this statute], M.G.L. 123A Section 12

8. Minnesota: Procedures for Commitment of Persons With Sexual Psychopathic Personalities and Sexually Dangerous Persons, Minnesota Statute Ann. Section 253B.02, subd. 18c & 253B.185; Procedures for Persons Mentally Ill and Dangerous to the Public, Minnesota Statutes Annotated Section 253B.18

9. Missouri: Sexually Violent Predators, Civil Commitment, Missouri Revised Statutes Section 632.480 et seq.

10. New Jersey: Sexually Violent Predator Act, New Jersey Statute Section 30: 4-27.24-41

11. North Dakota: Commitment of Sexually Dangerous Individuals, North Dakota Century Code Section 25-03.3-01-21

12. South Carolina: Sexually Violent Predator Act, South Carolina Code Annotated Section 44-48-10

13. Texas: Civil Commitment of Sexually Violent Predators, Texas Health and Safety Code Section 841.001

14. Virginia: Civil Commitment of Sexually Violent Predators, Virginia Code Annotated Section 37.1-70.9

15. Washington: Sexually Violent Predators, Revised Code of Washington Section 71.09.020

16. Wisconsin: Sexually Violent Persons, Wisconsin Statutes Section 980.01 et seq.

Given that Virginia's law had yet to be enacted and, like a one-time passed but later repealed law in Oklahoma, may never be implemented, I have chosen not to include Virginia's law in further discussions in this chapter. In that way, the discussion about how these laws are actually being implemented remains clear rather than speculative.

The reader may note that many states with "sexual predator" laws are not listed above. This is because that term is used in some states to refer to a community notification law for sex offenders (e.g., Colorado: Sexually Violent Predator, Colorado Revised Statutes [C.R.S.] 18-3-414.5 [1999], and Community Notification Concerning Sexually Violent Predators, C.R.S. 16-13-901 [1999]; Ohio: Sexual Predators, Ohio Revised Code Annotated, Section 2950.09 [1999]) or to a sex offender registration law (e.g., Indiana: Determination That a Person Is a Sexually Violent Predator, Burns Indiana Code Annotated Section 35-38-1-7.5 [Supp. 1999]) and not to a civil commitment law. That is one reason, among three, I will not use the term "sexual predator law" in this book to describe sex offender civil commitment statutes. The other two reasons are that (1) the phrase is not part of the legal language of some of the civil commitment laws (see enumeration above), and (2) the phrase carries a pejorative meaning that seems unnecessary within scientific and professional discourse.

Different Types of Assessments

This section describes the statutory framework for the situations under which clinicians can be considered qualified to conduct sex offender civil commitment evaluations. Statutory portions pertaining to when clinicians may be called upon, and under what circumstances, are delineated here, by concentrating on the stages at which civil commitment evaluations are conducted.

There are essentially two stages during which assessments are mandated by sex offender civil commitment laws. The first involves the precommitment process of determining who should and should not be committed. The second stage pertains to the reassessments of people who have already been committed, to see if their commitment status should be altered, either by being moved to a lesser restrictive environment (e.g., into the community under supervision) or by being fully discharged from their commitment. How each state goes about the selection procedures, however, differs significantly.

Precommitment

First, there is the issue of the various stages of assessment-enacted precommitment. There are essentially two potential precommitment stages, with each involving more than one evaluator.

Prereferral Assessments

Possible referral agencies in all but one state (i.e., Massachusetts) have interpreted their law as requiring some type of prereferral evaluation. Massachusetts has enacted its law without any prescreening (i.e., evaluation) of cases referred to prosecutors. The Department of Corrections in that state simply notifies relevant prosecutors of impending prison releases of all potentially eligible sex offenders (Tim App, personal communication, September 2000). The selection process in that state for which cases are pursued for commitment and which are not is left up to whatever procedures the prosecutors choose to employ.

Beyond that one state, some type of screening of possible referrals invariably occurs. How that is done differs considerably. About half of the statutes are explicit in defining the referral process (i.e., Florida, Iowa, Kansas, Missouri, New Jersey, South Carolina, and Texas). These laws typically describe and cause the development and the implementation of a "multidisciplinary team" that has the statutory responsibility for deciding which cases are to be referred to a prosecutor. This procedure of using a multidisciplinary team is not invariably the case. New Jersey's referral process, for instance, ultimately rests on the opinions of individual psychiatrists.

In contrast, the other half of the laws are silent about how a decision is to be made to refer a case to a prosecutor (i.e., Arizona, California, Illinois, Minnesota, North Dakota, Washington, and Wisconsin). Laws in this category typically describe which state agency has the responsibility for making referrals, but not the mechanics of how the decision making is to be performed (e.g., Wisconsin). Referral procedures under those circumstances are completely designed by the responsible agency. Finally, there is a variant where the state agency is not told in what manner the decision is to made, but is statutorily mandated to include considerations of certain characteristics (e.g., the use of certain assessment instrumentation), such as in California.

California's law seems unique in another way. Within that law, a second independent set of evaluations is mandated before any case can be referred to a prosecutor. This subsequent evaluation process necessarily involves at least two separate and independent evaluators who must agree on recommending commitment. If agreement between the evaluators is lacking in this regard, another two evaluators become employed in the same task.

Texas' law also stands out as unique concerning the prereferral evaluation process. Besides the initial use of a multidisciplinary team, the statute also mandates that an individual evaluator must assess the subject (separately), and must do so with an interview and with an examination of specified characteristics.

Interesting to note is that under all circumstances, the ultimate decision to pursue commitment is made by prosecutors, not by evaluators or any agency with referral responsibility. This is true even in California, where two different departments and at least three different evaluators have been involved, all with the same recommendation, prior to the referral. It may vary from jurisdiction to jurisdiction whether or not prosecutors are limited in what cases they can pursue by the requirement of a formal referral before a petition can be filed, but the situation is clear that prosecutors are not mandated by statute to file commitment petitions in all referred cases.

This latter fact has led to a second set of pre-probable cause evaluations being conducted in some states, beyond the prereferral procedures. (A probable cause hearing, within the civil commitment realm, is a legal process during which a judge determines whether or not there is sufficient reason to detain an individual for further evaluation concerning the possible commitment. Such a hearing is quite usual in sex offender civil commitment procedures, apparently being required in all but Texas.) In some states (e.g., Iowa, Washington), prosecutors quite regularly hire evaluators to assess referred cases, as a sort of second opinion about the likelihood a referred case really meets commitment criteria. Under these circumstances, the attorneys hold their decisions about filing commitment petitions in abeyance until they receive the results from those second assessments. In other states (e.g., Florida, Wisconsin), this process of obtaining a pre-petition "second opinion" occurs only rarely, such as when a prosecutor has doubts about the appropriateness of a specific referral or the attorney is looking for a "better witness." "Second opinion" procedures at this stage of the commitment process have never been practiced in some states (e.g., North Dakota).

On a rare basis, defense attorneys hire evaluators specifically to perform complete assessments of petition respondents before a probable cause hearing (e.g., as has occurred in Iowa). This apparently reflects an atypical defense strategy, in terms of its rarity, but simultaneously indicates another occasion when evaluators can be called on to perform a civil commitment assessment.

Post-Probable Cause, Precommitment Assessments

Once probable cause is found, the legal procedures involving evaluators become no more uniform across the states. The greatest degree of agreement is that in all states the respondent is entitled to hire an evaluator of his[1] choice, in addition to any other evaluator working on the case. The manner by which the courts and the prosecutors are involved with the selection of evaluators varies greatly.

The courts sometimes actively appoint their own evaluators, such as is true in Arizona and Minnesota. In the former state, for instance, the courts effectively maintain a list of people the courts consider qualified from which an evaluator is selected per case. This type of evaluator is clearly the court's expert. A variant on this is where the courts need to designate who will serve as an evaluator of the respondent (i.e., the subject of the petition), but the assigned evaluator is clearly under the employ of the office of the prosecuting attorney. This situation exists in Iowa, for instance, where the court designates an evaluator who is "deemed to be professionally qualified to conduct such an examination" upon the motion of the assistant attorney general. The same or similar statutory language exists in Kansas, Massachusetts, and South Carolina.

In other states, the courts do not directly participate in the selection of evaluators, but the examiners are also not defense counsel or prosecutor hired. These evaluators might best be labeled "statutorily appointed." This occurs in states where evaluators are assigned through a statutory mandate to an employing designated agency. This is the most common statutory structure concerning evaluators beyond the defense's right to hire its own. The specific examples are the following:

1. Department of Children and Family Services in Florida

2. Department of Human Services in Illinois

3. Department of Mental Health in Missouri

4. Department of Human Services in New Jersey

5. Department of Human Services in North Dakota

6. Department of Social and Health Services in Washington

7. Department of Health and Family Services in Wisconsin

California may also be viewed as included in this category, though that state really has no statutorily mandated evaluators (or evaluations) at this stage separate from the prereferral evaluation. The same examiners typically serve in both capacities without performing another assessment.

The reader may note that no current statute specifically allows *only* the clearly adversarial process of each side hiring its own evaluator, with the concomitant "battle of the experts" during the commitment hearing. This does not mean that such an adversarial process does not exist, as it clearly does everywhere. In Arizona, for instance, where the courts appoint their own experts, the statute also allows for the defense to hire its own and, if it does, for the prosecution to hire its own. In Washington, where prosecutors have historically shown the greatest degree of denying prosecution for referred cases, and the concomitant filing of petitions only where they believe they have a strongly supportive expert witness, defense attorneys have countered with very strong stands of their own, using a "battle of the experts" approach on numerous occasions.

There is one other varying statutory characteristic concerning the precommitment evaluation stage of interest here. This pertains to the number of evaluators required to be assessing the same subject. In California and Massachusetts, the law is very clear in mandating that at least two evaluators be involved. North Dakota's law has been interpreted and implemented in the same way. Some states effectively employ two independent evaluators though they are not mandated by statute to do so. In these cases, there is one evaluator within the Department of Corrections (i.e., DOC; the referring agency) and one from the mental health/social service department as described above. The first evaluator is involved, however, only because the DOC has chosen to address its referral responsibility through that procedure (e.g., Wisconsin). In contrast, some laws require only one evaluator (beyond a multidisciplinary team), and only one is typically involved beyond whatever the attorneys may do on their own (e.g., Florida, South Carolina).

Postcommitment

All of the statutes mandate that there be at least annual assessments concerning whether or not the person should remain committed. These are often called periodic reexaminations. In most cases, the department in custody of the individual has the responsibility to generate periodic reexamination reports (i.e., Arizona, California, Illinois, Massachusetts, Missouri, New Jersey, North Dakota, Washington, and Wisconsin). The other laws are less specific as to who will conduct these assessments, usually using the more generic phrase of a "qualified professional person" in describing who will do this task (e.g., Florida, Kansas, South Carolina). How one becomes so designated is not specified in these laws.

Who Is Allowed to Do These Evaluations

Precommitment

There are basically three ways to be considered qualified to perform and testify about sex offender civil commitment evaluations. The first is to be employed by one of the above enumerated state agencies or a referring state agency (such as a DOC) and to meet its rules for qualification (e.g., be a licensed psychologist or psychiatrist with a background in assessing sex offenders). Illinois, North Dakota, and Wisconsin are examples of such jurisdictions. When compared across the states, this is clearly one of the two largest categories of who is allowed to be a civil commitment evaluator.

The second category consists of the people who are under contract with the relevant state agency to perform these assessments but are specifically not employees of any state agency. California's law is the most explicit in this regard, stating that the evaluators cannot be state employees. (This is in stark contrast to the first category above where the evaluators must be state employees.) Florida functions in the same way.

The remaining evaluators consist of the people who are privately hired by defense and/or prosecuting attorneys. In theory, these can be anyone the attorneys believe will be viewed as sufficiently qualified by the courts. In practice, these are typically psychologists and psychiatrists with a background working with sex offenders or at least violent criminals of varied types. Relative to the number of states and petitions involving sex offender civil commitments, there seem to be a surprisingly small number of evaluators falling into this category. A common finding is that the same people do their civil commitment work in multiple states. There are experts of other types and from other fields who are occasionally brought to testify during commitment hearings about statistical matters, research study results, or ethical standards, but these people do not conduct direct assessments of the commitment subjects.

Postcommitment

Conducting postcommitment reexaminations means you need to be one of two types of people, except in Texas. One common scenario is that you work for the facility that has custody of the committed person, have been determined by that facility as qualified to conduct these examinations, and have been so designated. About half of all periodic reexaminations are performed by such people (e.g., California, Illinois, North Dakota, Washington). The other possibility is that you are hired privately by one of the attorneys involved in the case. Basic to this appointment is that the courts accept you as a "qualified professional," an undefined term in many statutes (e.g., Florida, Iowa, Kansas, South Carolina).

Texas has a unique postcommitment reexamination procedure, probably reflective of its distinctive form of civil commitment. Unlike other states, a sex offender civil commitment in Texas is necessarily of an outpatient nature. There is no inpatient facility to which committed individuals go. Periodic reports to be submitted to the committing courts are still required. The writers of these reports are specifically case managers and the people who are conducting the subjects' mandated treatment, not evaluators who are independent from the management or treatment of the committed people. Given that the commitment discharge criteria still involve the assessment of a meaningful change in the person's "behavioral abnormality," however, the content of the periodic reexaminations may not differ much from those in other states.

The Overall Criteria for Commitment

The defining characteristics of the recent generation of sex offender civil commitment laws are the commitment criteria. Across the country, there are essentially four criteria (except in North Dakota where there are only three) with variations on common themes. These criteria are described below in some detail, as they serve as the context for what most of the rest of this book addresses. In essence, the commitment criteria serve as the "referral questions" to be addressed in the evaluations.

Again, the caveat is offered that evaluators should ensure they have the most recent copy of the law under which they are working rather than relying on something printed below, which may have become outdated.

The criteria are divided below into two types: (1) the person's legal status, of concern specifically to prosecutors, and (2) issues more directly for the evaluators. Issues within each category are explicated in the idea that evaluators will well comprehend the parameters under which they are working

The Legal Status Criteria

In virtually all states, two of the four commitment criteria pertain to aspects of the legal status of the subject. These criteria can be, and quite typically are, addressed by prosecutors without the use of clinicians of any type, evaluators or otherwise. North Dakota's law is distinctly different from the others in regards to criteria of this type and, hence, is not included in the summary statements in this section.

Sexual "Conviction"

The first of the criteria is that the person has been involved in one of a few specified legal procedures following a charge for a relevant sexual offense (a concept described separately below). Without a formal legal charge for a relevant sexual offense, followed by one of the four outcomes, there can be no civil commitment (in all but North Dakota). Those possible four outcomes are described below:

1. In all states, the process of being convicted for a relevant sexual offense qualifies as meeting this criterion. (California represents the only variant compared with the other states in this regard, as the subject's conviction history must have involved at least two victims, something that could have been true simultaneously or at separate times in his history.)

2. With rare exception (i.e., Arizona, Massachusetts), someone who was adjudicated not guilty by reason of insanity following a charge for a relevant sex offense also meets this commitment criterion.

3. About half of the states explicitly include people adjudicated delinquent following such a charge as well, meaning that about half of the states allow for the sex offender civil commitment of juveniles (e.g., Massachusetts, New Jersey, Wisconsin).

4. Finally, a fourth type of individual is sometimes specified as meeting this criterion. This is the person who was charged with a relevant sexual offense but has been found incompetent to stand trial for that charge, and the court (following a motion from a prosecutor) decides through a trial-like procedure that the person did commit the sexual act underlying the legal charge (e.g., Kansas, Washington).

North Dakota's law simply requires the demonstration that the person has "engaged in sexually predatory conduct" some time in his history. That statute does not specify the type of evidence necessary to make this proof.

Scheduled Release

In most states, a person is potentially eligible for commitment only if he is in the process of being released from some type of incarcerated environment. Incarcerated environments include prisons, forensic hospitals, and juvenile detention/treatment facilities, depending on the commitment criteria for eligibility as described in the section above. Statutory exceptions to the necessity for a scheduled release from incarceration exist in two ways. In Minnesota, North Dakota, and Wisconsin, the laws apparently allow the commitment of someone who may never have been incarcerated based on a sexual offense, though I am aware of only North Dakota actually enacting a commitment procedure against someone who was in such a situation. The other exception exists in Iowa and Washington, as described below in the section Recent Overt Act.

One potentially thorny issue for evaluators is that the most recent incarceration (no matter where it is) may or may not need to be related to a relevant sexual offense. Evaluators can find themselves assessing people with historical sexual convictions, who are about to be released from prison this time for clearly nonsexual criminality (e.g., Florida, Iowa), and whose last recorded sexual offense was many years before their more recent nonsexual crime. This situation can make the use of certain risk assessment instrumentation difficult (see Chapter 5). Most statutes, however, require that the incarceration soon to end be directly related to the relevant sexual offense (the latter serving as the cause for incarceration, or its proximate cause with only a probation/supervised release revocation in between).

The timing of a commitment petition apparently must occur before the person is actually released from his incarceration. Most statutes specify a time period before the scheduled release when this must happen (e.g., within 90 days of anticipated release, in Wisconsin).

The point made here about the above two commitment criteria (concerning the required "conviction" and scheduled release from incarceration) is that evaluators do not typically need to address them. Although there can be administrative reasons to use examiners during a prereferral evaluation process to review the application of these criteria to specific cases, this seems solely of use during that stage. Prosecutors typically can address evidentiary needs related to these commitment criteria with documentation and without evaluators during probable cause and final commitment hearings.

Recent Overt Act

As mentioned above, two statutes use one additional concept in defining situations in which a person becomes eligible for commitment based on his legal status. In Iowa and Washington, the statutory phrase "recent overt act" seems to cover situations involving commitment eligibility for which the person

1. has been convicted (or adjudicated insane or delinquent) of a sexually violent offense in the past,

2. has been incarcerated and subsequently released for that "conviction," and

3. has committed "any act that has either caused harm of a sexually violent nature or creates a reasonable apprehension of such harm."

Under these circumstances in these two states, prosecutors can potentially file petitions for commitment even if the subjects are not about to be released from incarceration based directly on a "conviction" for a sexually violent offense. (Although California's law also includes the phrase "recent overt act," its definition is different and only serves within the context of specifying that an individual's "danger to the health and safety of others" does not "require proof of a recent overt act while the offender is in custody.")

Proving the existence of a "recent overt act" may be something for which prosecutors need the testimony of evaluators, though this is not at all certain. Through the time this book was written, there had been no cases in Iowa and only a tiny number of cases in Washington in which this issue was raised. Hence, there is very little case experience to pass on to the reader for guidance in addressing this concept.

Sexually Violent Offenses

Each of the statutes offers a description of crimes of relevance to the commitment process, what are typically referred to as "sexually violent." (The only two states not currently using this phrase are Minnesota and North Dakota. These states use the phrases "harmful sexual conduct" and "sexually predatory conduct," respectively.) These definitions almost always involve an enumeration of specific types of sexual crimes. There are various language differences and verbal nuances in these lists across the states. Examiners working within each state need to become familiar with that state's specific definitional list. A conceptual summary is offered for what behaviors are of potential relevance in assessing a subject's risk.

The statutory lists of what constitutes a relevant sexual act are written as specific sexual offenses and statute numbers (except in North Dakota, where more general descriptions of the different relevant acts are listed). Conceptually, any physical contact of a sexual nature involving a child counts. Most if not all unwanted physical contact of a sexual nature with an adult counts as well, though some states draw the threshold above groping and unwanted touching of body parts (as long as the victim is an adult and no other force or threat of force was employed). Sexual contact that specifically resulted from the use of a weapon seems to count no matter the age of the victim.

States differ far more on the extent to which sexually victimizing behavior devoid of physical contact counts. Iowa, for instance, includes the act of publicly exposing one's genitals to unsuspecting persons. Arizona includes that process only if the victim was a child. Wisconsin is more restrictive still in this regard, including only a nonphysical crime if it involved a child and the process of enticing (or attempting to entice) that child into a different location for purposes harmful to the child, including exposing one's genitals to the child. I know of no commitment law that includes in its list of defined sexually violent acts obscene phone calling, peeping in windows, or other such crimes if enacted against an adult.

Included among the typical types of offenses that define "sexually violent" are a small number of sexual crimes that are unique compared with what other states list. For instance, Iowa's definition includes "sexual contact with a corpse." Minnesota includes "living off or sharing earnings of a minor prostitute," "incestuous marriage," "disseminating to a minor matter harmful to a minor," and "possession of child pornography." Such idiosyncrasies are the basis for the caveat to evaluators that they need to become familiar with the state law under which they are working.

These lists of crimes that define "sexually violent acts" serve two purposes within each law, both of which are relevant to the commitment criteria. The subject must have committed and been "convicted" for one (or more) of the stated acts to be eligible for commitment based on his legal status. The other purpose is to define the types of acts that set the parameters for the person's assessed risk. The degree of likelihood for the enactment of any of the listed crimes is what evaluators attempt to assess.

Concerning the former purpose, virtually all of the sex offender civil commitment laws take into consideration that plea bargains can change the title of a crime for which the person is ultimately convicted. The term "sexual violence" is therefore additionally defined in virtually all jurisdictions (except California and, of course, North Dakota) with specified acts that have resulted in a conviction for any of certain nonsexual charges where the underlying behavior involved a "sexual" condition. Specifically, the crime for which the person was ultimately convicted needs to represent an act that was "sexually motivated." Typical examples of nonsexual crimes that can be found to be "sexually motivated" are murder and kidnapping.

Sexual motivation is typically defined in one of two ways, exemplified by Florida's wording ("one of the purposes for which the defendant committed the crime was for sexual gratification") and that of Illinois ("one of the purposes for an act is for the actor's sexual arousal or gratification"). Minnesota uses a unique description ("if the conduct was motivated by the person's sexual impulses or was part of a pattern of behavior that had criminal sexual conduct as a goal"), but essentially appears to be addressing the same underlying point. For evaluators assessing risk, this segment of definitions of sexual violence does not alter the types of acts of importance, but simply serves as acknowledgment that the criminal justice system does not need to prosecute sexually criminal acts with a sexual charge for the act to be considered relevant.

Clinical Commitment Criteria

All current sex offender civil commitment statutes include two commitment criteria that effectively require a mental health professional's assessment and testimony. The first involves a certain type of mental condition. The second requires a specific type of risk. Given that the assessment of these criteria are, in effect, what the rest of this book addresses, these criteria are described in state-by-state detail. Even so, the recommendation is made that evaluators ensure the following description is still current for whichever jurisdiction an assessment is to be conducted.

The Requisite Mental Condition

As is typical in the forensic application of professional mental health practices, the legal specifications of the mental condition to be assessed in sex offender civil commitments and our more typical psychiatric nomenclature do not match. Legislatures typically devised their own concepts, and then required clinicians to make assessments of those concepts.

The most commonly devised term of this type in the sex offender civil commitment arena is "mental abnormality." That term exists in the laws of eight states: Florida, Iowa, Kansas, Massachusetts, Missouri, New Jersey, South Carolina, and Washington, or over half the commitment states. The term's statutory definition is virtually the same across all of those states: "a congenital or acquired condition affecting the emotional [, cognitive] or volitional capacity which predisposes the person to commit sexually violent acts [in a degree constituting such person a menace to the health and safety of others]." The bracketed phrases represent the only variations among the definitions in the enumerated states.

In all of these statutes except Missouri's, there is also one other phrase defining the requisite mental condition: "or personality disorder." The term personality disorder is left completely undefined in all seven of those states except for Massachusetts. Presumably, evaluators are left to interpret the term significantly in keeping with the same diagnostic phrase in the *Diagnostic and Statistical Manual*, 4th edition (*DSM-IV*; American Psychiatric Association, 1994). In the Massachusetts statute, however, the term personality disorder is defined as "a congenital or acquired physical or mental condition that results in a general lack of power to control sexual impulses." This is obviously quite different from the *DSM-IV* definition of a concept with the same name.

Four statutes use another term familiar from the *DSM-IV*, but again with a differing definition. Instead of "mental abnormality or personality disorder," the statutes in the states of Arizona, California, Illinois, and Wisconsin use the phrase "[diagnosed] mental disorder" to describe the mental condition required for commitment. The legal phrase "mental disorder" clearly is not synonymous with the *DSM-IV* concept. In the latter three states, the definition of this phrase is virtually identical to that given above for mental abnormality: "a congenital or acquired condition affecting the emotional or volitional capacity that predisposes the person to engage in acts of sexual violence [in a degree constituting the person a menace to the health and safety of others]."

Arizona's definition uses other specific diagnostic terms from the *DSM-IV* to define "mental disorder." In that state, the term means "a paraphilia, personality disorder or conduct disorder or any combination of paraphilia, personality disorder and conduct disorder [that predisposes the person to commit sexual acts to such a degree as to render the person a danger to the health and safety of others]."

The Minnesota and North Dakota statutes share this attribute. Minnesota's commitment process (under its Sexually Dangerous Person statute) necessitates the demonstration that the person "has manifested a sexual, personality, or other mental disorder or dysfunction." Likewise, North Dakota does not give an overall name for the requisite mental condition, but describes it as "a congenital or acquired condition that is manifested by a sexual disorder, a personality disorder or other mental disorder or dysfunction."

The Texas law again stands out as unique, though this time only in its terminology. That statute uses the term "behavioral abnormality," though its definition should now sound familiar: "a congenital or acquired condition that, by affecting a person's emotional or volitional capacity, predisposes the person to commit a sexually violent offense, to the extent that the person becomes a menace to the health and safety of another person."

With the above detail, the reader can see that there are essentially two kinds of definitions of the mental condition required for commitment across the states, both of which include the need (except in Minnesota and North Dakota) to "predispose" the person to commit certain sexual acts. The first type uses some variation on the theme of an acquired or congenital condition that predisposes the person to commit a criminal sexual act. The second involves actual *DSM-IV* diagnostic categories such as sexual disorder, paraphilia, and/or personality disorder.

"Acquired or congenital . . ."

The commonality and centrality of the initial definitional phrase "acquired or congenital condition affecting the emotional, [cognitive] or volitional capacity" necessitate further investigation of the proper interpretation of these words. Breaking this phrase down into two components makes this easier.

The first reaction people have to the introductory segment, "acquired or congenital," is "what else is there?" Indeed, as pertains to mental conditions (or even behavioral conditions, to use the Texan term), there does not seem to be anything else possible. From that perspective, this phrase is essentially not useful in differentiating one mental condition from another. The only argument in court about this phrase appears to be in trying to define a specific mental condition as *either* congenital *or* acquired. For at least most relevant diagnoses of mental conditions (e.g., pedophilia, antisocial personality disorder), our knowledge about etiological factors is probably too minimal for an evaluator to answer questions of this type with certainty except to say that both factors likely play a role. Hence, the proper answer to the question about whether a specific diagnosis is either acquired or congenital is yes.

"Emotional or volitional capacity . . ."

The second component has been more problematic in some states: "affecting the emotional or volitional capacity." (New Jersey's law is the only one that also lists "cognitive" within the phrase "emotional or volitional capacity.") Based in logic, one could again raise the question of what mental condition does not affect the emotional or volitional capacity (especially if one adds New Jersey's inclusion of cognitive capacity, though it is not at all clear how cognitive is different from volitional). From that perspective, this phrase is again viewed as all-inclusive and essentially not useful in differentiating one condition from another.

In some jurisdictions, however, there has been a great deal of struggle concerning what the concept of "affecting . . . volitional capacity" means (e.g., Arizona, California, Kansas). The defense side of the argument offers the interpretation that the individual with such a condition must be unable (meaning completely unable) to control his actions. The reason why this represents the defense perspective is that most, if not virtually all, diagnostic conditions in the *DSM-IV* would fail to meet this test. This failure, if accepted by the courts, means that the respondent cannot have the requisite mental condition, and hence, should not be committed.

The prosecution side to this argument, and typically the perspective of evaluators who sometimes opine a respondent meets criteria, is that "affecting . . . volitional capacity" means that the person's mental condition causes an impairment in his decision-making ability where those decisions are directly related to actions he chooses. This impairment is a matter of degree, measured neither as completely negating volitional control nor as leaving the capacity functioning fully intact. Of high importance, the U.S. Supreme Court is currently reviewing the issue of the meaning of volitional capacity based in a case stemming from Kansas.

At least until the Supreme Court decides this case, it can be said that describing the relevant impairment can be tricky. There are many traps into which evaluators can fall when testifying about this concept. To exemplify these, consider describing impairment as the following:

1. *Demonstrated by the fact the person did something criminal, maybe even because criminality was repetitive.* This explication can become uncomfortable when asked if people such as Mohandas Gandhi, Martin Luther King, Jr., and Nelson Mandela shared this same impairment. One needs to be prepared to delineate the difference between civil disobedience, representing an actively chosen method for political change, and criminal conduct that has no other motive besides self-gain. Although this differentiation can be made, the counterargument is that what one person labels as civil disobedience is easily labeled by another as criminal activity—it is all a matter of perspective. As the debate ensues, the issue of clearly defining impairment can become lost.

2. *A type of compulsion.* Countering this definition are questions about whether or not the subject ever demonstrated some control over his criminal sexual interests. Situations such as in an institution's visiting room when another person's child visitor was near the subject can be raised. If the subject did not reach out and touch the child, then presumably some control was demonstrated. The evaluator needs to be able to describe a meaningful difference between "compulsion" and inability to stop oneself from doing an act. Although such a difference exists, this can be difficult for an evaluator to explain if not prepared ahead of time to do so. There may also be some individuals for whom the use of the word *compulsion* truly fits, but evaluators are cautioned against using this term without being able to specify its defining details.

3. *A lessening of "free will."* Discussions of "free will" can easily be heard by judges and jurors as reflecting the evaluator's religious beliefs, whether intended to reflect such beliefs or not. No matter how articulate an evaluator explains the concept of impairment in terms of free will, that explanation may be lost on the audience who fundamentally disagrees with the religious underpinnings.

So what is a meaningful way to describe the impairment represented by a diagnosed mental condition? There may very well be more than one manner to do this, but at least one is as follows. The evaluator starts with the basic way in which everyone makes decisions. We essentially formulate a decision equation in our heads. We consider everything we know about the pros and cons of one action versus another, with some considerations being weighed far more heavily than others. For instance, we may choose to accelerate at a yellow light to go through it under some circumstances, but not if we see a police car at the intersection. The situational consideration of the presence of the police car is so important that our desire to keep driving along through the yellow light is outweighed; it does not become of utmost importance in deciding what we will do.

Likewise, when we learn of relevant considerations that we did not know of before, we add them to our decision-making process. For instance, a child may not initially consider that touching something hot will cause pain, but this is a lesson typically learned quickly upon experience. In future decisions of a similar type, the child will tend to consider that fact. In adulthood, a similar process typically occurs, where we continue to refine our decision-making process by learning what the different parameters are, along with what the multiple options are for obtaining what we want. For example, we may find that a physical labor job is not as rewarding to us as a desk job (or vice versa), where both can serve adequately to give us the money we need. Overall, our decision-making process reflects adaptations to changing circumstances, and it considers different behavioral options accordingly.

Using this descriptive context, the relevant impairment can be defined. There were three components to the decision-making process delineated above. The first was the simple process of using "equations" in our heads. People who are afflicted with paraphilias and personality disorders (the most common relevant diagnoses among sex offenders who are civilly committed) probably have no deficit in this area. They can typically formulate a list of pros and cons and make decisions using the same method as the rest of us.

The second and third areas, however, are where impairments can be found. The issue of learning from experience (i.e., the second issue above) is crucial when it comes to personality disorders. Virtually by definition, these chronic conditions represent a person's deficit in ability to learn from experience, at least within certain realms. For instance, an antisocial personality disordered individual tends to see the negative outcomes from his (antisocial) acts as reflective of other people's doings, not his own. The victim "asked for it" and so should not have reported the perpetrator to the police. The judge was unfair. Witnesses lied on the stand. Any variety of attributions is made that serve to diminish the person's ability to learn that his actions caused him an undesired outcome. Without that process of self-attribution, there is no learning to cause future changes in his "mental equation" except perhaps how better not to get caught. The person's willingness to repeat the same behaviors does not reflect the experiential updating characteristic of the rest of us.

The third area reflects the realm of impairment more typical to the paraphiliac individual. This concerns options he believes are available to him. Let us look at the options for sexual gratification of the pedophile who also has a preference for children versus adult sexual partners. This person is only somewhat sexually interested in adults. Most of his desired sexual contacts are illegal. He can look at photographic depictions of children all he wants, to which he may masturbate. Watching children's television shows also represents an option for him. Actual sexual contact with a child, however, is an option that contains a potential high cost of facing legal consequences (even forgetting empathic issues about the children's well-being). Now let's add that this person feels he lacks the social skills to obtain a willing adult sexual partner but still feels strong needs for sexual contact with another person. The likelihood for having sexual contact with an adult does not seem very great to him. What options does he therefore consider realistic? The only option he views as viable is to have sexual contact with a child. His choosing this option can occur despite the fact that he takes full responsibility for the choice and his subsequent behavior (i.e., he is not personality disordered, and has learned to associate his actions with outcomes), and he is fully aware of the potential legal consequences for such an act. In other words, this "mental equation" may result in a "negative" outcome in his head, but it is still the option he favors over the very limited set of possibilities he considers. The person may very well have learned from prior (direct and vicarious) experiences, and incorporated that learning into his decision-making process, but he shows a deficit in his decision-making process as indicated in the limited options he considers. If the person repetitively limits his perceived options based on a continuing type of sexual desire, then this process represents impairment in his decision making. Paraphilias often signal this type of impairment.

Another way to phrase this same perspective on volitional impairment is that the person's desire for sexual contact involving children and/or violence is sufficiently strong that it overwhelms the individual's ability to consider various options and consequences. The strength of this desire, although not "irresistible" (to borrow an old legal concept, from the phrase "irresistible impulse"), becomes the basis for his deciding to sacrifice concerns for the consequences of his actions to himself and others. It is not the desire per se that is the problem, but the strength of the desire relative to other actively considered options.

Of course, an evaluation subject can be impaired in both ways, typically reflected by his being diagnosed with both paraphiliac and personality disorder conditions. No matter the diagnoses in a given case, however, the evaluator needs to be prepared to describe what constitutes the "volitional" impairment of that individual.

One other topic needs to be mentioned in this section. As stated above, there are arguments sometimes made that the legal phrase "affecting . . . volitional control" suggests an "utter lack of power to control the person's sexual impulses" (a phrase quoted from Minnesota's Sexual Psychopathic Personality commitment law). Although the attorneys can ask questions along this nature as much as they see fit, evaluators are cautioned against using this type of definition. Even in Minnesota, this phrase comes from one (older) type of sex offender civil commitment law, but not the commitment law of the type being delineated here. (The latter is Minnesota's "Sexually Dangerous Person." According to the other Minnesota law, the law's title and main term "'sexual psychopathic personality' means the existence in any person of such conditions of emotional instability, or impulsiveness of behavior, or lack of customary standards of good judgment, or failure to appreciate the consequences of personal acts, or a combination of any of these conditions, which render the person irresponsible for personal conduct with respect to sexual matters, if the person has evidenced, by a habitual course of misconduct in sexual matters, an utter lack of power to control the person's sexual impulses and, as a result, is dangerous to other persons." The sexually dangerous person is someone who "[1] has engaged in a course of harmful sexual conduct . . . ; [2] has manifested a sexual, personality, or other mental disorder or dysfunction; and [3] as a result, is likely to engage in acts of harmful sexual conduct.") In the more relevant latter statute, the explicitly stated phrase "it is not necessary to prove that the person has an inability to control the person's sexual impulses" demonstrates the impropriety of applying an all-or-none interpretation to "volitional capacity" when working within that statute. None of the recent vintage sex offender civil commitment laws (as enumerated above) is known to indicate otherwise.

"That predisposes the person to commit . . . "

In all but two of the current statutes (i.e., in Minnesota and North Dakota), the requisite mental condition is defined with the inclusion of a phrase in keeping with the rubric to this section. This phrase is the first within the definitions of the mental condition needed for commitment that is clearly differentiating among diagnostic categories. (As mentioned above, the laws in Minnesota and North Dakota do not use generic phrases such as "acquired or congenital" or "emotional of volitional capacity," but employ diagnostic terms instead. Hence, the requisite mental conditions for commitment under those laws are already more defined, through this point in the analysis, than those in the other state statutes.) The otherwise rather generically defined mental conditions must show a specific type of connection to sexual offending based on this phrase. This connection is not necessarily in terms of the likelihood for acting on a desire (though potentially overlapping the issue of likelihood), but rather that the diagnosed condition is directly (at least partially) responsible for the subject's drive toward sexual offending.

The main concerns here for evaluators are defining one's interpretation of the term "predispose" and, concomitantly, differentiating between "predisposing" and the concept of prediction. In dictionary terms, *predisposition* indicates an inclination or tendency, a predilection or susceptibility. Using an interpretation along these lines means that the requisite mental condition for civil commitment must (in all but Minnesota and North Dakota) have the attribute specifically of involving an inclination, tendency, predilection, or susceptibility toward committing one or more of certain enumerated sex crimes called sexually violent. (The definition of this last term is described below.)

There are two clarifications needed for that definition, however. The first one involves confusion between "predisposition" and the "assessment of risk."

Predisposition is sometimes described by evaluators as a component of their risk assessment. Although it may be appropriate to consider a subject's "sexually violent" inclinations as a segment of the risk being assessed, the process of defining the concept of "predisposition" in risk-related terms is not. The statutory inclusion of the term "predispose" is specifically within the definition of the required mental condition for commitment. The degree of risk the subject must represent to meet commitment criteria is defined separately (in terms described in the next section). Predisposition simply implies an inclination, not to what degree that inclination exists or to what degree of overall risk the person represents for acting on that tendency.

In the courtroom, this difference can be explained descriptively as well as metaphorically. Using the former approach, predisposition can be described as something inherent to the individual, inside the individual no matter where he finds himself. Predictions, on the other hand, represent something other people state about him, based on their assessments of him, which include his predisposition.

Metaphorically, an evaluator can describe the difference between (1) an alcoholic's strong urges to drink alcohol, sometimes more than other times, but always stemming from inside the person, and (2) a prediction that the person will or will not drink alcohol again. The latter, when professionally done, takes into consideration the degree to which the person acknowledges a problem with alcohol, and whether the person still goes to bars, still spends time with friends who drink whenever they are together, is in some type of ongoing alcohol abuse treatment, has someone to call who will help when the pressure gets particularly strong, and so on. In other words, the prediction process involves reviewing the applicability of risk factors and protective factors.

The second clarification needed concerning predisposition is that most statutes (i.e., 9 of the 15, these 9 being Arizona, California, Iowa, Kansas, Massachusetts, Missouri, North Dakota, Texas, and Washington) include one more phrase within their definition of the requisite mental condition. That phrase is either of the type "to such a degree as to render the person a danger to the health and safety of others" or "to the extent that the person becomes a menace to the health and safety of another person." These phrases, as part of the definitions of "mental abnormality" or similar concept, refer to the extent to which the person is predisposed to commit certain crimes. It appears from these phrases that for someone (in the listed states except North Dakota) to be considered as meeting the criteria for commitment, the person's predisposition needs to be related to some degree of likelihood for actually acting on that tendency. (North Dakota's law does not include the concept of predisposition.) To the extent to which this degree of likelihood simply means "something above zero," these phrases do not seem to add much to the existing concept of predisposition.

Risk for Sexual Violence

For someone to be committed under any of the statutes, the person's relevant mental condition must be related to a specified degree of risk for committing one (or more) sexually violent act. A description of the specific acts that constitute the sexually violent is offered below. In this section, the issue of the degree of risk is explicated.

Twelve of the statutes use the term "likely" to denote the degree of risk needed for commitment. In only 2 of those 12 laws is the term defined (i.e., Iowa and Washington), both by the phrase "more likely than not." Missouri's statute uses that latter phrase right away, rather than defining the commitment risk threshold in two steps. The remaining two states, Illinois and Wisconsin, use the undefined phrase "substantial probability" to define their risk thresholds.

Evaluators typically interpret the phrase "more likely than not" as meaning 50+%. The other terms, however, are not anywhere near as easily interpreted. Even a state supreme court's interpretation does not always clarify matters for evaluators about what these terms mean. For instance, the Wisconsin Supreme Court ruled that "substantial probability" means "much more likely to occur than not to occur." It seems a good bet that this is beyond 50+% (an interpretation of just the segment "more likely than not"), but by how much remains unclear.

In the 10 states where the term "likely" is used without any further definition, the lack of clarity is quite problematic. Some people interpret the term as synonymous with "more likely than not." Others make the interpretation using the term "probable" (an interpretation made by the Florida Supreme Court, for instance), which is by no means necessarily equated with "more likely than not." Still others say the term "likely" varies in its meaning depending on the degree of injury that would be expected to a victim. For instance, the percentage "likelihood" needed for commitment for someone who kills his victims is viewed as significantly lower than for someone who "only" touches children's buttocks over their clothes. A fourth interpretation consistently views "likely" as metaphorically the degree of likelihood for an airplane crashing when you would no longer get on the plane, a figure quite regularly conceived as significantly below "more likely than not."

Given the lack of clarity in the statutory risk descriptions, there are few absolutely correct ways for evaluators to interpret these legal terms. At the same time, there are some guidelines that can be delineated.

Recommended is the avoidance of being so vague in one's own interpretation that related opinions become meaningless. If one says, "I cannot define what 'likely' means" and then goes on to state that the subject meets criteria, the flaw in logic will be exposed easily. How can one come to believe that someone meets criteria if one has no idea what the commitment criteria mean? Cross-examination along this thread will leave the examiner tied up in knots, and ultimately make struggle worthless. To do sex offender civil commitment assessments, an examiner needs to have some type of working interpretation of the statutory terms.

That does not mean that evaluators should feign exactness and clarity where little exists. Some evaluators have done this through interpreting the term "likely" or "substantial probability" by attaching a specific percentage to it. The phrase "more likely than not" seems naturally to coincide with a percentage, though actually with a minimum threshold rather than with a percentage per se (i.e., anywhere over 50%, not specifically 50%). Concepts such as likely and substantial probability do not lend themselves to percentages as easily. Evaluators are cautioned against attributing such numerical exactness to a legal concept where none seems obvious.

There are two reasons for this. The first is that judges and jurors can perceive an evaluator who makes such definitive interpretations about legal concepts (i.e., concepts outside the evaluator's area of expertise) as acting inappropriately. The definitions of unclear legal concepts are not naturally part of evaluators' expertise. (Defining more obvious phrases, such as "more likely than not," as representing a threshold of 50+% does not seem to call for legal expertise.) This perception negatively affects the degree to which the expert's testimony will be influential to the triers of fact.

The second reason to avoid using arbitrary percentages as one's interpretation of a legal concept is that such exactness suggests that the science underlying the examiner's opinion is also that exact. When that erroneous idea is exposed, the evaluator's credibility may suffer greatly, even if the evaluator willingly and deliberately brings this out during direct examination. There is a significant risk that once jurors or judges hear an evaluator acknowledge the lack of exactness available in risk assessments based on today's science, they will be confused about why the examiner "pretended" to be exact in an area beyond the evaluator's expertise. From such confusion can arise questions about whether the examiner really understands the evaluation task at all.

There is a third guideline of importance. This pertains to the question of whether one really needs to have a fixed concept of "likely" at all. Might it be most appropriate to allow the interpretation of the term to vary depending on the seriousness of the potential crime (i.e., degree of injury to the victim)? In that way, what constitutes "likely" for an offender who tortures and murders his victims then could be much lower than what "likely" would mean for someone who "merely" touches children. This approach typically makes sense when viewed from the perspective that the seriousness of the crime matters and needs to be considered (beyond the simple differentiation of sex crimes listed in the statutes as sexually violent versus everything else that is not listed).

The problem with this "sliding scale" approach is that no one listening to testimony stemming from that approach will understand what the testimony means. To illustrate, does an opinion of "meets criteria" mean the subject is highly likely to do a low-injury offense, of low likelihood for doing a highly injurious crime, highly likely to commit a moderately injurious offense, or of moderate likelihood for enacting a highly injurious crime? Likewise, opinion testimony from different evaluators may very well differ only because of unspoken and potentially even unknown biases in how the different evaluators view different sex crimes, as opposed to more objective merits of the case. The recommendation is made that such communication problems should be avoided.

In theory, to salvage the sliding scale approach, a group of evaluators could get together and collectively define different thresholds for what "likely" means depending on specified types of predicted sex crimes and thereby avoid the confusion just mentioned. Although this has been discussed in at least one setting to date (i.e., among certain psychiatrists in New Jersey), the collective multithreshold approach has not gained much support.

Ultimately, the courts will decide what constitutes "likely" and similar terms. Evaluators would be amiss, however, to believe that the working definitions they use do not help shape that ultimate legal opinion. Appellate courts review lower court testimony and react to the information given in the transcripts. Expert witness testimony is considered along with everything else. Sometimes our influence is beyond the local courtroom and specific hearing in which we are testifying. This is another reason that examiners need to be as clear as they can about their understanding of the law, without overstating the exactness of that understanding.

In summary, you cannot suggest complete ignorance about what the legal term means, and you probably should not use a sliding scale, but you cannot be exact in your interpretation either. So, how can you usefully interpret the statutory language?

Consultations with others, both other evaluators and attorneys, can help an evaluator derive a meaningful interpretation. You will likely not get definitional clarity from these consultations, but some degree of grounding around a reasonable understanding is probable. Ultimately, one needs to decide on a descriptive interpretation, a working definition that seems reasonable and basically in keeping with what other evaluators (from the same state) are using. The description can be in terms of "high risk," "more likely than not," "much more likely than not" (each of these phrases has been employed by appellate courts in different states— Minnesota, Washington, and Wisconsin), or similar concepts. Although descriptive phrases such as these may not seem much more exact than using the original statutory term as it was, the attempt to delineate your understanding of your task makes your testimony more meaningful to jurors and judges. They can then decide if they agree or disagree with your working definition and the concomitant opinion you offer.

The Issue of "Predatory" Offending

Within the commitment criteria for six states (California, Iowa, Missouri, North Dakota, Texas, and Washington) is the term "predatory." (The Kansas law initially included this term, but legislation changed that.) In these six cases, the word "predatory" is used as a qualifier to the type of sexual acts for which the person is a "likely" (or "more likely than not") risk. Five of the six jurisdictions define the term similarly, using words such as Missouri's "acts directed towards strangers or individuals with whom relationships have been established or promoted for the primary purpose of victimization." North Dakota's law, being the exception among the six, employs the term within its definition of relevant sexual conduct rather than defining the term independently.

The usual evaluator interpretation of the defining phrase for "predatory" is that purely incestuous offenders are excluded from commitment eligibility. Also excluded are offenders who take sexual advantage of existing relationships (with children or adults), but whose relationships formed and continued to exist for reasons other than perpetration of a sexual crime. These people may be viewed as having the requisite mental condition and a risk for sexual reoffending beyond the statutory threshold, but still not be assessed as meeting commitment criteria due to the nature of the relationships in which the person's crimes occur.

The typical manner by which evaluators assess the "predatory" component to subjects' risk is to view the subjects' past patterns of known sexual offending. This is because the "predatory" nature of someone's future sexual criminality is not something that has been researched directly. In general, we do know that people tend to repeat past patterns of behavior when enacting similar acts, though there can be variability (e.g., Hanson & Bussière, 1998). Unless there is a pertinent reason in a specific case to think otherwise, this approach of looking at past behavior in assessing the concept of "predatory" appears to be the current examiners' standard.

Also coupled with this approach is the use of research results from actuarial risk assessment instrumentation (discussed in Chapter 5). The research-based outcome from the use of those scales offers some guidance in this matter, to the extent that the types of crimes counted as recidivist matches a statutory definition of "predatory" sexual offenses.

The Issue of Lesser Restrictive Alternatives

The final issue covered in this chapter is one that matters in only a small number of states during the precommitment phase (vs. the reexamination phase). As the background for understanding the topic of lesser restrictive alternatives, one needs first to be aware that every state (except Texas) maintains a secure facility to which committed people are typically housed and treated. It is against this backdrop that the concept of lesser restrictive alternatives comes into play.

How it comes into play, however, differs in the few states in which it matters during the earlier commitment stages. In Washington, precommitment evaluators are responsible for assessing if subjects can be managed effectively under lesser restrictive conditions in the community. If assessed as meaningfully possible, then the recommendation for commitment may not be appropriate (based on case law) despite all other criteria being met. This is apparently because of the last phrase in the statutory commitment criteria: "if not confined in a secure facility." Whether or not the imagined lesser restrictive conditions actually can be mandated and implemented is a matter for the courts to address.

In Arizona, the consideration of a lesser restrictive alternative to a secure facility commitment occurs during both precommitment and postcommitment adjudication, but only before disposition. Respondents can ask to be assessed for a lesser restrictive alternative before their commitment hearing, with the assessment being conducted in a program conjoint to the secure treatment unit at the Arizona State Hospital. This assessment is statutorily the same as that which occurs when the person requests the committing court to consider an initial outpatient commitment for the subject, or when an inpatient petitions the court for a lesser restrictive alternative to an existing secure facility commitment. The statutory commitment criteria themselves, however, are not necessarily interpreted (to the best of my knowledge) as taking lesser restrictive alternatives into consideration. That is basically saved for a dispositional phase of the commitment process.

The Illinois statute functions in a way similar to Arizona's. If a committing court wishes to consider a "supervised release" initial commitment order, the court has the option of ordering an evaluative report from the department specifically for that purpose. A dispositional hearing is convened after that report is submitted for the purpose of determining if the person goes to the secure facility (as an inpatient) or goes directly to a supervised release setting under the same type of commitment (as an outpatient). Wisconsin (previous to 1998) used to have this same postcommitment dispositional structure, but legislative changes deleted that option.

As mentioned above, there is one unique law when it comes to the issue of lesser restrictive alternatives: that in Texas. In Texas, a commitment is necessarily as an "outpatient," with that terminology written into the statute. There are many possible conditions imposed on the person as part of that outpatient commitment, the final imposed list being based on both statutory and nonstatutory considerations, all at the judge's discretion. Evaluators potentially from both sides present input in this regard. Only during the court's consideration of conditions to be imposed is there any discussion of "lesser restrictive alternatives." The final imposed conditions then become enforced through the criminal code (as a newly committed felony with potential imprisonment), rather than through revocation of a supervised release civil commitment to a hospital setting. In other words, unlike all of the other 14 states, failure within a "lesser restrictive alternative" in Texas can lead to imprisonment instead of secure hospitalization.

The other statutes quite explicitly state, or at least effectively negate, the option that an initial commitment can be to anywhere else but a secure facility. In these states (e.g., Missouri, South Carolina), the issue of lesser restrictive alternatives does not have applicability until the person has been committed to the secure facility and has later petitioned for this consideration. The evaluative considerations for this reexamination of subjects' commitments will be discussed later in this book.

Summary Comments

In reviewing the 15 relevant statutes, many similarities were found in defining the evaluators' task. Basically, all of the laws require (1) a diagnostic formulation, usually involving the additional issue to be addressed of a specific type of predisposition, along with (2) an assessment of risk for certain types of sexual offending. The risk thresholds for commitment are not exactly the same across the laws, with the most common threshold ("likely") being described with possibly the least clear term among the phrases used. No statute specifies any time frame for the risk being assessed. The task for examinations concerning least restrictive alternatives involves the same two issues, a diagnosis and risk assessment, though also with considerations probably best described under the rubric of risk management. The general finding was that all states except Texas place their committed individuals initially in secure facilities, so risk management considerations are not regularly reviewed at the time of commitment.

Overall, the basic referral questions for evaluators involve diagnostic and risk assessment considerations. The bulk of the remainder of this book therefore concentrates on those two issues.

Note

1. The use of male pronouns in this book reflects three facts: (1) A vast majority of convicted sex offenders are male; (2) only a tiny number of women have been assessed, and even a tinier number referred, for a potential civil commitment to date; and (3) virtually all of the research cited in this book was conducted solely with male respondents. Although it can be argued that a more accurate representation of sex offenders would use the pronoun combination of "he or she," this combination was believed more cumbersome to the reader than useful.

CHAPTER 2

Procedures for Conducting the Assessment

Franklin: Have you ever thought, Headmaster, that your standards might perhaps be a little out of date?

Headmaster: Of course they're out of date. Standards are always out of date. That is what makes them standards.

— Alan Bennett, *Forty Years On*

The previous chapter delineated the components of the sex offender civil commitment evaluation "referral questions." This chapter describes the general procedures by which evaluators should go about the task of answering those questions.

National Standards

Early in the process of the implementation of these civil commitment laws, there was no clearly explicated set of national standards setting forth all procedures for these types of evaluations. Examiners employed the generally accepted methods employed for other types of forensic assessments. These procedures represented carryovers from "older times." More recently, there have been to date two groups that have worked on developing some standards specific to this area.

The first group was a set of 10 people, each working in and representing one of nine states with active civil commitment laws (with two representatives from Illinois; see list below). During the initial formation of the proposed standards (in September 1999), the other states did not send representatives to participate.

Their input was solicited, and typically obtained later, in response to the proposed standards (in November 1999). The result involved a proposed set of standards divided into three segments: (1) procedural issues, (2) the assessment of the requisite mental condition, and (3) the risk assessment. The final proposed standards follow:

I. Procedural Issues

The overall philosophy underlying these procedures is that the relevant diagnostic assessment and risk assessment both be multidimensional and following the ethical guidelines of relevant professional organizations. Specific recommended standards in this area include the following:

1. All persons being employed in performing an evaluation relevant to a sex offender civil commitment and/or its continuance must have some identified competence with all procedures employed (i.e., training specific to this type of assessment). Areas considered relevant to competence include

   a. knowledge, training, and/or experience of forensic evaluations;

   b. knowledge of characteristics and/or treatment of sex offenders;

   c. diagnostic assessment; and

   d. risk assessment.

2. The assessment must include a face-to-face contact with the evaluation subject if the person is willing.

3. The assessment should use a variety of sources for information if possible, though ethical considerations may preclude soliciting information from the subject's victims.

4. The evaluation is completed with timeliness as defined within the specific state.

5. All information that substantiated the basis for one or more opinions must be preserved for reasonable future reference related to appeals, treatment needs, and reexaminations. This does not mean that the evaluator needs to store all such information or any redundant pieces of information, but that the evaluator needs to be certain that all such information remains reasonably available for future use.

6. All procedures employed are in accord with ethical principles of one's own relevant professional organizations such as the American Psychological Association (including the "Specialty Guidelines for Forensic Psychologists"; Committee on Ethical Guidelines for Forensic Psychologists, 1991), the American Psychiatric Association, and the Association for the Treatment of Sexual Abusers.

II. Concerning the Assessment of the Requisite Mental Condition

In assessing for the requisite mental condition relevant to commitment, the following represent the standards proposed:

1. The evaluator needs to provide a description or foundation for how any diagnosed mental conditions meet the standard for the requisite legally delineated mental condition.

2. Diagnoses need to be determined through professionally accepted procedures, including the use of structured methods when possible.

3. Psychological tests can be considered appropriate for use in the assessment of diagnostic conditions.

4. The evaluator must make use of current diagnostic standards for opinions concerning a subject's mental condition.

III. Concerning the Risk Assessment

In assessing for the degree of risk represented by the subject of the possible civil commitment, the following represent the standards proposed:

1. The evaluator must under common evaluation circumstances use some set of actuarial instruments, these being derived through scientific methods, where instruction is obtainable through distanced learning (e.g., Internet, teleconferencing). Exceptions to the use of actuarial instruments need to be based on reasoned scientific argument, such as the lack of applicability of the available instruments to the specific case or a very short expected life span for the subject. (A subject's expected life span affects the applicability of instruments designed to assess risk related to time periods such as 5, 10, or 15 years. Without taking into consideration an apparent fact that a specific subject is not likely to live even 5 years, interpretations of risk instrumentation assessing longer-term risk would be inappropriate.) In situations involving any exception, it is incumbent upon the evaluator to state the reason that actuarial instrumentation was not employed.

2. The evaluator's choice of risk assessment instrumentation needs to be reasonably related to the subject and task.

3. The evaluator has the responsibility of staying abreast of current scientific knowledge related to the proper selection of risk assessment instrumentation.

4. Where there is empirical support to conclude that there are multiple dimensions to be assessed, then the evaluator needs to cover each of the relevant dimensions through the instrumentation chosen (e.g., the potentially separate recidivism dimensions of sexual deviance and antisocial/violent personality traits should both be assessed as part of a risk assessment concerned with recidivism).

5. The presentation of opinions related to risk should be phrased in terms of whether or not the person meets the state's legal threshold, and not through the use of a specific percentage of likelihood for reoffending. This standard allows for testimony of an opinion of the type "beyond the statutory threshold of 50%," as long as that testimony does not go on to state an exact percentage likelihood for the individual's risk.

6. No psychological test (e.g., Rorschach Inkblot Test) should be employed specifically for this type of risk assessment unless empirical evidence of its specific utility relative to this type of risk assessment is also reported.

7. General psychometric instrumentation beyond psychological tests may be used for testing for (a) dynamic risk factors or (b) other research-demonstrated risk factors.

8. The evaluator must be prepared to present the full set of factual bases for risk assessment opinions offered. Correspondingly, the recommendation is made for the full set of factual bases to be included in written reports, including the results found per risk assessment instrument employed.

This proposed set of standards (developed most directly by Cathi Harris from Arizona, Amy Phenix from California, Karen Parker from Florida, Barry Levitt and Phil Riedda from Illinois, Harry Hoberman from Minnesota, Lauretta Walker from Missouri, Joseph Belanger from North Dakota, Roy Luepnitz from Texas, and myself from Wisconsin) was never submitted to any national professional body for consideration as standards to be promoted by the organization.

The reason for this was the expressed fear by representatives of one of the nonparticipating states that any set of standards would become just another tool used by cross-examining attorneys to eviscerate evaluators who employed something other than a standard procedure even for good reason. Lacking a clear consensus to promote the proposed set of standards to a national organization, coupled with the fact that the group of states' representatives did not have a formal organizational leader (i.e., someone in the position to finalize decisions that did not represent consensus), the group lacked the ability to proceed.

Around the same time, the Association for the Treatment of Sexual Abusers (ATSA) assigned the task of reviewing sex offender civil commitment laws and their concomitant evaluation procedures to an internal Policy Committee. After about a year and one-half (David D'Amora, personal communication, September 2000), the Policy Committee finalized its work and presented a draft policy to the ATSA Board of Directors. Just before this book was completed, the board completed soliciting other input concerning the draft policy, and adopted the policy. The segment of the policy pertaining to sex offender civil commitment evaluations, titled "Risk Assessment," is copied below:

The Association for the Treatment of Sexual Abusers recommends that assessments of an individual in a civil commitment proceeding be based on the best available scientific knowledge, including the use of current, validated risk assessment instruments. Professionals performing such evaluations should be well trained, qualified and experienced in the evaluation and treatment of sexual offenders and should follow established ethical and professional guidelines.

To most accurately evaluate the risk of future sexual violence, the evaluator should include the best available actuarial instruments that have been validated as risk predictors for the population to which they will be administered. An actuarial instrument is a system for assessing risk using specific factors, with specific scoring rules, which indicates placement for an individual within a certain risk group. The evaluator's choice of risk assessment instrumentation needs to be reasonably related to the subject and task. No psychological test (e.g., Rorschach Inkblot Test, MMPI, MSI) should be employed specifically for this type of assessment unless scientific evidence of its validity relative to this type of assessment has been established.

The reader may note a strong similarity in the two sets of standards. The changing membership of the ATSA Policy Committee and the members of the ATSA Board of Directors never included any of the state representatives listed for the first set of guidelines. At least some members of the Policy Committee, however, became aware of that earlier proposal before the committee finalized its draft, with that earlier proposal then having some influence on the committee's work.

Besides these two works, one from an international organization, apparently no other national or international organization for mental health professionals has offered anything similar. The American Psychiatric Association has instead taken a rather strong stance against these commitment laws and, in the process, most everything involved with their implementation (Zonana, Abel, Bradford, Hoge, & Metzer, 1999). People willing to conduct commitment evaluations are therefore given no guidance from that organization. The American Psychological Association also has not assisted to any degree, having taken no formal position about any aspect of these laws or their implementation procedures.

All recommendations within this book for evaluative procedures are therefore in keeping with the two sets of national standards described above. Although future sets of standards may contain minor differences from the above, these standards appear to represent the clearest sets of guidelines to date for how sex offender civil commitment evaluations should be performed.

Standard Procedures for Gathering Information

All assessments start through a process of gathering relevant information. The only potential difference between sex offender civil commitment evaluation procedures and other forensic assessments is what constitutes pertinent information. Civil commitment evaluations potentially involve information from throughout the subject's lifetime, from potentially all life spheres, and inclusive potentially even of physiological data along with psychological and sociological facts and figures. To say that "the person's whole life is on trial" during a civil commitment assessment may not be an exaggeration. Although other types of forensic evaluations may use information from the person's early life (such as to score a Psychopathy

Checklist–Revised [PCL–R] for sentencing purposes), court testimony in these civil commitment hearings quite regularly goes into detail about the person's behavior before age 15, the details of his lifelong criminal history, his sexual practices from throughout his life, and so on, far more so than seems to be true for other types of "trials."

With that as a guiding perspective, each of the sections listed below includes recommendations for how to gather and organize subjects' lifetime worth of information, the data necessary for a comprehensive sex offender civil commitment evaluation:

1. Records

2. The clinical interview, including the issue of informed consent and competence to proceed

3. Collateral interviews

4. Physiological assessments

5. Risk assessment instrumentation

6. Psychological tests

7. Professional consultations

Finally, at the end of this chapter is a brief discussion of a few pertinent ethical issues, though the main discussion of ethical matters occurs in Chapter 10.

Records: Paper, Paper, and More Paper

If there is one rule about sex offender civil commitment evaluations no matter the jurisdiction, it is that they involve a lot of records, often with many duplicates of those same records both within any given set and collectively of the complete set. In addition, the simple weight of records for any given case continues to multiply as the case progresses through the commitment process, both through the active pursuit of missing pieces of information by the examiner and through witness depositions caused by the attorneys. With someone's complete life history of potential relevance (to both diagnostic and risk assessment concerns), there seems no reason to decline any document detailing an aspect of the subject's life. None should ever be rejected prior to being reviewed.

On the other hand, as will be discussed in detail in Chapter 5, there are many times when "more" is simply "more." More paper (i.e., more data) does not at all equate with a "better" or "more accurate" clinical assessment (Grove, Zald, Lebow, Snitz, & Nelson, 2000). Conversely, if you are missing a crucial piece of information, the stacks of other documents still can fail in making the assessment "good enough."

Gathering as complete a set of records as possible from which to begin a sex offender civil commitment evaluation can be the most important step an examiner takes. Obtaining all desired records, however, can be problematic. Some records may no longer exist (e.g., juvenile records for an elderly man). Likewise, effective requests for some documents require the subject's signed authorization, a circumstance of little likelihood (except for defense-hired evaluators). Fortunately, the commitment criteria of most of these statutes virtually guarantees that at least one clear set of records should be available (precommitment) for use by evaluators. The subject of these proceedings quite regularly comes from an incarcerated facility. That facility, or set of facilities (such as prisons within a department of corrections; DOC), will have obtained, developed, and maintained a significant and eminently useful set of records concerning each subject potentially or actually referred for commitment. The commitment statutes or other pertinent laws regularly make these records available to court- or statutorily appointed and prosecution-hired evaluators.

Useful records can quite regularly be obtained from a second source, the prosecutors of the subject's past criminal offenses. The information in prosecutor files often overlaps with DOC records, but many times the prosecutors also have documents beyond the DOC set. Such documents may describe details of what a victim claimed, of police investigations, of anticipated witness testimony (through "Minutes of Testimony" documents even in cases where no trial actually occurred), of transcripts of actual testimony including the subject's words at a sentencing hearing, and of the negotiations resulting in plea bargains. People hired by defense attorneys will also potentially have access to files that contain a host of similarly useful information. Defense attorney files may not be available to an examiner hired by a prosecutor or working for a state department, at least without authorization from the subject and attorney.

Despite the best of evaluators' efforts, there are frequently some records not used by evaluators in commitment assessments because they were not obtainable. For instance, mental health and medical treatment records from outside the facility in which the subject has been incarcerated are commonly absent from the documents reviewed by examiners. This is regularly because signed authorization is needed to obtain them and such authorization was not given. A court order can theoretically be used to gain access to otherwise confidential records for the purpose of a civil commitment evaluation, though obtaining a court order for such a purpose does not appear to be common practice.

Some jurisdictions allow relatively easy access to school records, though in other places any type of records from juvenile years can be near impossible to obtain. (The common exception occurs in those states that allow for the commitment of a juvenile, a situation in which many juvenile records systematically become available from the referring facility.) Even with signed authorization, military records are still not easy to acquire, especially within the time frame in which the evaluation report is often needed.

As stated above, sometimes "more" is just "more," and not really of any use. At the same time, it seems important for evaluators to be aware of any shortcomings in their information-gathering process. To avoid potential gaps in what is known about a subject, some evaluators fight to obtain every piece of paper potentially available, from juvenile records to military records to outpatient treatment records. Although such efforts, when described on the witness stand, tend to give a positive impression of the expert's comprehensiveness, it is not clear that some of these hard-to-obtain pieces of information help significantly in the assessment.

Whether someone had a juvenile criminal record or not is typically of importance, especially if any of that criminality was sexual in nature. What grades he obtained in early elementary school, however, is not typically of significance. The subject's early vaccination record is irrelevant. Not every juvenile record offers great potential utility, but some do. With differentiations of this type, the issue for an examiner is how best to concentrate efforts on obtaining the needed information and not waste time gathering relatively useless records.

Most often, the document of great value in regards to juvenile history, military history, and other potentially difficult-to-find pieces of information is the presentence investigation. The detail of what is covered in a presentence investigation varies across jurisdictions and even within jurisdictions across investigators, but those documents typically make statements that at least allow an evaluator to know if there is something more worth searching for in an area or not. For instance, the investigation report may make the blunt statement that the person has no juvenile criminal history, indicating that further pursuit of juvenile records will likely not be worth the effort. Likewise, statements in those reports such as the person received an honorable discharge without any disciplinary actions from his military experience strongly suggest there is not much to pursue further in this regard. Of course, conclusions about the reliability of the recorded information from these reports is left to the user, and the user does need to note from where the presentence writer obtained the information in making reliability conclusions. (Information about the subject's military history may have come solely from the subject's unverified self-report, making the information far more suspect than if it were verified more officially, for instance.) The main point, though, is that some documents are worth fighting for more than others. Access to presentence investigation reports by evaluators varies across jurisdictions, with some jurisdictions allowing easy access and others only allowing access by specific court order. The recommendation is that evaluators attempt to obtain this document in all cases, even if a court order is needed for access.

Organizing the Information

Once evaluators have gathered all of the paper likely to become available, the process of extracting useful information begins. The process of doing this is regularly the most time-consuming segment of a comprehensive sex offender civil commitment evaluation.

Simply reading through the records to glean what they say is rarely effective or appropriate while doing a complete commitment assessment. First of all, the volume of records being reviewed typically prohibits a brief meaningful understanding of how the reported actions, time frames, interventions, relationships, risk factors, protective factors, and the host of other categories of information making up a subject's life affect diagnostic and risk assessment considerations.

Second, evaluators need to be able to testify about their results with supportive detail for all opinions drawn (see proposed standards above), with that testimony oftentimes being months after the assessment was conducted. With numerous intervening evaluations performed, evaluators' memories for these details are not likely to be reliable or complete. Instead, these data need to be retrievable without requiring the repeated review of all documents.

Third, legal proceedings involving the requirement to share one's case notes (i.e., discovery procedures) also mandate that one's thinking about a case be recorded in some fashion that is transferable to a nonclinician. This latter issue, coupled with the need to save records of one's data and conclusions from a case, appears included in the "national standards" above. To accomplish these tasks, evaluators need to spend a very significant portion of their assessment time separating out useful information from the nonuseful, and doing so in a way that organizes and records the data for future reference.

There appear to be three different manners by which this organization is done around the country, all effective relative to the issues enumerated above. The methods are to

1. take extensive notes of the records, as one reviews them;

2. use Post-it notes or similar "bookmarks" with different categorical descriptive labels, and keep all relevant pages in some organized way; and/or

3. record all relevant information and its source(s) in the body of the evaluation final report.

Each of these methods has its pros and cons, and each can be effective, as described in the next few paragraphs.

The first procedure, taking extensive notes as one goes through the pile of documents, is one of the more time-consuming methods listed. When using this style of records review, the examiner transcribes material by quoting it (or electronically scanning it) into a template used for organizing the information into pertinent categories. For instance, a police investigation report may contain numerous statements by an interviewed victim that the examiner then quotes in a "Legal History" section of the informational or organizational template. Official legal charges would also be recorded (such as from a Presentence Investigation Report) under the same organizational rubric. Data concerning the subject's alcohol abuse history, however, would be recorded in a separate section titled something like "Substance Abuse History." With a predetermined set of categories serving as the organizational tool, the evaluator goes through the complete set of documents recording all information considered potentially useful. Suggested rubrics for such a template are as follows:

1. Demographics,

2. Legal History (including both charged and uncharged offenses),

3. Institutional Adjustment,

4. Supervised Release Experience,

5. Employment,

6. Substance Use/Abuse,

7. General Diagnostic Information,

8. Treatment Participation and Benefit,

9. Aftercare Plans, and

10. Risk Assessment Instrumentation Information.

Recommended to be included in the process of recording information is the source for that information (e.g., "1982 Presentence Investigation," "2/4/95 Admission Psychological Report"). This can be accomplished by recording the document as you go, by making a master list of sources you number and then use just the numbers in your notes (including potentially Bates stamped numbers, if the records you are reviewing were previously stamped in this fashion. Bates stamps are a consecutive set of numbers for the purpose of indicating what documents exist relevant to a legal proceeding; these numbers commonly are stamped by an attorney for discovery purposes), or by using an Excel format in your computerized note taking, such that you type in the name and date of the document only once, and then copy the information where you need to elsewhere in your note file.

However you accomplish this lengthy process, the subject's pertinent life history is recorded in a rather comprehensive and categorized way. Recommended as well is that this process include (1) chronological ordering of entries per category, so as to make reviewing of the person's life history in any given area all the easier and more meaningful, and (2) multiple entries of any information under different rubrics that pertain to more than one area. All of this organization can facilitate a very effective experience on the witness stand, given that virtually any important information becomes readily retrievable within moments. Examiners need not spend time looking through pages and pages of records to find the answer to questions involving detail.

This organizational process takes a lot of time. To its credit, however, the evaluator has everything summarized at a glance, with this information ready for easy retrieval no matter how lengthy the postponement of anticipated court procedures. Once information is compiled in this way, diagnostic and risk assessment procedures also follow rather easily to the extent that the case materials allow them.

The second procedure, that of using labeled Post-it notes or bookmarks within the stack of records, avoids the extensive note taking described above. This informational sorting method is the most rapid process among the three. Evaluators can potentially write only a relatively small set of notes as they go through the records, instead marking where types of information can be found at some later date. When the evaluator then needs to summarize the existing information of one type, the examiner looks through each document labeled as containing information of that category.

The pros to this approach certainly include the relative quickness in which records can be reviewed and assessments can therefore be conducted. A relative weakness to this approach is that the lack of enumerated information supportive to one's opinions means a potentially more awkward and less professional appearance when testifying as one flips through a large stack of pages trying to find the supportive sources.

The third method, using one's report to summarize all relevant information, can actually be done separately from the above procedures, or coupled with either one. When done independently, the evaluator goes through records essentially with an accompanying final report template. As potentially pertinent information is found in documents, the evaluator records the findings (initially in general ways) parenthetically along with its source document name and date under the rubric of relevance in the report. When all documents have been reviewed using this procedure, the report is organized to read more coherently, resulting in an organized summary of the records. Rubrics such as "Social History," "Legal History," "Treatment Participation," "Other Diagnostic Considerations," and "Risk Considerations" can serve to facilitate the recording of information into meaningful sections. (See Chapter 8 for details of suggested report organization and content.) The report is not written into final form, of course, until all other information is gathered, such as from the interviews of the subject and collateral individuals.

The advantages of this approach are that it both summarizes information and facilitates the simultaneous writing of a final report. This organization is also quite useful on the witness stand. The downside to this approach includes that these reports tend to be quite lengthy, in a way that attorneys, judges, and other readers find tedious and too detailed. In addition, as will be described in Chapter 8, submitting a report with so much detail can actually open the door for a more problematic set of cross-examination questions about all of the different points made or alleged. Each statement of fact and allegation can become the subject of questioning point by point, ultimately leading to a good deal of obfuscation of what the truly important points were among the other life details.

As mentioned, these three different approaches to organizing assessment information are not mutually exclusive. In addition, which one is superior to the other can depend on the circumstances, priorities, and memory skills of the evaluator. Hence, no specific recommendation for one procedure over another is made here, except to emphasize the initial statement that true shortcuts are usually not worth taking.

The Clinical Interview

Within the ethical guidelines for both psychologists and psychiatrists is the idea that all assessments must involve at least the offer to the subject of an evaluation interview. (This ethical point and the potential issues that arise if the subject turns down the offer are discussed in Chapter 9. In this chapter, the assumption will be made that an interview was offered to and accepted by the evaluation subject.) This section describes aspects of the interviewing process of special significance within sex offender civil commitment evaluations.

Timing of the Interview

The recommendation is strongly made here that interviews occur only after the examiner has reviewed at least virtually all relevant documents. This may not be an evaluator's normal method of doing clinical interviews. In fact, under other circumstances, the argument can be made that an interview should be conducted before any documents have been reviewed, to ensure that the examiner obtains a "fresh" impression of the subject that is "untainted" by what other people have written. Within the context of sex offender civil commitment evaluations, however, this trust in the utility and accuracy of our clinical impression is very significantly misguided.

There are three reasons behind this statement. First, for an examiner to find out the details of the person's thinking, feeling, and behaviors relative to his historical sexual offending, the evaluator needs to know what has been reported about the person. Depending on the subject to tell us all of those details for each and every crime alleged about him without our asking the comprehensive set of questions is a foolhardy endeavor. Issues of memory, willingness to talk about embarrassing events, and straightforward deception all come into play even during the best of interviews. Without the evaluator having a complete idea of what others have recorded about the subject, the interview is very unlikely to produce much useful information while still giving the impression of having been fruitful due to the examiner's ignorance of topics not covered well enough.

The second reason for the recommendation is that too strong a reliance on our impressions of an individual without grounding in factual history leaves us open to being most positively influenced by the person's abilities to convince us of characteristics he actually lacks. If we are not sufficiently prepared, we can more easily perceive sincerity, empathy, remorse, and the like where they do not exist, simply because the person is practiced in feigning those presentations. The fact is that the set of people who become subjects of these commitment evaluations includes significant numbers of highly psychopathic individuals. If an evaluator assumes he or she has the "natural" clinical skill to detect deception of this type without being grounded in the subject's factual history, that examiner is likely to fall prey to that deception rather regularly. Of course, if the evaluator fights against that fault by regularly viewing a great many characteristics of subjects' interview behaviors as signaling deception, then that bias will also be faulty. This whole problem can be minimized by knowing the person's recorded history well before entering the interview room.

Finally, though probably foremost, research results suggest a third rationale for the above recommendation. There is reason to believe that clinical interview information can actually detract from the accuracy of our final risk assessments (e.g., Grove et al., 2000), at least as compared to judgments made without such information. Given that the interview portion of risk assessment procedures may actually be their weakest link, it seems clear that evaluators should not deliberately increase the subjectivity or randomness of the information gathered through the interview by not having a well-informed life history of the individual first.

Informed Consent

Under general circumstances, clinicians begin an evaluation interview with an attempt to obtain what is typically termed "informed consent." The actual parameters of what is meant and practiced here may differ across situations and clinicians, but the common concept is that the subject has come to understand (1) the purpose of the interview and (2) the potential risks and benefits to participating in the interview and (3) has made a reasoned decision to participate. Examiners go through a process of obtaining informed consent before clinical interviews for both ethical and legalistic reasons. Under most sex offender civil commitment evaluation circumstances, the issue of informed consent is not different, though there may be an exception.

First, to explain that difference, the sex offender civil commitment informed consent process needs to be detailed. This is most often done both orally and in writing. Before any interview questions are asked, the examiner orally presents information intended to inform the subject of needed details upon which the subject can meaningfully make a decision between participating or not. Recommended components of that oral presentation include the following:

1. The purpose of the interview, that is, being part of a larger assessment of the subject as concerns his possible sex offender civil commitment

2. What a sex offender civil commitment potentially entails in the relevant state

3. The professional status of the evaluator and who the evaluator is working for (potentially including a statement that the evaluator is not working either for the subject or against the subject)

4. That the person has a right to participate in the interview and a right not to do so (There are some places where the person may be required to participate by court order. This issue will be addressed later.)

5. That if the person chooses to answer the examiner's questions, the subject still does not have to answer all of the examiner's questions

6. That the person can decide not to answer any of the examiner's questions, but can still choose to tell or show the examiner whatever the person wishes while the examiner simply listens and takes notes

7. That no matter to what degree the person chooses to participate in the interview, the examiner will still be writing an evaluation report based on available information and to whom that report will be circulated

8. That anything the person says in talking to the examiner should not be thought of as confidential (unless the examiner is working for a defense attorney, in a circumstance in which the attorney can truly "bury" the examiner's information and findings, and the information shared does not fall under a legal requirement for reporting such as exist in some child abuse reporting laws)

9. That the subject's decision about participating in the interview will not be interpreted as psychologically meaningful (i.e., a decision to decline will not be interpreted as meaning the person is trying to hide something, and a decision to participate will not be interpreted as meaning he was open about himself)

Items 8 and 9 are the ones that, to my knowledge, give evaluators the most trouble.

Concerning no. 8, for instance, the simple act of saying that the interview information is not private does not, in my view, adequately describe the more than occasional experience of subjects of sex offender civil commitment assessments. Evaluators often end up testifying about the commitment assessments. In doing so, the examiners quite frequently refer to comments the person made during his interview. The fact is that virtually anyone can be sitting in the courtroom during such testimony, including representatives of the media who can then print and broadcast reports of what the subject said during his interview. This possible eventuality goes way beyond what most people think of when simply told by an evaluator, "This is not confidential." The same is true relative to the fact that the subject's family members, victims, parole officer, and other people of significance can be listening in the courtroom as well. To obtain truly informed consent, the recommendation is made that evaluators spend some time describing this potential eventuality, even if the examiner is afraid that the subject would decline the interview when the lack of privacy is truly explicated (a reason I have heard for avoiding offering this type of information). Balancing this full disclosure about the lack of confidentiality by the examiner can also be statements that the person's life history details are likely to come out in the courtroom anyway. The subject may prefer to take the opportunity to describe his viewpoints instead of letting others speak for him.

Item 9 above actually contrasts with how some evaluators practice. Some examiners believe it is appropriate to interpret a subject's participation decision as psychologically meaningful, especially if the person has not obtained advice from an attorney about what to do (and therefore the decision was truly the subject's, and not reflective of legal advice).

There are three problems with this latter approach. First, there may very well be psychological meaning behind the decision, but what that meaning is typically remains unknown. If the person declines to participate, how do we know that he is trying to avoid disclosure, versus (1) feeling too afraid to face his legal circumstances, (2) lacking understanding of the potential benefits to his participating, (3) acknowledging to himself that there is nothing he can say that differs significantly from what the evaluator already knows from the records (so why spend time confirming those things), (4) following someone else's advice despite his own judgment, (5) being fatalistic about his chances to avoid the negative outcome from the assessment, or (6) reacting to what he perceives as the examiner's desire not to have to do an interview and wishing not to annoy the examiner in order to obtain a better recommendation?

A psychological interpretation of the subject's declining the interview may reflect more of a bias in the examiner than reality in the subject. Likewise, a similar list of possibilities concerning why a person may agree to participating in an interview can be constructed, again showing the impropriety of making psychological attributions to this decision.

Second, some subjects have conferred with their attorneys with the result of obtaining a recommendation about interview participation. The subject may decide to follow that advice simply with the logic that the attorney knows more about these kinds of things than does the subject. There may actually be things the subject would like to tell the evaluator that do not get said due to legal advice. This will remain unknown to the evaluator who simply hears that the subject declines the interview.

Finally, the practice in some courts is not to permit any testimony by evaluators stating that the person declined participating in the assessment interview. The stated rationale by judges making such rulings is that the information is more prejudicial than probative for the jury to hear (when a jury is involved). If the evaluator cannot even testify that the person declined an interview, what does the evaluator do with the fact that this was considered an important piece of information in deriving the expert's opinions?

In light of these considerations, evaluators are encouraged not to make psychological interpretations of subject's decisions about interview participation. Once avoiding such interpretations becomes the standard for one's practice, then informing the subject of this fact becomes a natural part of the informed consent process. In that way, the subject is at least being told that he should not be considering that factor in his participation decision.

After the oral presentation concerning informed consent issues, it is recommended that evaluators present all subjects (who are able to read) a copy of an informed consent form that reiterates these same points. At the bottom of the form, there should be a space for the signatures of the subject and the examiner, along with the current date. The suggestion is made that evaluators attempt to obtain subjects' consent in writing before proceeding with the interview (and then co-sign as having witnessed the signature). This signature can go a long way in the courtroom when the subject claims you never told him all the things you did, or if he declined the interview, that you never even offered him an interview (both of these concerns not being hypothetical examples to me). Finally, although the examiner keeps the signed copy of the informed consent form, the evaluator might also consider giving a blank copy to the subject for his own records of what he signed.

An example of an informed consent form is available in Appendix B. This portrayal is not meant to represent the only style for such a form, but is simply to facilitate an examiner's development and use of such a form without "reinventing the wheel."

The Issue of Competence to Proceed

In some states, the process described above for informed consent may not be totally sufficient. For those states, there exists a need for the person to be competent potentially to give consent and, potentially separately, to proceed in the legal process. These types of competence exist despite the fact that the potential commitment is involuntary and entails a type of impaired mental functioning.

Which states actually have laws that include these issues of competence is beyond me to say. Such laws clearly exist in Illinois and Wisconsin, where the sex offender civil commitment statutes plainly give respondents (to a commitment petition) what is referred to as "all constitutional rights available to a defendant in a criminal proceeding." Competence to proceed is a criminal defendant right in both of these jurisdictions, such that evaluators should be cognizant that an interviewee may need to be competent before an interview proceeds. The legal meaningfulness of this concept may be more of an open question in other states. For instance, North Dakota's law makes reference to "the respondent's guardian" in one section (Chapter 25-03.3-10), possibly referring to an earlier section describing procedures for a minor "who is a witness or otherwise involved in the proceeding," thereby potentially including the respondent.

Conversely, numerous states specifically allow for the civil commitment of someone who has already been adjudicated incompetent to proceed to trial under one specific circumstance. That situation must involve a relevant sexual charge given a court has also ruled, concomitantly or independently, that it is beyond reasonable doubt that the person committed the underlying criminal sexual act (e.g., Arizona, Kansas). In these jurisdictions and under at least this circumstance, a respondent's competence does not appear to be a relevant issue.

Finally, there is what the laws state, and then there is the evaluator's ethical issue. Should one proceed with an interview knowing full well that the subject clearly lacks an understanding of his legal situation, of what is happening to him, and the potential costs (and benefits) to him for what he might say? The law may allow it, but our professional ethics may have something more to say on the matter. This issue is discussed further in Chapter 9.

Contents of the Interview

Delineating all of the details of good interviewing technique is beyond the scope of this book. The material covered in this section solely pertains to the recommended content for sex offender civil commitment assessment interviews.

One way to conceptualize the required content for interview questions is to view the desired end product of knowledge from the interview. There are basically four components to that end product:

1. Verification (and lack thereof) of the information previously gleaned from documents and collateral interviews

2. Evaluative information concerning what the person gained from previous treatment

3. Scoring of risk assessment instruments and psychological tests

4. Current emotional and cognitive functioning (a category that may or may not be subsumed in Categories 1 and 3)

The evaluator uses information of the first (and last) kind(s) ultimately to determine diagnoses. Categories 2 and 3 (excluding some psychological tests) pertain most specifically to the risk assessment portion of the evaluation. Because current risk assessment instruments are heavily weighted toward documented historical—versus interview—data, the interview questioning format does not typically affect this category much (though there are categories where self-reported information matters). Likewise, any paper-and-pencil psychological testing can be administered irrelevant of the interview structure, so the topic of psychological tests is addressed below as a separate topic (except the PCL–R, which is discussed in this section). That leaves Categories 1 and 2 from the above list as relevant for choosing one's interview format.

Imposing some degree of structure to one's interview ensures covering the needed topics. There are different structures an evaluator can use.

One is simply to go through the informational categories of one's notes (if one used a note-taking structure that allows this). In other words, the evaluator starts with a rubric such as "Legal History" and asks details about each and every entry under that heading. When this topic is covered, questioning is done in the second category, and so on. This is a very direct method for ensuring that the respondent has had a chance to verify or disagree with any significant piece of information obtained from his records. The potential problem with solely using this approach is that areas beyond the subject's records may not be covered.

A different approach is to employ a structure from more general use, but one that also seems to apply well under these circumstances. Such an example is the semistructured interview for the PCL–R (Hare, 1991). Given that this interviewing structure pertains to a psychological test that both is useful for sex offender civil commitment evaluations (both diagnostically and in the risk assessment) and is more generally based in work with criminal populations, this structure is highly recommended as one evaluators consider.

This structure emphasizes the person's criminal history, interpersonal relationships, degree and types of violence, and emotional life, all areas of potential relevance to a commitment assessment. The PCL–R interview alone, however, does not contain questions specific to sexual history beyond some basic details. Evaluators employing this interview structure might consider adding questions about paraphiliac interests and practices. A skilled examiner using the PCL–R structure will also need to interweave questions to verify documented history beyond what the interview structure might otherwise entail, though the interview's "semistructured" format actually allows this without great efforts.

In addition, general interview structures do not cover the detailed assessment of a person's treatment benefit. Hence, adding a second structure to the first, one designed specifically for this purpose, seems wise. One suggestion in this regard is the Relapse Prevention Interview (R. Beckett, D. Fisher, R. Mann, and D. Thornton, as described in Eldridge, 1998; see Appendix A). This 19-item (numbered 1a-10b) interview delves into the details of how the offender understands his offense cycle, how he might intervene in that cycle in the future, and what steps he has taken to ensure that such interventions take place. These items can be used with people who have gone through treatment as well as those who have not, as there is no specific reference to treatment programming. Hence, this interview structure can be used with all civil commitment subjects.

If you are working in a setting in which you can obtain both pre- and posttreatment (or current within-treatment) measures, another format presents itself. The structure of a risk assessment instrument called the Violence Risk Scale–Sex Offender (VRS–SO; Wong, Olver, Wilde, Nicholaichuk, & Gordon, 2000) includes many such items. The benefit of using this structure is that research has been conducted supportive to the predictive validity of the change scores from these items, at least as far as short-term violent recidivism is concerned. Although the outcome of violent recidivism is not of specific interest compared with the commitment criteria (involving sexual violence, not general violence), the fact that research exists concerning the meaning of this type of information at all is a plus.

Recording the Subject's Responses

Many evaluators record interview responses on pages of notes separate from everything else. There is nothing wrong with this. A different approach to be considered is to record the interview responses in between the evaluator's notes taken from the documents reviewed, with interview answers being recorded under each rubric of relevance. For instance, when legal history matters are being discussed, the subject's descriptions of what transpired can be recorded immediately beneath the documented history. If the interviewer is using a computer to record the responses, ease at differentiating the interview information from the documented data can be facilitated through the use of italics for all interview information. By recording everything within its own category as one goes through the interview, integrating this information with the documented history in one's assessment, report, and testimony becomes very easy.

Collateral Interviews

Gathering information from people familiar with the evaluation subject is useful, to a point. Commonly contacted people within sex offender civil commitment evaluations are treatment staff, community supervision agents (such as parole and probation agents), and previous evaluators. Less common are the subject's family members, sex partners, and ex-lovers. Rarely are the subject's victims contacted.

Sometimes one or more of these people have invaluable information. At other times, the information obtained is too tainted with bias to be useful. Although the general recommendation is made that evaluators consider collateral interviewing in all of their cases, there are times when the credibility of such information may be discounted before it is even obtained. For example, the offender's brother who was convicted as an accomplice to sexual offending, but who has always denied any involvement in such crimes, is likely to offer little that the evaluator can take as truthful. If he denies that the evaluation subject ever did anything wrong, the examiner would likely find that information as not meaningful. If the brother goes to the other extreme, and paints the picture that the subject was involved in lots of criminal behavior (while continuing to deny any such behavior himself), and thereby paints himself as an innocent victim, this, too, will not likely be found meaningful.

Finally, if the brother states that, yes, his brother was generally a good guy, but he did this one crime, what meaning is that going to have? In an a priori knowable way, some informational sources can be discounted even before contact is made.

The most valuable information, from any collateral source, is factual and behavioral in nature, versus impressionistic. If the person can tell you facts and specific behaviors by the subject, this information can fill in gaps for both diagnostic and risk assessment concerns. This is especially true if one can obtain a second source (including the subject himself, during his interview) of the veracity of the report. For this reason, the recommendation is made that collateral interviewing be done before the subject's interview.

On the other hand, there are circumstances when this chronological ordering will not occur despite one's best efforts. The subject's early behavioral history, for instance, is often not well recorded in documents available to the evaluator, but can sometimes be obtained through collateral interviews and then used to document diagnostic criteria (such as the before-age-15 behaviors for antisocial personality disorder), psychological test scoring (such as on the PCL–R), and risk assessment instrumentation scoring.

Certain diagnostic information may best be investigated through interviewing the subject's sexual partners (e.g., wife, ex-wife, ex-live in). The subject's paraphiliac behaviors, for instance, may be well-known to these people. Sexually sadistic behaviors fall into this category, where the ex-partners may have been regularly required to participate in scripts of painful, humiliating, and/or injurious sexual practices.

Interviews with supervising agents can result in a great deal of information about how the subject interacts with authority and rules; his willingness to state lies, deceive, and manipulate; and his general aggressiveness in settings beyond the incarcerated (i.e., the one in which the assessment may be occurring).

Problems can develop quickly in trying to use impressionistic (vs. factual and behavioral) information. Family members may be sugarcoating what they portray out of loyalty to the subject. Conversely, they may see the subject as the cause of all of their problems in life, and wish him harm. Treatment personnel can (and often do) show the same extremes, from thinking that their efforts have had enormous positive effect to perceiving the person as the devil incarnate. Under many circumstances, extreme impressions may reflect at least as much about the people reporting them as they do about the subject himself. Of course, when the reported impressions reflect accurately about the subject and when they do not can be a very problematic differentiation for the evaluator. That difficulty suggests that evaluators should not put much trust in unverified information of this type when anything more reliable is available.

Although the topic of conducting the risk assessment will be addressed in later chapters, there are a couple of related points to be mentioned here. The above caveat about not paying much attention to other people's impressions has an empirical basis within the context of a risk assessment. Treatment personnel, for instance, quite regularly develop and report impressions about subjects' treatment progress, but the impressions even among trained staff and even when solicited in a structured way may be poorly related to actual recidivist outcomes (e.g., Seto & Barbaree, 1999).

Apparently, people's impressions are unduly influenced by apparent "honesty," suggestions of remorse, and so on, when in fact these impressions (whether accurate or not concerning the issue of honesty or remorse) are not related to actual recidivism. This may be all the more true when the subjects are even relatively psychopathic (i.e., not necessarily fully psychopathic as defined by the PCL–R) (Marquis, Abracen, & Looman, 2001).

Evaluators probably need to remember the above facts when it comes to their own interview impressions. Examiners looking for signs of remorse, truthfulness, and so forth during interviews may simply be setting themselves up to be influenced by impressions that are, at best, not related to recidivism risk (Grove et al., 2000).

Physiological Assessments

Some evaluators employ procedures to obtain more objective data (i.e., beyond people's reports) through the use of physiological measurements of the subject. There are currently three options in this regard: (1) the penile plethysmograph (PPG), (2) the Abel's Assessment of Sexual Interests (ASI), and (3) the polygraph.

The PPG is a device designed to assess a subject's sexual interests through direct measurement of penile reactions while the person is watching and/or listening to a set of stimuli. The potential utility of PPG results is in both the diagnostic and risk assessment portions of the evaluation. Deviant sexual interests can be interpreted as clear support for a paraphiliac diagnosis. Likewise, based on the meta-analytic results from Hanson and Bussière (1998) and the research by Rice and Harris (1997), there seems significant reason to believe that deviant PPG results are meaningful when assessing the risk for sexual recidivism. This latter use is discussed in more detail in Chapter 7. (For a far more comprehensive discussion about the validity and reliability of the PPG, see Harris, Rice, Quinsey, Chaplin, & Earls, 1992.)

The ASI, or Abel Screen as it is sometimes called, represents an alternative method to the PPG (and self-reports) for assessing someone's sexual interests. The subject looks at certain pictorial stimuli while the device measures the relative degree of time the person spends glancing at certain aspects of those pictures. Relative differences in these times is interpreted to mean relative differences in (and absolute degrees of) sexual interest. The ASI is rarely used in sex offender civil commitment assessments, and then typically along with, rather than instead of, the PPG. (This information is known from personal communications in 1999 and 2000 with Timothy App, Joseph Belanger, Timothy Budz, George Bukowski, Austin DesLauriers, Richard Gowdy, Steven Gray, Harry Hoberman, Stephen Huot, Geoffrey McKee, Gene Messer, Marie Molett, Karen Parker, Joanne Roux, Robert Wheeler, Phillip Witt, and others.) Two factors combine to cause this paucity of use: (1) expense and (2) lack of research indicating its predictive value (Sachsenmaier & Peters, in press).

The third physiological instrument is the polygraph. Polygraphs are also rarely administered specifically within sex offender civil commitment evaluations, though examiners seem quite willing to use the results from such testing if found among the documents reviewed (the same series of personal communications from 1999 and 2000 listed in the prior paragraph). The actual utility of polygraph assessments for civil commitment evaluators is not so much the demonstration of honesty versus deception, but in the contents of the pre- and posttesting interviews of the subjects. It is during those interviews that many subjects disclose information not otherwise recorded.

At the time this book was written, a vast majority of pretrial civil commitment evaluations did not employ any physiological assessment or even an attempt in this regard (Doren, 1999b). The reasons for this are likely multiple, and probably include a view of lack of utility, expense, and the general lack of easy availability.

The postcommitment reexamination assessment process appears to differ in this regard, however. PPG assessments are relatively common within the commitment treatment programs, such that reexaminers often have such data available. Polygraph assessments seem to be becoming more widely used within those programs as well (e.g., in Wisconsin's curriculum, where it is employed as one measure of the person's readiness for certain treatment programming). Because reexaminers are not typically barred from reviewing any treatment information, polygraph results are sometimes available for, and used in, postcommitment evaluations.

Risk Assessment Instrumentation

The two sets of proposed national standards quoted at the beginning of this chapter both make mention that the use of actuarial risk assessment instruments is expected in sex offender civil commitment evaluations unless there is an empirically based reason against their use in a specific case. Such reasons include (1) a type of subject who is a member of a large class to which the application of the instruments has never been researched (e.g., female sex offenders, very young offenders) and (2) a type of subject who belongs to a very small subset of sex offenders where there is also empirical reason to believe that category of offenders has different characteristics indicating risk as compared to the more typical sex offenders (e.g., sexual sadists, especially who have killed victims; Grubin, 1994; Warren, Hazelwood, & Dietz, 1996). Besides these types of special cases, the proposed standards seem to be quite clear in their intention.

The details of what instruments exist, how to choose from among them, their validity, and so on will be discussed in Chapter 5. Let it suffice here to say that evaluators should expect to gather the information necessary to score the selected instruments as part of the procedures delineated above.

Psychological Tests

Most psychologists spent a great deal of time in graduate school and during internship learning the tools of the trade that most distinguish psychologists from other mental health professionals: psychological tests. The fact is, however, that in virtually all cases, psychological tests fail to show a research-supported relationship to sexual recidivism (e.g., Hanson & Bussière, 1998). There are only two known exceptions to this (beyond the PPG). One has been mentioned before, the PCL–R. This test, scored by the evaluator without handing anything over to the subject for his responses, has consistently shown predictive value for general violent recidivism (e.g., Dempster, 1999), and sexual recidivism more particularly (e.g., Rice, Harris, & Quinsey, 1990; Rice, Quinsey, & Harris, 1991).

The second psychological test of potential predictive utility is the Minnesota Multiphasic Personality Inventory (MMPI; Hathaway & McKinley, 1983), but this statement is made with caveats. In actuality, there is only evidence that two scales may be of use in this regard, Scales 4 and 5 (Hanson & Bussière, 1998). Scale 4 was found to show statistical significance in their meta-analysis, but not to a degree that is clinically meaningful. Scale 5's empirical results were found somewhat more impressive, but the number of relevant studies and sample sizes has been minimal (i.e., three studies involving a total of 239 subjects). Finally, given that (1) the MMPI is a rather lengthy test to use only to extract one or two scale scores, and (2) there are no clear guidelines for interpreting what scores on either scale equate to what degree of sexual recidivism risk, there seems little reason to use the MMPI as part of the risk assessment in a sex offender civil commitment evaluation.

Evaluators are not, of course, precluded from using any variety of psychological tests to assist in the examination's diagnostic segment. Extrapolating beyond the diagnostic process to employing psychological test results (beyond the PCL–R and certain scales of the MMPI) within the risk assessment, however, is strongly discouraged. Evaluators may be tempted by "theorized" relationships between certain psychological variables (e.g., depression, substance abuse history) and a subject's sexual recidivism likelihood, but empirical results do not support the predictive application of psychometric variables in support of such theories.

Professional Consultations

Once all case data gathering has been completed, there is still one more source of information of potential utility: the professional consultation. Unlike the earlier stages of data gathering, this procedure is designed to ensure that the examiner's interpretation of those data has been accurate.

Professional consultations can be very brief or in great detail. The real point of a consultation is to assist the evaluator in looking at the existing data appropriately. Issues discussed with another professional can therefore surround legal matters (i.e., the interpretation of statutory language), diagnostic issues, and/or risk assessment concerns.

Selection of the professional with whom to consult matters. Obviously, the more experienced with the relevant issue, the better. Other considerations exist, however, such as any known biases the person may have (e.g., diagnosing sexual sadism far more frequently than others doing the same work under the same circumstances; strong avoidance to finding that commitment criteria are met even when most everyone else agrees the criteria are met).

The information shared during a professional consultation can also affect the conference outcome with the best of consultants. If one feels particularly uncertain about what information may be relevant to share and what may not, the evaluator may wish to do the consultation in writing (which happens naturally if done by e-mail) so as to preserve for the record what information actually was transmitted within the consultation. In that way, later determinations of what may have been important can be compared with what was actually communicated.

The evaluator may debate about whether or not a professional consultation is always needed. After all, some cases will seem very clearly to fall one way or the other, and concerns about diagnostic and/or risk assessment issues can be quite minor. On the other hand, a professional consultation may fall into the category of something that never hurts, and always is viewed positively by judges and juries.

Ethical Considerations

Not described in this chapter were certain circumstances that could easily raise ethical concerns for an evaluator. For instance, what if the subject turns down the option of being interviewed? Can the evaluation be conducted anyway? What about those times when the courts order the person to participate in the evaluation interview? Are the rules under such circumstances different? Should the evaluator refuse to do such an interview? Finally, what about interviewing a subject's victims, or the victims' family members or therapists? Should not the evaluator attempt to gain the valuable information the victims possess beyond what was recorded in police reports?

These are all very important issues, deserving of ethical consideration. This chapter was devoted purely to how information can be gathered, however, and not the ethical issues that underlie the recommendations. Each of the above ethical concerns is discussed instead in Chapter 9.

Summary Comments

This chapter described the general procedures by which sex offender civil commitment assessments are conducted. The issue of national standards was first reviewed as a guidepost for what evaluators need to do. What records to obtain and how to organize the information available were discussed next. Numerous recommendations and issues concerning the evaluation interview were then delineated. Finally, the issue of what testing should be performed was also covered.

In total, this chapter was meant to give an overall information gathering structure for a sex offender civil commitment assessment. The remainder of this book addresses details of how to analyze the data obtained once the information-gathering process has been completed.

CHAPTER 3

Diagnostic Issues Within Sex Offender Civil Commitment Assessments

Defining Relevant Paraphilias

Who steals my purse steals trash; 'tis something, nothing;
'Twas mine, 'tis his, and has been slave to thousands;
But he that filches from me my good name
Robs me of that which not enriches him,
And makes me poor indeed.

— William Shakespeare

Defending the Labels We Use

Some diagnostic labels that clinicians employ do not seem to diminish the people to whom they are applied. Depression, for instance, tends to elicit more sympathy and understanding from others than a pejorative attribution. The diagnoses common to sex offender civil commitment evaluations are different, however. Paraphilias and personality disorders are often seen as descriptions of how the person is "perverted" or "bad." Adding that issue to the fact that these diagnoses are at the heart of one of the two clinical criteria for commitment, and one can see why these diagnoses can represent areas of strong examination during commitment hearing testimony.

Defending diagnoses from the *Diagnostic and Statistical Manual*, 4th edition (*DSM-IV*; American Psychiatric Association, 1994) in court, even when properly made, is not necessarily an easy task. Consider the following illustrative cross-examination:

Attorney: Doctor, you diagnosed my client as having a paraphilia related to raping, correct?

Witness: Yes.

Attorney: And you supposedly used the *DSM-IV* to make that diagnosis?

Witness: Yes.

Attorney: But there is no paraphilia diagnosis listed in the *DSM-IV* for raping, is there doctor?

Witness: There is, though it is not listed out separately.

Attorney: On what page is it, this paraphilia diagnosis of yours?

Witness: It is not a paraphilia of mine, and it is listed as "Paraphilia Not Otherwise Specified, NOS," on page 532.

Attorney: Well, let's take a look at page 532. It says [quotes the paragraph on NOS]. There is nothing listed saying "rape" or "rape-related" or "nonconsent" there, is there doctor?

Witness: No, there is not, but that list just represents examples, not a comprehensive list; all representing types of paraphilia that are less commonly found than those disorders are listed individually on the earlier pages.

Attorney: So listed disorders such as necrophilia, sex with corpses, and urophilia, sex involving urine, are less common than, say, pedophilia?

Witness: Yes, apparently.

Attorney: A rape-related paraphilia is not even named in this list of less common diagnoses. So a paraphilia related to raping must be even less common than necrophilia and urophilia, right doctor?

Witness: I do not know if that is true.

Attorney: So, to use this category, you could make up anything and call it paraphilia NOS, couldn't you doctor?

Witness: No, it needs to meet the description of a paraphilia, as described on pages 522-523.

Attorney: So now we are going to pages 522-523. [Turns pages.] Okay. This is the main part you mean, where it says "recurrent, intense sexually arousing fantasies, sexual urges, or behaviors generally involving 1) nonhuman objects, 2) the suffering or humiliation of oneself or one's partner, or 3) children or other nonconsenting persons, that occur over a period of at least 6 months," is that correct?

Witness: Yes.

Attorney: Let's explore this a bit shall we. You say you relied on this phrase in defining the paraphilia you gave to my client?

Witness: I used that phrase in a definitional way for the paraphilia your client was diagnosed by me.

Attorney: In your interview with my client, did he tell you anything about his sexual fantasies or sexual urges?

Witness: Yes.

Attorney: Did anything he said in that regard meet this description?

Witness: No. He described only fantasies and urges involving adult consensual sexuality.

Attorney: Did the records you reviewed suggest he has ever said he has other types of sexual fantasies or urges?

Witness: No.

Attorney: So you are now down to the "behavior" component, correct? You diagnosed this disorder just because of your interpretation of his behavior?

Witness: The diagnosis was based solely on his overt recorded behavior.

Attorney: In this list of types of behavior, on page 523, there is nothing that says "rape" or "rape-related," is there doctor?

Witness: The phrase "or other nonconsenting persons" is interpreted that way.

Attorney: Interpreted by whom?

Witness: By me.

Attorney: So now we are back to your diagnosis, and not something listed in the manual, aren't we doctor?

Witness: That is not correct. I have also received training about this interpretation of the manual. I was just being clear in my answer to your last question that the diagnostic process for this respondent within my evaluation of him was my responsibility.

Attorney: I see. I am glad you are taking responsibility for this, given that it is beyond anything the manual says. So, you are saying that you diagnosed a paraphilia based on the parts of this listed phrase, the parts that say "behavior involving . . . nonconsenting persons," is that correct doctor?

Witness: Yes, in part.

Attorney: It seems obvious that all rape, by definition, involves a "nonconsenting" person. So what you are saying is that all rapists have this diagnosis of yours, that the diagnosis you are using is simply a fancy way of saying someone has been convicted of rape; isn't that essentially what you are saying, doctor?

The expert witness' answers above were technically correct, though the impression to the judge and/or jury may still have been that diagnosis offered was anything but soundly based in the *DSM-IV*.

To address situations such as the above, this chapter and the next are designed to explicate relevant definitional and application details of the *DSM-IV* and make recommendations for the practitioner within the context of sex offender civil commitment evaluations. This chapter will cover the issue of why diagnoses need to be made; shortcomings of the *DSM-IV* within the context of sex offender civil commitment evaluations; the issue of criteria versus guidelines; *DSM-IV* definitional problems for *paraphilia*; the diagnosis of *paraphilia, not otherwise specified, nonconsent*; other relevant types of paraphilia NOS; thresholds for diagnosing a paraphilia; and the descriptive language we use.

This chapter and the next assume the reader has both basic diagnostic skills and an understanding of how to employ the *DSM-IV* under general diagnostic circumstances. In addition, these chapters were designed to facilitate responding to direct and cross-examination questions of a very detailed nature. That is why there will sometimes be a lengthy discourse on what may appear to be a minor point. During testimony, when one needs to defend an application of the *DSM-IV*, these issues can feel like anything but minor.

Why Diagnose at All?

Diagnoses generally serve to communicate the existence of a syndrome, or set of symptoms, to another professional. The extrapolation into the forensic arena is not always comfortable or easy, as exemplified above. Should evaluators attempt to make diagnoses knowing that the purpose for doing so is different from the clinically typical one?

A simple answer is that commitment statutes require the determination of whether or not a certain type of mental condition exists in the subject. Psychiatric diagnoses facilitate that determination. In some states, in fact, the commitment criteria specify diagnostic labels with which we are familiar from the *DSM-IV* (e.g., North Dakota; see Chapter 1). In most states, however, the statutory terms do not even resemble *DSM-IV* language. Maybe it would be better in those jurisdictions not to diagnose commitment subjects but only to describe their psychological attributes.

This "safe" position cannot be viewed as meaningful once an evaluator begins testimony, however. Once an evaluator begins to describe a subject's psychological attributes, any attorney can take the evaluator through *DSM-IV* diagnostic criteria, and effectively force a diagnosis to be made or rejected. I have already seen one judge use this technique in dealing with a reluctant expert witness. Avoiding the diagnostic process simply delays the inevitable, if one's work is to be given any credibility in the courtroom at all.

In effect, these laws all specifically *require* that the examiners determine each offender's mental condition related to his sexual offending. (See Chapter 1 for details.) This is as it should be, given that the ostensible purpose for these laws (beyond protection of the public) is to provide treatment for mental conditions that are driving people to reoffend sexually. To address this legal requirement, clinicians quite regularly depend on the *DSM-IV*.

Shortcomings of the *DSM-IV*

The *DSM-IV* clearly serves in the United States as the generally accepted diagnostic manual of psychiatric disorders despite a rare view to the contrary (e.g., Campbell, 1999). Even so, the unfortunate reality is that the *DSM-IV* often leaves the clinician without sufficient guidance for diagnostic situations common to incarcerated sex offenders. As a group, these offenders bring their own unique characteristics and circumstances to diagnostic scrutiny, characteristics that the *DSM-IV* often delineates too ambiguously or not at all.

In addition, clinicians typically have been trained to address diagnostic issues with conceptual, versus semantic, definitional clarity. Within the courtroom setting, however, there is a strong tendency for each diagnostic proclamation to be scrutinized (during cross-examination) using the words from the *DSM-IV* rather than a general conceptualization offered by the clinician. There are basically two ways to address this type of questioning. The first is to stick with the conceptualization model of diagnoses, answering detailed questions of semantics by declining to accept that method for understanding the *DSM-IV*. This issue is discussed in detail below.

The second approach is to know the details of the manual's wording better than the questioner. The former approach has the shortcoming of potentially appearing vague and evasive, as proper as the approach may be from a professional training perspective. The latter is what is more often employed in sex offender civil commitment evaluation work. Even so, one can take the latter approach too far (i.e., be too literal in the semantic interpretation), as discussed in the following section.

The Issue of Criteria Versus Guidelines

One of the major issues in applying the *DSM-IV* to sex offenders is the process of deciding when a relevant set of definitional criteria is met. Clarity and consistency in such thresholds facilitate everything for which the diagnostic process exists, from delineating research samples to designing effective treatment protocols. The diagnostic criteria in the *DSM-IV*, however, apparently do not lend themselves to the implementation of exact definitional standards. The "criteria" are not meant to represent a mechanically applied enumeration of definitional characteristics, as stated in that manual:

> The specific diagnostic criteria included in DSM-IV are meant to serve as guidelines to be informed by clinical judgment and are not meant to be used in a cookbook fashion. For example, the exercise of clinical judgment may justify giving a certain diagnosis to an individual even though the clinical presentation falls just short of meeting the full criteria for the diagnosis as long as the symptoms that are present are persistent and severe. On the other hand, lack of familiarity with DSM-IV or excessively flexible and idiosyncratic application of DSM-IV criteria or conventions substantially reduces its utility as a common language for communication. (p. xxiii)

The need for the application of guidelines, versus strict criteria, can be illustrated with an actual case. The offender was convicted of sexually assaulting five different children orally, vaginally, and anally on a repetitive basis for "only" 5 consecutive months. The diagnostic criteria for *pedophilia* include that the fantasies, urges, and/or behavior need to have occurred for "at least 6 months." This perpetrator never acknowledged sexual fantasies or urges involving sexual contact with children, though he did plead guilty to the multiple criminal charges stemming from his conduct. His having been arrested after a reported 5-month period of offending interrupted his ability to continue to enact sexual behaviors with minors beyond the manual's 6-month threshold. There was apparently no other reason for his terminating such behavior, as there was no suggestion he was stopping or even slowing down on his own. This man's twice-weekly offenses over the 5-month period were viewed as falling sufficiently into the category of "persistent and severe" so as to represent a paraphilia despite the criteria of "at least 6 months."

As the *DSM-IV* states, clinicians need to use this license for going beyond the enumerated characteristics for a diagnosis quite carefully. Hunches and guesses do not belong in the final determination of diagnostic formulations, no matter how strongly one "feels" one is right, especially in the serious realm of sex offender civil commitments.

DSM-IV Definitional Problems for Paraphilia

To understand the problems inherent to the application of paraphilia diagnoses within sex offender civil commitment assessments, one needs first to become aware of the details of the *DSM-IV*'s set of definitional characteristics. There are four different segments of the diagnostic manual's definition of paraphilia. Each of these definitional aspects can be problematic when applied to sex offenders under commitment circumstances. The phrases include

1. the initial definitional segment "recurrent, intense sexually arousing fantasies, sexual urges, or behaviors" (American Psychiatric Association, 1994, p. 522);

2. the second segment, "generally involving 1) nonhuman objects, 2) the suffering or humiliation of oneself or one's partner, or 3) children or other nonconsenting persons" (pp. 522-523);

3. the third factor, that these things have occurred "over a period of at least 6 months" (p. 523); and

4. the last consideration, that "the behavior, sexual urges, or fantasies cause clinically significant distress or impairment in social, occupational, or other important areas of functioning" (p. 523).

Each of these areas is discussed below in detail. The suggestion is made for readers not interested in more than a global understanding of the potential diagnostic issues that they may wish to be selective in perusing the following discourse. The degree of detail in the following, although viewed as necessary by some readers, may lead others to speculate on whether this writer deserves a *DSM-IV* diagnosis of obsessive-compulsive disorder. In defense, I suggest that it is long experience in court rather than (at least just) personal proclivities that have led me to such a detailed examination of the meaning of specific words within the diagnostic manual.

"Recurrent, intense sexually arousing fantasies, sexual urges, or behaviors . . ."

There appears to be a set of overlapping difficulties inherent in understanding this definitional phrase:

a. What does the phrase "recurrent, intense sexually arousing" modify ("fantasies" only, or "fantasies, sexual urges, or behaviors")?

b. If the answer to "a" includes "behaviors," what does "intense . . . behaviors" mean?

c. If the answer to "a" includes only "fantasies," then what does it mean for "behaviors" to remain without a modifier?

Evaluators need to be clear in their understanding of these issues to answer the detailed, sometimes obfuscating questions of cross-examiners in the courtroom. Otherwise, one's application of the *DSM-IV* can be made to look to have been without sufficient understanding. The credibility of one's testimony goes away quickly under such circumstances.

"Recurrent, intense sexually arousing . . ."

A colleague of mine pursued an answer to the first question by writing to the DSM-IV Sexual Disorders Work Group, because these were the people who originated the phrase (Donald Hands, personal communication, 1997). He obtained two responses from the set of writers, both of which concluded that "recurrent, intense sexually arousing" modifies only the word "fantasies" and not "sexual urges, or behaviors" (Chester W. Schmidt, personal communication, 1997; Thomas N. Wise, personal communication, 1997). This answer addresses the first question above, and nullifies question "b" above as well (concerning what "intense . . . behaviors" would mean). Unfortunately, this "official" response still seems problematic.

If the phrase "recurrent, intense sexually arousing" modifies only the word "fantasies," then the rest of this first segment is the otherwise unmodified ". . . sexual urges, or behaviors." Sexual urges seems clear enough, but what does it mean to leave the word "behaviors" unmodified?

One reasonable way to eliminate this quandary is to interpret the phrase "sexual urges, or behaviors" as "sexual urges or sexual behaviors." By eliminating the comma separating the modifier "sexual" from the word "behaviors," it allows the adjective to modify "behaviors." The new phrase effectively becomes equivalent to "sexual urges and/or behaviors."

This interpretation avoids both problems described above and seems to be the best option available. This solution may seem obvious to some readers. The reader should be aware, however, that the writers of the *DSM* apparently did not intend this reinterpretation. Besides the two writers' statements concerning Dr. Hands's inquiry that specify otherwise, the *DSM-IV* itself repeats the same apparent error later in its text in a different, but even more clear manner. In the phrase "The behavior, sexual urges, or fantasies cause clinically significant distress" (p. 523), the *DSM-IV* quite specifically avoids using the word "sexual" to modify the word "behavior."

Looking for alternative guidance from the rest of the definitional phrase does not facilitate clarification: "(behaviors) generally involving 1) nonhuman objects, 2) suffering or humiliation of oneself or one's partner, or 3) children or other nonconsenting persons." "Behaviors generally involving 1) nonhuman objects" includes actions like hitting a ball with a baseball bat and reading one's mail. Similarly, "behaviors generally involving . . . 2) the suffering or humiliation of oneself or one's partner" includes some altruistic or wartime actions. Likewise, "behaviors generally involving . . . 3) children or other nonconsenting persons" includes general parenting or standard procedures by mental health clinicians with involuntary patients. Clearly, none of these types of behaviors represents a sexual disorder or paraphilia.

If we take these written phrases literally, the *DSM-IV* leaves us in a quandary. The term "behaviors" needs some type of adjective specifying the sexual aspect or intent necessary for a paraphilia. On the other hand, modifying "behaviors" with the word "intense" also leaves the interpretation unclear. There is no clearly appropriate manner to interpret the existing phrases. I conclude that the only reasonable application of the relevant phrase uses "sexual" as a modifier to "behavior," irrelevant of the current wording in the manual.

" . . . Generally involving 1) nonhuman objects, 2) the suffering or humiliation of oneself or one's partner, or 3) children or other nonconsenting persons."

Two of the three components to this phrase can be problematic when applied to sex offenders within the context of a civil commitment assessment. The initial segment, concerning "nonhuman objects," is not typically an issue under these circumstances because fantasies, urges, and behaviors of this type do not fall into the category of what the civil commitment laws describe as sexually violent or sexually predatory offenses. The other two phrases, however, raise important questions.

"The suffering or humiliation of oneself or one's partner . . . "

The most common interpretation of this second component pertains to masochistic or sadistic interests. In some cases, the diagnosis of *sexual sadism*, for instance, based on repetitive behavior alone, is quite straightforward, such as where repetitive sexual torture of victims is found with obvious increases in the offender's sexual arousal.

The issue inherent in this phrase becomes evident when one considers the example of the repetitive rapist (a phrase that may itself be considered as significantly redundant) without obvious signs of torturing coupled with arousal. Rape *victims* quite regularly *experience* suffering and humiliation. Does this mean that virtually all rapists who repeat their offenses over more than a 6-month period are paraphiliacs? Or is the point of this phrase to represent the *desired intention* of the perpetrator? This latter interpretation, although possibly more commonsensical, does not lend itself to simple differentiation of paraphiliacs from nonparaphiliacs.

Clearly, "recurrent, intense sexually arousing fantasies" and "sexual urges" specifically toward raping involve the intention of the perpetrator to inflict physical and/or psychological harm. The inclusion of repetitive "behaviors" of this type in the paraphilia definition, however, blurs this distinction. Repetitive sexual assaults may or may not involve the perpetrator's intention specifically to inflict pain or humiliation. Many rapists do not reportedly see their actions as even constituting rape, no less with the express purpose to inflict pain (Groth & Birnbaum, 1979). Some rapists view their actions as a means of seduction, for instance.

Others simply feel entitled to indulge themselves and do not think about, or care about, the victim's feelings.

On the other hand, some rapists are clearly driven by a desire to inflict pain and injury. Within this last category, there are at least two subtypes: those obtaining sexual arousal from that process and those obtaining only emotional gratification through the physical expression of rage (Prentky & Knight, 1991).

Two case examples demonstrate the potentially independent relationship between victim experience and perpetrator intent inherent in making a paraphiliac diagnosis. The first situation involves

1. the person who only has sexual encounters with other people in a way that those partners experience as consensual,

2. the partners experience no suffering or humiliation, but

3. the person frequently fantasizes that his partners are experiencing such suffering during those sexual encounters in order to increase his sexual arousal, and

4. he experiences emotional distress from that set of fantasies.

This person would not be considered a rapist, but he may very well be viewed as paraphiliac. His internal experience would likely be considered of sufficient relevance irrelevant of the experience of his sexual partners.

In contrast, a second category of circumstances would be the following:

1. the individual's fantasies only involve what he considers consensual sexual encounters with other people, but

2. at least some of his partners experience some type of physical and/or psychological suffering during actual sexual contact,

3. he becomes increasingly aroused sexually through what he experiences as a "seduction process," and

4. he experiences some type of impairment in social functioning because of that repetitive type of sexual contact.

An example of this kind of person is a "date rapist" who views a *repetitive* segment of his sexual encounters simply as part of the "standard dating ritual" where women are supposed to say no but really mean yes and just wish to be "seduced." If he finds that he regularly cannot continue "dating" women he wants to due to his behavior, or if he is eventually arrested and convicted for such a sexual crime, he is experiencing some social impairment caused by his actions. From his internal perspective, he does not see himself as having had the intention specifically of causing psychological or physical suffering to his partners. Yet, besides potentially being convicted as a rapist, he can be viewed as meeting criteria for a *DSM-IV* paraphilia based on his repetitive behaviors and his concomitant sexual arousal. His sexual arousal pattern becomes the telltale sign of a paraphilia *given that it is specifically associated with a "partner's" nonconsensual status.*

To summarize, there are people who fantasize about inflicting suffering to others but do not enact the fantasies, and there are people who use thinking errors to avoid knowing they are inflicting suffering. In neither of these situations does the victim's experience of pain or humiliation become the sole determinant of the existence of a paraphilia in the subject. For a paraphilia to be diagnosed using the phrase "suffering or humiliation of . . . one's partner," there appears to need to exist some connection between that victim's suffering *and* either the intention *or* the arousal of the perpetrator. Of course, the process of obtaining reliable measures during a civil commitment assessment of an offender's intentions and arousal patterns is often problematic.

"Children or other nonconsenting persons . . ."

There are two issues raised by this phrase. The first pertains to the interpretation of the word "children." Different definitions for this word include the following:

1. Anyone under the legal age of consent (e.g., age 15, 16, 17, or 18, depending on jurisdiction)

2. Anyone yet to reach puberty (which the *DSM-IV* operationalizes as "generally age 13 years or younger")

3. Anyone still under the legal guardianship of an adult

These definitions differ in their nature, ranging across (1) legal, (2) biological, and (3) social perspectives. (A fourth alternative, the psychological definition of "children," probably can be viewed as fitting under the second segment of this section's rubric phrase; that is the segment "nonconsenting persons.") When an evaluator is attempting to apply the concept of "children" victims to situations caused by some sex offenders, the different perspectives enumerated can be far more than semantic. Clear contradictions can develop.

For instance, use of the "legal age of consent" interpretation means that any offender who repetitively seeks and/or has sexual contact with underage, postpubescent adolescents (and who suffers emotional distress or social impairment such as imprisonment because of that process) would properly be diagnosed as paraphiliac. Use of the biological definition (i.e., puberty), however, would contradict this conclusion. Similarly, an adult who repetitively seeks sexual contact with underage youngsters who have run away from adult supervision and are prostituting themselves to survive does not meet the third (social) definition, but still meets at least the first (legal), if not also the second (biological) definition. These illustrations are not hypothetical, but represent actual case examples.

Differences in a perpetrator's victims' life circumstances and physical development may be significantly affected by an offender's availability of victims and his assessment of his legal risk more than a clearly intended result stemming from his sexual preference. Apparently, crossover in victim age categories and gender is rather common (Abel, Becker, Cunningham-Rathner, Mittelman, & Rouleau, 1988; Ahlmeyer, English, & Simons, 1998). Making distinctions for diagnostic purposes based on fixed thresholds and concepts concerning what constitutes "children" may therefore be artificial and improper.

Based on this perspective, the recommendation is made that evaluators' interpretation of the word "children" specifically for diagnostic purposes include any of the above. Rather than concentrate on issues of victims' breast or beard development; chronological age relative to legal definitions, which change from jurisdiction to jurisdiction; or the unfortunate circumstances making certain youngsters more vulnerable than others, emphasis should likely be given to the actions of the perpetrator. By using any of the above potential interpretations of "children," evaluators can then take into diagnostic consideration the seemingly critical degree of effort made by an individual to obtain sexual contact with children, and the repetition of such actions.

The second concern within the phrase "children or other nonconsenting persons" is exactly how inclusive is the segment "other nonconsenting persons." Diagnostic categories such as exhibitionism and voyeurism obviously are contained within this category. Their defining criteria specifically include the "use" of "unsuspecting" (and therefore presumably nonconsenting) persons by the paraphiliac individual. But what about the person who repetitively fantasizes about, has urges toward, and overtly enacts rape behaviors? By definition, these fantasies, urges, and behaviors involve nonconsenting persons. Social impairment can easily occur through repetitive acts of this type, such as imprisonment and the loss of opportunities for emotionally intimate relationships. If the fantasies, urges, and behaviors continue for a period beyond 6 months, it would seem that the criteria for a paraphilia pertaining to rape is contained in the *DSM-IV* without being separately delineated in the manual. The issues with such a paraphilia are detailed later in this chapter.

"Over a period of at least 6 months"

This simple phrase involves far more than initially may meet the eye. Consider the following scenario. You are assessing a subject who quite repetitively coerced sexual contacts of almost all types with two stepchildren over a period of 3 months. He was arrested and jailed for a relatively short period of time, but released when the charges were dropped for evidentiary reasons. Upon reentering the home, he goes back to assaulting the children for another 2½ months until he is again arrested. This time he is convicted of one count of sexual abuse involving a child and is incarcerated. Your assessment is occurring during this person's incarceration. Does he meet the "at least 6 months" criterion for pedophilia? The recommended answer is yes, despite the technical details about how best to count "the 6 months."

Situations such as this are not rare among the cases reviewed for potential sex offender civil commitments. The "at least 6 months" fragment of the paraphilia definition seems simply to indicate that the relevant fantasies, urges, and/or behaviors have existed for at least the requisite time period. Upon application to specific case situations where basically only overt behavior is available for the examiner's review, however, the application of this simple interpretation can be tricky.

The following types of situations illustrate the potential issues that can arise:

1. The offender has sexual contact with a child once in January and then again once in September of the same year, versus sexual contact twice per week for that complete time period.

This first example pertains to the issue of what needs to have occurred during a consecutive period of at least 6 months: (1) a simple recurrence of the sexual fantasy, urge, or behavior or (2) a more continual process. This differentiation seems to speak to the strength of the paraphiliac drive and/or the availability of desired sexual partners (whether the child or someone else) more than whether or not this paraphiliac criterion has been met. The "at least 6 months" criterion seems to be met either way.

2. The offender has sexual contact with a child quite repetitively for 5 consecutive months before being arrested and imprisoned, with no known sexually deviant fantasies, urges, or behaviors prior to that time period.

The second example illustrates the potential diagnostic effect of a legally imposed incapacitation from sexual contact with children. Is 5 months of such behavior enough to meet this criterion or is 6 months mandatory despite what would have likely continued into the sixth and seventh months if the perpetrator had not been interrupted? Given the guideline nature of this criterion, this example would appear to meet the diagnostic threshold. (The discussion of various threshold issues occurs later in this chapter.)

3. The offender has sexual contact with a child a few times within the same month before being arrested and incarcerated for 2 years, with such sexual contact again occurring for a month postincarceration before again being arrested.

Third is the example involving (1) the interruption of overt sexual contact with children through incapacitation rather than by the perpetrator's choice, with (2) his choice again being demonstrated upon removal of that incapacitation. The overall time frame is beyond 6 months, but only when the focus is on the total time period involved. The time available to the offender to perpetrate his crimes is far less. Is this differentiation meaningful? The answer is, probably not. The offender is still seeking sexual contact with children with rapidity even when he just experienced significant "social impairment" for the same behavior. It does not make sense to give him "time off" due specifically to the consequences stemming from his paraphiliac behavior. Nor is this different conceptually from Example 1 above.

4. There is evidence of one or two highly ritualized, prolonged, sadistic rapes within a month and no known priors, with consideration of the research-based assumption that sadists tend to have developed their sexual fantasies over extended period of time prior to (and during) their overt behavioral enactment (Warren, Hazelwood, & Dietz, 1996).

Finally, there exists the far thornier issue of "what we know" about certain sex offenders in general as compared to the facts we have for a specific case. Knowledgeable clinicians may be well aware of what research *suggests* is true pertaining to an individual case, but going beyond a "rule out" or "provisional" diagnosis based on general research knowledge can be quite problematic for cases likely to be argued in a court of law. This is not to say it absolutely should not be done, but great care should be exercised in this regard. The diagnostician at least needs to be prepared to present the research supporting the conclusion. On the other hand, I recommend against making very significant assumptions concerning individual cases based solely on some general clinical lore for civil commitment diagnostic purposes.

Paraphilia, Not Otherwise Specified, Nonconsent

This category probably represents the most controversial among the commonly diagnosed conditions within the sex offender civil commitment realm. Although the existence of a paraphilia related to raping is debated by only a few people, issues exist in the lack of enumerated definitional criteria within the *DSM-IV*. These issues are described in detail below.

Demonstrating Its Existence

Clinicians conducting sex offender treatment probably have come upon one or more people who demonstrate all of the criteria for a rape-related paraphilia. These people experience sexual fantasies involving raping someone, feel urges in that direction, and have acted on those fantasies and urges by coercing others into sexual contact. For some of these offenders, these characteristics last for more than 6 months and lead to some obvious social impairment such as repetitive incarcerations.

Likewise, if one looks to potential authorities and research to determine if a rape-related paraphilia exists, these sources are not difficult to find. For instance, Nathaniel McConaghy (1999) states, "It would seem appropriate that rape be classified as an independent paraphilia, and it is discussed here as such." Gene Abel and colleagues listed "rape" as one of many paraphiliac conditions they researched and to which members of their sample acknowledged (Abel, Osborn, & Twigg, 1993). William Marshall and Howard Barbaree (1995) found that 30.8% of their rapist sample showed a deviant penile plethysmographic profile. Richard Laws has testified that "in the field of treating sex offenders, rape is recognized as a paraphilia by most . . . practitioners" (deposition given June 11, 1999, concerning *In re: Commitment of R. S.*, King County, Washington). Fred Berlin and Park Dietz have testified to the same effect (*In re: Commitment of G. T.*, Dane County, Wisconsin, 1997).

If there is no meaningful argument about whether or not there are some rapists who experience a paraphiliac condition specifically related to their sexual assaultiveness, why, then, is there no separately listed paraphilia of this type in the current diagnostic manual?

At least four reasons present themselves:

1. It was not believed that such a condition really exists.

2. There was fear that such an official diagnostic category could lead to widespread use of that diagnosis by rapists in attempts to be found not guilty by reason of insanity for their crimes.

3. There was strong opposition by those espousing a "feminist theory" concerning rape, such that the idea was unacceptable that rape might be associated with a pathological condition (vs. seen as an outgrowth of differential power relationships).

4. There was a desire to avoid naming a condition for some rapists, which might have then implied their having psychiatric/psychological treatment needs that would add competition for limited insurance dollars with existing types of preferred clientele.

Reportedly, the writers of the manual did not seriously debate whether or not the condition exists (Fred Berlin and Park Dietz, separately, in court testimony cited above). There reportedly was clear agreement that such a condition exists. Instead, legal ramifications and political concerns (issues 2 and 3 above) were reportedly given significant weight. In addition, it is not clear to what extent issue influenced the discussion (Park Dietz, personal communication, 1997).

In an attempt to put legal, political, and fiscal concerns aside, the real question that needs to be answered is to what degree there is evidence that demonstrates the existence of a paraphilia exemplified by the repetitive raping of others. Starting with objective data in answering this question seems best.

Such an objective demonstration of this condition potentially could occur with the physiological instrument called the penile plethysmograph (PPG). That tool assesses the degree to which a male is sexually aroused by listening to, looking at, and/or fantasizing about depictions of stimuli of concern (ranging from cooperative adult sexual contact to sexual contact with minors to violence).

In general, PPG physiological findings for rapists are not consistent for all groups of such offenders and under all conditions. One finding is that they do not get "turned on" by the violence depicted in the testing lab, at least not to the point that rapists can be differentiated from nonrapists (e.g., Baxter, Barbaree, & Marshall, 1986; Hall, 1989; Langevin, Paitich, & Russon, 1985). Other research, sometimes using particularly brutal depictions of rape against women, often does show some degree of differentiation between rapists and nonrapists in sexual arousal patterns involving physical violence (e.g., Marshall & Barbaree, 1995; Quinsey, Lalumière, Rice, & Harris, 1995), though not invariably (Eccles, Marshall, & Barbaree, 1994).

Such findings can be interpreted as demonstration of paraphiliac interests in rapists, though the extreme nature of the test stimuli may need to be employed in more PPG labs with replicated results before this interpretation is clear. On the other hand, PPG results showing that rapists demonstrate equal sexual arousal to rape and consensual sex, in contrast to what nonrapist controls show, is not uncommon (e.g., Abel, Barlow, Blanchard, & Guild, 1977; Quinsey & Chaplin, 1984).

Finally, there is the finding, or maybe described interpretation of data, that most rapists at least do not get "turned off" by any violence that accompanies the sexual component of raping, in contrast to what nonrapists show (e.g., Barbaree, Marshall, & Lanthier, 1979).

Overall, these findings suggest that, by using the PPG, men who rape can often, though not invariably, be differentiated from those who do not in either or both of two ways. Some rapists are demonstrably aroused to physical violence against women, in contrast to what nonrapists show. Other rapists may differ "only" through a lack of arousal inhibition to depictions of physical violence, situations in which nonrapists quickly lose their sexual arousal.

There are potentially two relevant diagnostic points to be made from these findings. One is that some rapists do not seem to experience a rape-related paraphilia. They are apparently not specifically aroused by the nonconsensual or violent nature of the interaction. (To draw this conclusion specifically from PPG results, one must assume that PPG data of this type are sufficiently related to the diagnoses of paraphilias, an assumption that is probably not fully correct. There are various reasons why a paraphiliac rapist may not demonstrate his deviant arousal pattern in a PPG: [1] Some people can suppress their deviant arousal on a PPG when they so desire, [2] some people may be so conditioned to pornography involving strongly violent content that the PPG testing stimuli are simply not strong enough to elicit a reaction, and/or [3] the testing situation, by its nature as artificial and full of distractions, may actually interfere with the arousal of some people. On the other hand, a finding of deviant arousal on a PPG occurs despite the countering reasons listed.)

The other diagnostic point is that some rapists clearly do show sexual arousal to violent and nonconsensual interactions. Of course, we do not need to determine that all rapists show arousal to violent or nonconsensual sexual encounters to demonstrate the existence of a rape-related paraphilia. Finding some cases throughout the physiological assessment literature strongly supports the existence of this paraphiliac condition.

Clinical writings on rapists also document some such cases, albeit without the employment of an objective assessment process. For instance, Groth and Birnbaum (1979), in their pivotal book *Men Who Rape*, describe some individuals who acknowledged repetitively sexually fantasizing about, and having desires toward, raping even while these individuals were already incarcerated for such sexual offending.

With such documentation in the professional literature, we need to come back again to the *DSM-IV* and its apparent omission. For whatever reasons, the *DSM-IV* failed to enumerate separately a paraphilia related to raping. Does this mean the *DSM-IV* totally omits such a condition?

No. The *DSM-IV* does include a paraphilia related to rape within its definitional paragraphs. Looking at the definitional phrases already described, we find "recurrent, intense, sexual fantasies, sexual urges, or behaviors generally involving ... nonconsenting persons that occur over a period of at least 6 months ... [and] ... cause clinically significant distress or impairment in social, occupational, or other important areas of functioning" (p. 523). This set of phrases clearly relates to defining characteristics of voyeurism and exhibitionism. The phrases also define a type of "nonconsent," however, that pertains to raping as well.

Exploring the above *DSM-IV* definitional phrase further specifically within the context of a civil commitment assessment, we should take note that evaluators do not typically enjoy the benefit of a fully honest disclosure of the subject's sexual fantasies and urges. Examiners most commonly need to rely on documentation of the subjects' behaviors alone instead. Concentrating on that sole avenue for *applying* the *DSM-IV* definition of paraphilia, the relevant definitional phrase becomes "behaviors generally involving . . . nonconsenting persons that occur over a period of at least 6 months . . . [and] the behavior[s] cause clinically significant distress or impairment in social, occupational, or other important areas of functioning."

The concept of "behaviors generally involving . . . nonconsenting persons" is met by definition of rapists' acts. Similarly, a meaningful degree of persistence of the sexual behavior pattern is typically documented for most rapists coming under a civil commitment assessment. This leaves only the final consideration in question, that of the "clinically significant distress or impairment in social, occupational, or other areas of functioning."

When perpetrators openly describe personal distress over their repetitive sexually assaultive behaviors, criteria for a paraphilia are clearly met. During initial periods of assessment for possible civil commitment (as opposed to during treatment), however, this type of acknowledgment is not likely. Instead, clinicians typically need to rely on the issue of impairment to the offender's functioning caused by his actions. Given that most rapists do not come under the civil commitment diagnostician's scrutiny until already suffering some of that impairment (such as incarceration), there is only one question remaining in this area. Was the offender aware that his "partners" were not consenting and that he was therefore at risk socially, occupationally, and legally?

At least two types of circumstances suggest why this question *may* be of importance. The first involves the rapist who became intoxicated or drugged before he raped. Can he be expected to have been sufficiently aware of the nonconsenting nature of his victim's participation in the sexual contact? If not, then a paraphilia diagnosis based on nonconsensual behavior alone would be inaccurate. On the other hand, the more frequently the offender perpetrated such crimes, the more evidence exists that he has a repetitive desire specifically for nonconsensual sexual contact, despite (and maybe enacted overtly because of) his intoxication.

The second scenario involves the "date rapist." Some of these people apparently do not see their actions as involving an unwilling partner. Intellectualized excuses (e.g., she really wanted intercourse despite saying no) and selective attention (to his wants vs. her expressions of emotional pain) reportedly relieve them of that awareness, even when they rape numerous women over a lengthy period of time. If that reported unawareness is an accurate representation of their experience (and not simply deceptive verbalized portrayals to examiners), can they be said to suffer a rape-related paraphilia? Does their behavior's repetitiveness suffice to suggest a paraphilia, as it would in meeting criteria for pedophilia if their victims were children? The general answer seems to be debatable, though some argument can be made from extrapolation of the PPG research cited above that the answer is in the affirmative. Likewise, caution should be exercised in simply believing offenders' self-reports that they were unaware of their victims' feelings: This type of deception by subjects of a forensic evaluation is quite common. On the other hand, within the world of sex offender civil commitment assessments, where documented clarity is much easier to defend in the courtroom than clinical speculation, making a paraphilia diagnosis under this circumstance is typically not recommended.

Despite the potential arguments to be made about the limits to what we know and the edges or thresholds for where a rape-related paraphilia begins, there does not appear to be a meaningful argument against the idea that at least some rapists clearly meet the *DSM-IV* criteria for a paraphilia. If the offender has repetitively and knowingly enacted sexual contact with nonconsenting persons over a period of at least 6 months (specifically for sexual arousal to the nonconsensual interaction), and that behavior has caused him significant impairment in social, occupational, or other areas of functioning, then criteria for a paraphilia are met.

As stated above, the *DSM-IV* does not offer an individually delineated diagnostic category for that paraphilia. Existing diagnostic categories do not capture the same type of sexual arousal pattern. Sexual sadism, for instance, involves "acts . . . in which the psychological or physical suffering (including humiliation) of the victim *is sexually exciting* to the person" (p. 530, emphasis added). This definition goes beyond what has been described here as pertaining to most rapists. In fact, only about 2% to 5% of incarcerated rapists are sexual sadists (Langevin, 1990). Similarly, frotteurism involves "touching and rubbing against a nonconsenting person" (p. 527), a definition that is clearly insufficient when applied to rapists who force sexual intercourse or other types of penetration onto their victims.

The only *DSM-IV* category that applies is the diagnosis of paraphilia, not otherwise specified (NOS), the category "for coding Paraphilias that do not meet the criteria for any of the specified categories" (p. 532). The usage of paraphilia NOS to define a paraphilia related to raping is in keeping with the conditions dictated (on p. 4) in the *DSM-IV*. Using an NOS category is also considered just as meaningful by the writers of the *DSM-IV* as using any of the individually listed diagnoses (Laurie McQueen, personal communication, September 2000). The only issue in employing this category is one other item mandated by the manual, the differentiation of this specific type of paraphilia from others also listed as NOS.

Some clinicians use the descriptor "rape" after paraphilia NOS to explicate the relevant type of mental disorder. This may be thought of as being borrowed from the older concept of "paraphilic rapism." Other diagnosticians view the proper nomenclature to be the term "nonconsent." Based on the fact that "rape" is a legal term, and "nonconsent" is more psychological in nature, the recommendation is made that only the latter term be used to describe a specific type of paraphilia NOS. The fact that the *DSM-IV* definitional phrase "or other non-consenting persons" includes this same descriptive term also suggests its appropriateness.

Determining Paraphilia NOS, Nonconsent From Overt Behavior Alone

As described above, not all rapists, even rapists who are repetitively caught for their crimes, are paraphiliacs. A clinician needs to review an individual's sexual fantasies, urges, and/or behaviors to see if a paraphilia diagnosis is appropriate. Under civil commitment assessment circumstances, the likelihood for obtaining truthful descriptions of the offender's fantasies and urges is not high. Hence, evaluators often need to rely solely on the documented behavior of the subject to determine diagnoses. In the case where paraphilia NOS, nonconsent is potentially applicable, the behavioral determination of the proper diagnosis can be problematic.

As described above, most rapists do not show deviant sexual arousal patterns during (at least typical) PPG testing. This suggests that the simple repetition of raping should not necessarily be thought of as demonstrating a paraphiliac condition. (As stated earlier in this chapter, there are various reasons why a PPG may show no deviant responding from a person who in actuality is paraphiliac. On the other hand, it seems clear that at least some rapists do not experience such a disorder.) So are there overt actions besides repetitive rapes that clinicians can use to make this determination?

The answer appears to be yes. There are numerous ways by which a person can demonstrate his paraphiliac interests during sexual assaults. The following is an enumeration of behaviors that may serve as indicators, beyond repetitive raping, of the presence of paraphilia NOS, nonconsent:

1. *Ejaculation or other clear signs of sexual arousal during events that are clearly nonconsensual.* There are two issues here, the combination of which being the true key to this aspect of diagnosing paraphilia NOS, nonconsent. The first pertains to the issue of sexual arousal of which ejaculation is one clear sign. (Ejaculation, as used here, is meant to include clear documentation of sustained arousal by the perpetrator. Ejaculation is far more likely to be documented directly than is the presence of an erection without ejaculation. Semen or "wetness" frequently gets recorded in victim, law enforcement, and medical reports. It seems reasonable to conclude, though not certainly true, that a victim's report of penetration by the perpetrator's penis indicates the offender was erect and aroused as well even without recorded ejaculation.) Ejaculation alone tells us only that the perpetrator was aroused and not by what. We do not know by the sole fact of ejaculation what aroused the offender.

The second component to this defining characteristic is that there is reason to believe the arousal pertained at least in part to the nonconsensual nature of the interaction. Just because the victim's report makes it absolutely clear that the victim was not consenting to the sexual contact, this does not mean that the rapist's arousal was caused in part by that nonconsensual component of what was happening. Many rapists, for instance, seem more interested in "beating up" on someone for the rewards violence brings than for purposes of sexual arousal (e.g., Barbaree, Seto, Serin, Amos, & Preston, 1994). In those cases, the offenders may not even be paying attention to the victim's plight, just their own aggressive desires. As noted above, distorted perceptions and expectations can even make the rapist not see that what he is doing is clearly nonconsensual. People referred to as "date rapists" frequently fit this description, where some of the offenders see the woman as simply being "coy" or "playing the game" or that the woman "led him on" so far and cannot really expect the man to stop before he is satisfied. The offender's being oblivious would seem to suggest that his arousal is not caused by the nonconsensual nature of the interaction. (So as not to be misinterpreted here, I wish to note that although some "date rapists" are truly oblivious to their victims' suffering, to the point of asking the victim for a subsequent date, other rapists simply use "dating" as an excuse to (a) get access and (b) decrease the chance the victim will report the assault. Not everyone labeled a "date rapist" was unaware of what he was doing.)

A different and still relatively common rape scenario involves what is clearly a nonconsensual attack by the offender, but one in which he does not specifically become sexually aroused (at least to the point of ejaculation). Rapists who fall into this category include those who are typologically classified as "vindictive" rapists (Prentky & Knight, 1991). Rape, in these cases, even repetitive raping, can simply represent a strong desire and willingness to hurt women as an expression of anger and rage rather than sexual interest per se.

Rather, the combination of both (a) ejaculation and (b) the recognition by the offender during the assault that what he was doing constituted a clear case of non-consenting sexual contact begins to constitute what it means to be a paraphiliac rapist. That recognition, of course, can occur through many means, including (but not limited to) the offender's paying attention to the victim's reaction, his perpetrating against a stranger, or his use (or implied use) of a weapon and/or "rape kit" (e.g., crow bar, ski mask, duct tape, scissors). The general clinical look here can be exemplified with a case study based solely on data recorded from various documents.

The offender's pattern was to find women who were complete strangers to him upon which he would make his attack. He did this process repetitively; despite having been caught, convicted, and imprisoned between some occasions. The victim's report in one such case included the comment that the offender had stated to her during his assault that he knew this was rape, and knew that she was going "to turn him in," but that he was going to rape her anyway.

He was recorded to have ejaculated many times over many hours of assaulting that specific victim. This fact was documented by the results of a medical examination of the victim's vagina and the fact that some of his semen was found in a bottle into which he had made the victim spit after oral copulation. In some of this perpetrator's other known rapes, he was reported to have made statements that acknowledged the nonconsensual nature of the contact with the women. He also was recorded to have ejaculated during every such assault.

2. Repetitive patterns of actions, as if scripts. Conceptually and diagnostically, it appears that individuals suffering from a paraphilia tend to have a set of fantasies that goes along with individuals' deviant behaviors. Within this presumption is the idea that someone who acts on his fantasies tends to follow them as closely as he feels he can under the circumstances in which either he finds himself or he can manufacture. Based on this view of sexual deviancy, people who have, and physi-cally act on, a paraphilia involving nonconsensual sexual contact typically carry with them a set of associated fantasies that guides their actions. Under circum-stances where the nonconsensual component of an overt interaction is very clear to the perpetrator during a rape, it seems reasonable to assume the person is already feeling sufficiently uninhibited behaviorally to enact at least some aspects of his related fantasies. A rape-related paraphiliac can therefore show such behavioral signs of ongoing rape fantasies.

To probe for signs of acted-out sexual fantasies, an evaluator needs to look for documented demonstration of a consistent pattern of behavioral characteristics by the offender across his sexual assaults. This can be thought of as the individualized signature of the offender's fantasies. If the documentation is good enough, the signature actually involves the complete set of details of how the assault occurred, from very near the beginning right through the point of how the offender separates from his victim. Such a pattern can include how the perpetrator

    a. set the victim up ("groomed the victim," if that concept is even applicable to the specific case);

    b. initiated his attack;

    c. made certain comments during the assault;

    d. had the victim do or say certain things;

    e. did certain acts, even in a certain order during the assault; and

    f. treated the victim after the assault itself ended.

For example, one offender showed a repetitive pattern of the following:

1. He made contact with an adult female stranger at a bus stop in a neighborhood where drug deals were not uncommon. He approached her with some pleasant small talk, stated he had some drugs, and asked if she would like to share them with him.

2. If she said yes, he walked with her supposedly toward "his garage" where they would be able to sit down and use the drugs. Once inside the garage, however, his previously very pleasant attitude suddenly and drastically changed. With a great deal of hostility and significant physical force, he grabbed the woman and threw her to the floor. He then made a statement that he was going to have sex with her, in language far more graphic.

3. He used "weapons of availability" to subdue the victim, including a brick and some wood.

4. He made various degrading comments to the women during the assaults, concentrating on personality attributes (vs. physical characteristics or "generic to women" comments).

5. He always forced the victims to undress completely, but he never removed any of his clothing completely.

6. He told the victims not to say a word during any of the time he was with them, enforcing that with a beating if they failed to comply.

7. His sexual assaults always went from forced fellatio to vaginal intercourse, even when he forced intercourse a second time with the same victim during the same assault.

8. He always brought and used a condom, during vaginal intercourse. He always ejaculated into the condom, at least during the first set of fellatio-intercourse interactions for each victim. (There was one victim to whom he did this set of sexual contacts twice, during which he did not use a condom the second time. He ejaculated the first time into the condom, sat with the victim for a short period of time, and then repeated the whole process again. During the second set of sexual contacts, he ejaculated inside her vagina without wearing a condom.)

9. After the assaults, he walked away with the victim's pants, which he left somewhere away from where the victim could easily obtain them.

There may be multiple ways to interpret this set of actions outside of the repetitive behavioral context. The fact that this individual showed this pattern repetitively, and showed only this pattern, however, speaks to the "script" that went behind his actions. One can reasonably argue that repetitive behavioral patterns concerning only one sexual scenario involves a fantasy the perpetrator holds dear. From that perspective, this man was repetitively acting out a fantasy about which he was clearly aroused.

The documentation available is many times not so complete as to describe each of these characteristics for each known rape. One does not necessarily need all of these features, however, to see a relevant pattern. For instance, some perpetrators do things specifically to emphasize the nonconsensual nature of the sexual contact during their crimes, without other associated features, while still simultaneously working toward their own sexual gratification. This fact alone, especially if repetitive across events, can serve as sufficient grounds to conclude there were behavioral signs of paraphiliac sexual interests.

Unlike the above behavioral descriptions, simple postassault comments of apology by the offender to the victim (e.g., unexplained statements such as "I'm sorry for what I did" or "I apologize for what happened") are not thought of as an indication of his deliberate intention for a nonconsensual interaction (for which he then expresses remorse). Clearly, these comments represent a *recognition* by the offender that what occurred was against the victim's will. Apologetic comments, however, often appear to be made for the express purpose of making the victim feel more sympathetic toward the perpetrator, and therefore less likely to turn him in to the authorities. Such comments by an offender may represent nothing more than final manipulations before separating from his victims. Under typical circumstances, there does not seem to be sufficient evidence to conclude that such statements demonstrate that the perpetrator regrets a paraphiliac condition he cannot sufficiently control, even though this may be true for some individuals.

3. *Where virtually all of the person's criminal behavior is sexual.* Some offenders show a lengthy list of numerous types of crimes. Psychopaths, for instance,

are in part defined by their "criminal versatility" (i.e., Item 20 on the Psychopathy Checklist–Revised; Hare, 1991), meaning there typically is no specialization of criminal interest. Paraphiliac rapists, however, tend to show at least a repetitive process of sexual assaults in their records (especially if allegations and self-reports are counted, and not just official charges and convictions). There may be other recorded criminal activity (and often is), but at least a significant portion of their criminal behavior is sexual in nature.

Putting this into other, more emphatic terms, the repetitively sexual nature of someone's criminal record is thought of as helping to differentiate the paraphiliac offender from the more general personality disordered criminal. Someone whose complete enumeration of offenses is solely and repetitively raping is likely to be someone whose criminal interests lie solely in that area. In contrast, an individual who is willing to take anything he can get from anyone, in any of various ways only one of which is sexual, is more likely to be personality disordered than suffering from a rape-related paraphilia. This difference in overall criminal record can assist in the determination of when a paraphilia may exist. Complicating the situation, of course, is that one diagnostic formulation does not negate the other, and people can suffer from both a paraphilia and a personality disorder.

4. *Raping when the victim had already been willing to have consensual sex.* Some offenders will show a pattern of altering what starts as a consensual sexual encounter to a nonconsensual interaction. This can occur with ongoing lovers, with acquaintances, or with otherwise "one-nighter" strangers. The process, especially when it constitutes a repetitive pattern, seems to be a strong sign that the offender is getting satisfaction from the nonconsensual sexual contact that the consensual interaction does not give him. Examples of this include the following:

a. The man who picks up a hitchhiker who agrees to have sex with him, only to pull a weapon on her anyway and make sexual demands of her

b. The man who picks up a patron in a bar who agrees to have sex with him, only later to beat the person and force unwanted sexual acts

c. The husband who starts having consensual sex with his wife, but frequently then forces her to do things for his sexual gratification she does not want to do (which also can be a sign of a strong sense of entitlement)

Conceptually, even just a single clear instance of behavior such as this where the perpetrator is not angry or being vengeful may appropriately raise the question of a nonconsent paraphilia. As a differentiating consideration, if the above type of behavior occurs only when the perpetrator is obviously very angry, there is possible reason to view the raping as related more to a desire to beat up (cause physical harm to) the victim than to getting sexually aroused through a nonconsensual interaction. Realistically, however, it seems unusual for someone to be repetitively very angry with people, to the point of raping, when those victims were consenting and cooperating sexual partners.

5. *Short time period after consequence before raping again.* One of the possible signs of a paraphiliac rapist as compared to other rapists appears to be that the former tends to repeat his sexual offending very soon after he is released from prison. The clinician experienced with sex offenders certainly knows some cases in which rapists repeated their same pattern of sexual offending within a small number of postincarceration weeks, sometimes despite the perpetrators' being on parole (or other community supervision). Conceptually, these "ex-cons" may literally be driven toward nonconsensual sexual contacts with others. The fact that they just experienced a significant period of incarceration does not ultimately alter their behavior even in the short run, when the memory of prison is still presumed to be fresh. The reoffenders, in effect, become willing to risk getting caught and going back to prison for an even longer term specifically to satisfy their sexual desire.

An example of this situation comes from the case described in no. 1 above. That individual repeated his same pattern of sexual offending within 6 weeks of his release from an extended prison stay. Three months later, he attempted to repeat the same type of crime again, only then getting caught for his apparently first postincarceration recidivist act. Paraphiliac rapists do not typically wait years to repeat their crimes.

There is one additional consideration here. Highly psychopathic offenders can also show a pattern of reoffending quickly after prison release. Their criminality may represent more about their impulsivity and disregard for others than specifically a deviant sexual arousal. Evaluators need to consider the degree to which the subject is psychopathic before concluding that rapid reoffending clearly indicates the presence of a paraphilia.

6. *Raping under circumstance with high likelihood for being caught.* This is an alternative conceptualization of the same issue just described above in no. 5. The situation under which someone rapes shows the care he demonstrates to avoid detection. The opportunistic nonparaphiliac rapist defines his circumstances by two factors: (a) victim availability and (b) the relative lack of detection by others. The vengeful, nonparaphiliac rapist may not take his likelihood for detection into high consideration at the time, but this is clearly due to his strong emotional and immediate desire to express his rage. There may be relatively little assault planning by either of these types of individuals. When someone shows he plans his offense (through a demonstrated repetitive pattern or script), but still does not take his potential for getting caught into significant consideration, this may be a sign of a paraphiliac interest in the activity. In the planning of his to-be-enacted fantasy, he has concentrated solely on what is of prime interest to him, his sexual excitement from a nonconsensual interaction.

An example of this type of behavior is the offender who repetitively had his stepdaughter visit him while in a secure facility (the young woman was accompanied by her mother). This stepdaughter, at the time of these visits in her midadolescence, had quite repetitively experienced his groping her and attempts to force more when they still lived together before he was incarcerated (though this was not known to the institution staff until much later). During the visitations, he put his hands on his stepdaughter in sexual ways despite being under the eyes of supervising staff.

Those visitations were, of course, terminated permanently after such events. (The young woman later stated that she had been afraid of her stepfather and was glad she did not "have to" visit him anymore.) The degree of determination by the offender despite the high likelihood for being caught was impressive.

Differentiating the paraphiliac rapist in this characteristic from the more general psychopathic rapist can be tricky. A factor to consider is the degree to which the assault was the result of enacted planning versus opportunistic without significant planning. Although paraphiliac rapists can take advantage of opportunities, they would seem more likely to work to create those opportunities and more likely to follow similar patterns of behavior across assaults than would more purely psychopathic individuals.

7. *Having concomitant cooperative sexual partners.* A naive but sometimes heard argument is that some people rape because they are without access to a cooperative sex partner. This is not a viewpoint commonly accepted by knowledgeable clinicians, at least beyond the effect of more direct etiological considerations such as *chronic* emotional loneliness (Seidman, Marshall, Hudson, & Robertson, 1994). A perpetrator's having a cooperative sex partner in his life during the same time that he is raping other women helps to eliminate this argument in any given case. When there is clearly a willing and available sex partner in the offender's life and he makes a practice of raping anyway, then the conclusion seems reasonable that sexual assaulting gave him something that his cooperative relationship did not.

There is one point to be made clear here. Clinically speaking, some men rape women mostly following arguments with their "cooperative" sex partner. The apparent motive in these assaults may therefore not be specifically sexual at all, but seems to stem from the men's taking out their anger and/or need for control in a situation that does not directly threaten the relationship with their usual partner. The main point here is that these men do not appear to rape when things are going smoothly in their preferred sexual relationship. Paraphiliac rapists, on the other hand, do not necessarily rape only in temporal association with upsetting events in their primary relationship.

8. *Various types of victims in "purely" sex offenders.* Pedophiles are potentially easily classified because of the repetitive age category of their victims. In contrast, although many rapists restrict their criminal sexual activity to adult women, this singularity does not by itself indicate the existence of a paraphilia. In fact, the sex offender who broadens the range of his possible victims to include adolescents and even children may more likely be the paraphiliac rapist. There appear to be two discriminating considerations here.

The first issue to be determined is whether or not the person who is "taking sex" from a wide variety of people is also taking other things as well. The more generally versatile, or even psychopathic, criminal will tend to take from others whatever he wishes, with sex potentially being just one of those things. Taking material goods and money may also highly rank in their repertoire. Paraphiliac rapists, however, would more typically show a pattern of just sexual criminality, as described in no. 3 above. Evaluators need to review the subject's degree of psychopathy to make the appropriate interpretation of varied types of victims.

If a rather purely sexual criminal pattern is found, a second issue needs to be considered. Within an offender's pattern of almost solely sexual crimes, with crimes against victims from multiple age categories, the clinician needs to differentiate the paraphiliac process from the more opportunistic nonparaphiliac offender. Sex offenders can pick on different age categories of victims because the victims' ages basically do not matter to him, just the opportunity for sexual gratification. On the other hand, the paraphiliac rapist may involve himself sexually with minors because of the greater ease in gaining access to a nonconsensual victim.

The specific behaviors shown by the perpetrator during his assaults on minors can be instrumental in making the motive differentiation. Admittedly, these details can be lacking in official reports, or considered unverified from victims' reports. Even so, evaluators can investigate records for details such as the following:

a. Clear demonstration of the minor victim's distress being shown during the assault during which the perpetrator continues his arousal and ejaculates. Examples of such victim behaviors include crying, attempts to yell, physical fighting, and pleading with the offender to stop.

b. Significant physical violence against the minor victim, beyond that which was necessary to gain compliance. (When this specific characteristic is found, further differentiation needs to be conducted. Concerning differentiating from a diagnosis of sexual sadism, see the next section. Differentiating from the more personality disordered chronically angry rapist who "solely" wishes to beat up the victim, the issue of reported anger expression is clearly of relevance.)

c. Covering the face of the victim during the assault, when doing so is not for the purpose of protecting the offender's identity. The concept here is that the perpetrator may not wish to see himself as being sexual with a child and is doing what he can to picture himself with an adult. (When the characteristic of covering the victim's face is found, a differentiation from sexual sadism should also be made, as sadists can do this same behavior but for a different reason: to inflict terror.)

d. Performing sexual acts that are clearly physically painful and potentially injurious to the victims. Included here are anal rapes, vaginal rapes in younger children, and fellatio involving gagging of the victim. (Again, a differentiation from sexual sadism needs to be made if this type of behavior is found, as sadists can do the same type of action.)

e. Sexually offending on victims who are asleep, or otherwise made unconscious or nonvolitional, such as through the use of drugs.

f. Offender vocalizations during the assault in keeping with a nonconsensual focus on what is happening. This category includes comments such as "I know you don't want this, but I'm going to do it anyway," "Go ahead and fight. It only makes it better for me," and "I know this is rape." In some cases, the perpetrator can even be voicing what he plans on doing to the victim, and that process of telling clearly increases his sexual arousal before the actual enactment of the stated plans.

The knowledgeable reader may note that many of these enumerated situations can also be signs of sexual sadism. This differentiation also needs to occur, and is described in a section below.

With some offenders, their use of adolescents and children as victims, instead of their most desired adult victims, is based on their lack of confidence or ability to gain access to nonconsensual adults. This can be because of the perpetrator's small physical stature, his lack of intelligence for planning a "successful" rape of an adult, a lack of self-confidence in dealing with adults in general, or the simple fear of getting turned in to the authorities. A pattern of using a weapon with adult victims, but no weapon to get minors to comply, would suggest these types of concerns on the part of the offender.

9. *Maintenance of a "rape kit."* A "rape kit" is a set of implements a perpetrator keeps available (e.g., in his car) for use in fulfilling his sexual fantasy involving a nonconsensual (and/or sadistic) interaction. The specific implements vary, but such kits can include rope, duct tape, handcuffs, blindfold, scissors (for cutting clothes away), condoms, blanket, weapons (e.g., a knife), and additionally for sadists, items specific to the infliction of pain (e.g., pliers, lighter). When an evaluator comes across documentation of a gathering of items such as these in a place from where an offender perpetrated a crime (e.g., in his car), the evaluator should seriously consider the existence of a paraphilia.

Some items will, of course, be more indicative than others. Whereas a blanket in the trunk of the offender's automobile can simply mean he went on a picnic the day before, a collection of handcuffs and rope can be harder to explain away. Likewise, the simple possession of a weapon in the glove compartment may be explained in a variety of ways (both legal and illegal), but the individual's keeping a weapon handy for no known purpose other than facilitating his sexual assaulting is an indication of the offender's planning in this regard. His pattern may look like he attacks in an opportunistic way, but these "spontaneous" assaults involve a planned and anticipated fantasy that is only looking for a situation in which it can be enacted (what Anna Salter has described as "planned spontaneity"; personal communication, 1998).

Absence of Contrary Signs

There are certain things that a sex offender may have done during his crimes that can serve as contraindications for the applicability of paraphilia NOS, nonconsent. Clinicians need to seek out evidence of these contrary signs along with the above indicative signs of the disorder. Such contrary characteristics include the following:

1. Interrupting his sexual assault when he realizes the victim is emotionally distressed.

2. A pattern of grooming victims that involves more of an emotional and/or sexual seduction than simply the process of gaining private access.

3. Comments by the offender vocalized during the assault indicating he views the interaction as consensual, or at least likely to result in an enjoyable encounter for the victim. An example of the latter is where the perpetrator talks about his being the victim's boyfriend, or after the attack sets a "date" for a later time and place.

4. Arguably, a clear sign of not paying attention to the victim, suggesting that the victim is being used more for a "masturbatory receptacle" rather than for the purpose of truly interacting with someone (in a nonconsensual way). (This last example is potentially debatable, as some paraphiliac rapists may simply enact their rape fantasy while raping, and in so doing not pay real attention to the actual victim.)

The reader is cautioned against viewing postassault treatment-related comments suggesting victim empathy by the perpetrator as contraindicating a paraphilia NOS, nonconsent. First of all, such comments are difficult to interpret as truly representing the emotional and cognitive state of empathy. Even more important, however, is that an offender can be quite empathic to the plight of his victims after his assaults while still obtaining a great deal of sexual gratification from their victimization during the assaults. Not all paraphiliac rapists are full-blown psychopaths and totally lacking in the capacity for empathy. In fact, their sensitivity to what victims are experiencing is *exactly* what heightens these offenders' sexual pleasure. The capacity for empathy is not a contraindication of the existence of paraphilia NOS, nonconsent.

For example, Anna Salter (personal communication, August 2001) relates the story of a young man with an extensive history of stalking and raping women who got a job in a video store. A 15-year-old comes into the store. While she is selecting a tape in the back, he puts a sign on the door that says, "Closed. Be right back." She brings her selection up to the counter, though he tells her that she has picked out an awful tape. She follows him to the back of the store where he is going to show her a better one. He pulls a knife, rapes her, and then sobs that he has really done it now. She gets up to leave. He apologizes again. He is behind her as she heads for the door. He stabs her in the head, gets her down and goes for her throat. She protects her throat and he stabs her in the chest. Then he stops, apologizes, cries some more. This cycle repeats itself before she eventually gets out of the store (which she does). As Dr. Salter related, "The moral of the story is that the labile affective states of many offenders can be independent of their motivations."

Differentiation From Sexual Sadism

Paraphilia NOS, nonconsent is different from sexual sadism. Sadism specifically involves sexual arousal to the infliction of physical and/or psychological pain to someone else, whereas paraphilia NOS, nonconsent does not. Trying to differentiate these conditions based on an offender's documented behaviors alone, however, can be problematic.

One reason for this difficulty is the apparent close relationship between these two disorders. One theoretical perspective, for instance, is that paraphilia NOS, nonconsent represents one condition along a continuum that includes sexual sadism further down the same path (Anna Salter, personal communication, 1997). These diagnostic categories may not represent separate taxonomic entities so much as different expressions of the same underlying condition, that involving sexual arousal to psychological distress of the "partner" and/or a strong emotional sense of control over that "partner's" life.

A second reason for this difficulty is that virtually any sexual assault involving sadistic elements is also going to involve some degree of sexual arousal by the offender specifically related to situations that are nonconsensual. That does not mean that these offenders are all aroused specifically to the nonconsensual aspect of the interaction, but rather that their arousal to the sadistic elements of their assault can be difficult to distinguish from the simultaneous nonconsensual nature of what they are doing to the victims.

Putting these two issues together, clinicians may best conceptualize the behavioral differentiation between paraphilia NOS, nonconsent and sexual sadism more as a matter of degree than kind. With this in mind, signs of the more extreme condition, sadism, may be thought of as more inclusive of the following, when accompanied by some type of arousal in the perpetrator:

a. mutilating the victim;

b. deliberately injuring, causing bleeding, or causing death to the victim (this latter example needs to be related to the person's sexual arousal, and not solely for the purpose of covering up a crime or due to panicking by the offender);

c. performing acts specifically and solely designed to terrorize the victim—this can include blindfolding the victim after the perpetrator has already been well seen (meaning the blindfold was not for the purpose of protecting the identity of the perpetrator) and/or making repetitive comments about how he plans on killing or injuring the victim even if no such actions are ever enacted;

d. choking the victim to near death, allowing the victim to recover, only to choke the victim again;

e. deliberately slowly inflicting physical pain to the victim after the victim has already been subdued—this can include using cigarettes to burn the victim, using salt to put into the victim's eyes, using pliers to twist and squeeze the nipples or testicles of the victim, or any variety of other similar ways to inflict significant pain, particular after the person has been bound and not just psychologically subdued;

f. forcing fellatio immediately after anal intercourse (Park Dietz, personal communication, 1997);

g. inserting inanimate objects into victims' orifices, and/or having them do this to themselves—these objects can include glass bottles, fruit, metal tools, broom handles, or almost anything that the offender has available;

h. forcing one victim to have sexual contact with another while the perpetrator does not participate physically;

i. forcing one victim to watch the sexual assault of another;

j. involving prolonged periods of assault, for many hours and sometimes for days (potentially including true captivity) versus minutes to an hour or two; and/or

k. taking "trophies" of the experience, meaning that the offender takes something with him from the assault (presumably to remember it by); these can include strands of hair, jewelry, photographs taken during the assault, a piece of clothing, or even a collection of the offender's own semen that he had the victim repetitively spit out after each time he ejaculated into the person's mouth.

This is not meant to be a comprehensive enumeration of what sadists do that the nonconsensual paraphiliacs tend not to do. Conceptually, this list can remind the clinician of the kinds of behaviors that tend to differentiate the two conditions.

With the totality of the above as a guide, readers may even find possible examples of paraphilia NOS, nonconsent in media reports. Although it is never recommended that clinicians diagnose people based solely on media reports, some reports can be intriguing in their descriptions. The following is one such example.

> Nancy [S.] thought she was going to see a video of her second child's birth when she pushed the play button. Instead, she discovered a recording that authorities say shows her estranged husband raping three unconscious women. . . . Steven [S.], a 39-year-old traveling businessman, allegedly used Rohypnol, the so-called date rape pill, to knock his victims out. Prosecutors said the tape shows him having sex with women from Texas, Arkansas and Missouri. He has been charged in the Texas and Arkansas cases. Nancy [S.] fought back tears as she talked about the tape she discovered June 13 after going to Steven [S.'s] home to pick up the video camera when he wasn't home. "First and foremost, it destroyed my family," said [S.], who is raising the couple's two daughters, who are 3 months old and nearly 5. "I've gone through a lot of hatred that he could be so cruel because he did this while I was pregnant with our second child. I don't think he had any regard for me, my daughters, women in general, that he could be so vile and so heinous." (Associated Press, July 29, 1997; reprinted with permission of The Associated Press)

Certain characteristics of this man seem prominent. Potential attributes of paraphilia NOS, nonconsent are suggested

a. by his known repetitive sexually assaultive behavior,

b. where overt signs of victim suffering could not have been significantly relevant for his sexual arousal during the assaults (thus ruling out sexual sadism),

c. with very clear incapacitation of the victim's ability to consent before the sexual contact,

d. that incapacitation being caused by something he brought with him on a regular basis (e.g., the Rohypnol, in this case a drug that can be viewed as part of his "rape kit"),

e. coupled with recordings of the assaults for playback (which indicate both the planned nature of the attacks, by having the camera available, and his anticipated arousal to reliving those events through viewing the tapes themselves).

Other Relevant Types of Paraphilia NOS

Besides paraphilia NOS, nonconsent, there are other subtypes of paraphilia NOS of potential relevance within sex offender civil commitment assessments. Possibly the most common of these is paraphilia NOS, sexually attracted to adolescents, or what is otherwise called hebephilia or ephebophilia by some authors.

Four issues concern this diagnosis within a sex offender civil commitment assessment. Three of these will be explored here. The fourth topic, concerning the definition of "adolescent," will not be discussed, as this would simply involve a reiteration of what was stated earlier concerning the definition of "children."

The first matter is whether it is "normal" and not pathological for adult males to be sexually aroused by adolescents. The advertising business has apparently sometimes thought so. Use of provocatively attired adolescent girls to promote products is not uncommon, for instance, in the famous (or maybe infamous) Calvin Klein advertisement using a youthful Brooke Shields. There was obviously the belief that the general consumer population contains enough adults attracted to a sexualized adolescent to make such a portrayal worth the spending of a great deal of advertising money.

In fact, there is some scientific evidence that such an attraction is not uncommon. In a PPG study by Barbaree and Marshall (1989), about one third of adult nonoffending men showed sexual arousal to adolescents as well as to adults (though generalization from this finding is problematic due to the small number of nonoffending subjects, $n = 22$, employed in this study). Although this is still a minority of men showing this pattern, this does not appear to be atypical.

Is there evidence that a paraphilia related to this attraction exists? After all, if such an attraction is itself not uncommon even among "the average nonoffending man," then can we say that the attraction represents a pathological condition?

The answer to that question lies in the degree to which someone is repetitively or chronically impaired by that attraction, not the attraction per se. Although a significant portion of adult men show sexual arousal to adolescents, there does not appear to be many who, as adults, selectively pursue sexual contact with adolescents. For those who do, getting legally prosecuted or otherwise punished (such as through losing one's significant adult relationship or losing one's job) can serve as the one-time event from which the person learns never to venture into sexual activity with adolescents again. Up to this point, there would be insufficient evidence of a paraphilia.

Some people do not stop acting in ways that cause repetitive negative effects of their attraction to adolescents at this point, however. Despite serious consequences to them (i.e., impairment) due to their earlier behavior, these people continue to seek sexual contact with adolescents. Consensual adult relationships may not be pursued at all. Sexual contact with adolescents repeatedly occurs despite the ongoing risk of legal consequences and inability to maintain such relationships on a long-term basis due to the adolescents' growing beyond the age range of interest. These people show the characteristics of hebephilia, more formally called paraphilia NOS, sexually attracted to adolescents.

When such a paraphilia exists, many times it is in someone who is otherwise also attracted to consensual adult sexual contact. On an occasion, one comes upon a case where the person seems only to be attracted to adolescents and not adults. If clinicians borrow from the *DSM-IV* model for diagnosing pedophilia, then one could add the descriptor "exclusive" or "nonexclusive" after paraphilia NOS, sexually attracted to adolescents to define a subject's condition more definitively.

For the record, there is evidence from objective research that the "exclusive" form of this condition does exist. In the same Barbaree and Marshall (1989) study mentioned above, there was a comment about one subject who had to be excluded from the rest of the analyses because his PPG results did not fit into the patterns shown by everyone else in that study. That person showed a very clear interest in adolescents and no other age group. Given that this was a study concerning the sexual interests of convicted child molesters, it seems that "exclusive hebephilia" is a relatively rare condition even among offenders involving underage people.

The final issue concerning this diagnosis is quite specific to the context of civil commitment laws. In some of the civil commitment states, the defining characteristics of what constitutes a *relevant* sex offense may have an upper victim age cutoff, such as 15 (e.g., in Washington State). This does not change the potential appropriateness of the diagnosis to an individual, but it can dramatically alter the degree to which the diagnosis can be viewed as "predisposing" or "causing" the person to commit "sexually violent acts" defined using that victim age threshold. For instance, even if a middle-aged person (1) continually seeks out 16-year-olds and no one else for sexual gratification, and (2) his doing so continually gets him into legal trouble when he resides in some states, and social trouble of a variety of other types no matter where he goes, this paraphiliac condition should not be viewed as causing the person to commit sexually violent offenses in certain states quite specifically because of his partner age preference.

Thresholds for Diagnosing a Paraphilia

General Issues

Diagnosing sex offenders can represent a kind of dilemma. On the one hand, clinicians, the general public, and the criminal justice system view these offenders as fully responsible for what they do. If we take the perspective that repetitive sexually assaultive behaviors against adults represents prima facie evidence of the existence of a mental disorder, we could be undermining the perspective that the offenders are personally responsible for what they do and the legal consequences thereof.

This situation is complicated by a difference in how rapists and child molesters are viewed. Societal agents seem to have formed an alliance to ensure that rapists are viewed as "evil" and not "sick" (or as other people would phrase the comparison, "bad," not "mad"). The clinician who diagnoses a mental disorder "to explain" a perpetrator's actions is open to ridicule and may very well lack credibility with the courts.

On the other hand, repetitive sexual assaults against children are quickly labeled as representing pedophilia by nonclinicians such as judges and the media, even beyond occasions where this diagnosis is clinically accurate. Clinicians risk little in making such a diagnosis when assessing a case of a repetitive child molester and, in fact, might risk more damage to their credibility when they do not make the diagnosis. As a society, we do not appear to have trouble viewing many child molesters as both "sick" *and* deserving of punishment.

Victims' ages may be the only behavioral difference between what some rapists and some child molesters do or even want to do. The process of determining when an offense-specific mental disorder exists, however, differs between the two types of offenders. To understand the proper threshold for diagnosing a paraphilia, we need to explore the bases for our dissimilar views concerning the two types of sex offenders.

The simplest explanation of this bias may be the general belief in society that any sexual attraction by an adult toward another adult is "normal," but toward a child is inherently "abnormal." If we are exploring the underpinnings of what constitutes a paraphilia from this perspective, then raping an adult is still understandable without invoking a mental disorder to explain the behavior (i.e., to have sex, albeit against the victim's desire). Likewise, having sexual contact with a child is a clear sign that "something" is wrong. Repetitive sexual contact with children makes is obvious that the something wrong is within the perpetrator's psyche.

Another perspective is based in feminist theory. That theory views raping as not even a crime involving a sexual motive, but a method by which those in socially dominant positions (typically men) use to maintain control over those in lesser power positions. Raping is viewed as a sociological versus psychological process and does not represent the manifestation of a diagnosable psychiatric condition. Child molestation, though still stemming from the same sociological process, may represent a diagnostic manifestation due to the degree of power differential that already exists between the adult perpetrator and the child victim. Adults do not typically need to enact various forcible rituals to maintain their dominance over children. Hence, the individual who repetitively has sexual contacts with children may very well have something amiss in his psyche, far more so than a sex offender doing the same actions solely with adults.

Societal beliefs and sociological theories aside, the real question for the civil commitment evaluator is what the scientific evidence is concerning paraphiliac diagnoses for rapists and child molesters, and at what thresholds for each. People doing civil commitment evaluations should bring as much science to the process as possible, and not just be responding to general societal beliefs or intriguing theories.

Fortunately, there is some congruence between the layperson's view of reality and relevant empirical information. What the general societal belief and feminist theory espouse seems somewhat supported by the research data.

The Threshold for Pedophilia

The easiest demonstration of this fact comes from PPG studies. A child molester does not need to have been caught more than 2 or 3 times before the PPG research would indicate a very strong likelihood (i.e., 80% or more) that he is pedophiliac (Freund & Watson, 1991). This is especially true if at least two of the victims were boys (Freund & Watson, 1991, 1992). An evaluating clinician can conclude with confidence that the simple act of repeating child sexual contact (i.e., with different victims) implies at least some degree of pedophiliac sexual arousal in the perpetrator. This makes one type of threshold for diagnosing pedophilia based on offender behavior alone rather easy to define. With two different boy victims, or three child victims of any gender combination, there is a high likelihood for the person to be pedophiliac.

Two other threshold matters beyond the number of different victims need to be mentioned here:

1. The *DSM-IV* states that pedophilia should not be diagnosed for someone who is still under 16 years of age. This threshold, as it is written, seems clear enough. What about the situation of the 17- or 18-year-old who (a) committed various sexual offenses when he was 14 against children who were 4 to 6 years old, (b) was caught by the judicial system, and (c) was incarcerated in a juvenile correctional institution during the intervening years since he was 14? Now that he is over 16, is a diagnosis of pedophilia appropriate given that it would be based solely on behavioral information from before he was 16? In one sex offender civil commitment case in Wisconsin, a judge decided this did not make sense to him, such that he did not find reason to detain the respondent further, specifying that as one of the reasons (*In re: Commitment of R. P.*, Rock County, June 14, 1996).

The judge's reasoning was that if someone's behavior does not constitute a specific disorder before the person was a certain age, and the person does not exhibit any more such behavior (albeit with lack of opportunity), then the person's getting older does not "all of a sudden" mean that the same old behavior now becomes the basis for a disorder. Using this logic, one is left with the conclusion that an evaluator needs to have some kind of evidence of pedophilia from after the person's 16th birthday to make that diagnosis.

On the other hand, there is a flaw in the logic. The judge made the assumption that the "criteria" for pedophilia listed in the *DSM-IV* were hard-and-fast rules. If one sees them instead as guidelines, as described in the manual itself, then there can certainly be cases in which a diagnosis of pedophilia is appropriate even before the person turns 16. Studies of juvenile offenders have found, for instance, that the age of onset of sexual deviance of various types ranged from 13 to 15.5 years, with some beginning as early as 10 years old (see Abel et al., 1993, for this review).

No clear thresholds are available in this regard, in part because sizable PPG studies involving juveniles are far more rare, and in part because juveniles may give more deviant-looking profiles than adults in general (Hunter, Goodwin, & Becker, 1994). Hence, the reader is cautioned against making a diagnosis of pedophilia with someone under age 16 (or using solely the same information for someone a couple of years older) unless the behavior was clearly sexual, frequent, over a relatively lengthy period of time, and involved victims who were not only much younger than the subject but also not even close to the same emotional level as the subject.

2. Is it appropriate to diagnose pedophilia for someone who demonstrated a very clear pedophiliac pattern or behavior (and maybe also voiced fantasies and urges) before he was incarcerated, but who has been imprisoned for a significant number of years during which he has not been known to do anything related to pedophilic interests? This is an absolutely common scenario within the sex offender civil commitment realm.

Fortunately, the answer is a straightforward affirmative, for various reasons. First, this is true according to some writers of that section of the manual (Park Dietz, personal communication, 1995; Thomas Wise, personal communication, 1995).

Second, pedophilia is not known to "go into remission" (fancy words for "go away") on its own. Third, even if the person participated in treatment during his incarceration, there is little reason to believe that he does not still suffer from the symptoms of the disorder. After all, treatment as it is implemented today is not viewed as a cure for the disorder. Finally, incarceration is not known to have a negative impact on deviant arousal. In fact, offenders often maintain or increase their paraphiliac arousal during incarceration through the pairing of deviant fantasies and masturbation.

The Threshold for Paraphilia NOS, Nonconsent

Attempts to follow the same type of behavioral definition model based again only on PPG research results to define the threshold for pedophilia have not worked well for sex offenders who solely attack adults. This situation is not for lack of trying to find such results, as such research studies have been performed many times (see the reviews by Hall, Shondrick, & Hirschman, 1993, and Lalumière & Quinsey, 1992). The results indicate that there are some rapists who show clear sexual arousal to depictions of rape in the PPG laboratories (e.g., Earls & Proulx, 1987) and some who show about equal interest in rape and consensual sex (e.g., Barbaree et al., 1979). Importantly, a significant proportion of rapists apparently do not show a different PPG pattern from nonrapists (e.g., Baxter, Barbaree, & Marshall, 1986; Marshall & Barbaree, 1995; Murphy, Krisak, Stalgaitis, & Anderson, 1984).

Buried in these apparently null findings, however, are two key issues. First, from the Marshall and Barbaree (1995) study, about 30% of the subjects did show some sexual arousal to depictions of rape. The existence of some sadists, and some rapists who are aroused by the nonconsensual nature of the laboratory rape vignettes, was clearly documented in this study, along with other criminals with the same deviant sexual interests who had never been convicted for a sexual offense.

Second, despite the fact that most rapists do not show the telltale PPG spike indicative of increased arousal to rape depictions in these studies, there are clear indications that most rapists also do not show the inhibition of sexual arousal inherent to the arousal patterns of most nonoffending adult males (e.g., Barbaree, 1990). Most adult males lose their sexual arousal once violence is added to an otherwise consensual sexual encounter. That is not true for most rapists. Although most rapists may not get specifically turned on by raping, they do not get turned off by their violence either. The point is that a lack of inhibition may not fall into the same category as a positive attraction. As Howard Barbaree has stated, "Any failure to inhibit may be regarded as a failure or as a 'pathology' of some kind, but it is not in my view a paraphilia" (personal communication, August 1998).

Overall, it appears that we cannot state a numerical threshold for defining a rape-related paraphilia using PPG research results in the same way that pedophilia can be defined. The research simply does not support such a numerical definition. Conceptually, a strongly demonstrated proclivity toward repeated raping seems like it must matter in diagnosing a rape-related paraphilia. Defining a specific numerical threshold for the existence of the disorder, however, is not supported by the PPG data.

The lack of behavioral frequency threshold for defining a rape-related paraphilia means that other factors must be considered for that purpose (given that in the civil commitment arena, the evaluator will rarely assess someone willing to describe rape-related sexual fantasies and urges). As described earlier in this chapter, there are numerous behavioral signs of such disorders during the crimes such people commit.

Although evaluators might prefer exact thresholds for how many of what specific signs are needed to diagnose this type of paraphilia, this lack of clarity is not really any different from what is found for other *DSM-IV* diagnostic categories (e.g., *alcohol abuse, schizophrenia, specific phobia*). Our lack of empirically based information in this regard simply represents the current state of our knowledge.

The Descriptive Language We Use

Diagnosable mental disorders represent conditions that can fall anywhere along the continuum from short-term states to more chronic traits. For instance, the *DSM-IV* defines (1) *adjustment disorders* in terms of short-term responses to situational stressors, but (2) *mental retardation* as basically a lifelong condition.

Corresponding to this continuum is a logistical variation in how the diagnosed conditions are described. At one end, we say that someone is *suffering from* the condition, such as an adjustment disorder or alcohol intoxication. At the other end, we say that someone "is defined by" the condition, with statements about someone *being* mentally retarded or personality disordered.

Given our societal bias toward seeing sex offenders as representing a trait related to their offending, and even being defined by these potentially infrequent behaviors, mental health clinicians need to be very cautious in how they describe *DSM-IV* diagnoses involving sexually offending individuals. Labels such as "sex offender" and "sexually violent predator" (or the like) are already in the courtroom, leaving their indelible effect. Evaluators need not contribute to the use of pejorative phraseology unnecessarily in how we describe some of our own profession's labels. While still being clearly descriptive, we should avoid defining commitment subjects effectively as simply the embodiment of a disorder. Metaphorically, we know that being diagnosed with cancer is conceptually different from being defined by one's cancerous condition. To use the latter way of describing a condition undermines the rest of the person's being. With this perspective in mind, the recommendation is made that evaluators describe diagnostic formulations in terms such as (using pedophilia, for example) "I diagnosed Mr. X with pedophilia," as opposed to "Mr. X is pedophilic."

Summary Comments

This chapter covered the myriad of fine details related to paraphilias commonly diagnosed for sex offenders undergoing civil commitment evaluations. Although the *DSM-IV* offers an overall structure of use in making these diagnoses, application of that structure to incarcerated and/or nonforthcoming individuals was found problematic. Much discussion was made concerning the "NOS, nonconsent" diagnosis due to the issues inherent to diagnosing some rapists in particular. Definitional guidelines were offered for that diagnosis for addressing the common situation in which relevant sexual fantasies and urges are denied by the subject while his recorded behavior seems contrasting to that self-report. Finally, behavioral thresholds for meeting criteria for some paraphilias were described, with only pedophilia being found potentially to offer numerical thresholds based on existing research.

Overall, this chapter may have covered far more detail than some evaluators wished in describing the application of paraphiliac diagnoses to the civil commitment arena. On the other hand, experience has taught me that a great deal of questioning in the courtroom can focus on exactly the minutia delineated herein. It is hoped that people interested in understanding these fine points of the forensic diagnostic process obtained what they sought.

CHAPTER 4

Diagnostic Issues Within Sex Offender Civil Commitment Assessments

Diagnostic Issues Beyond the Paraphilias

When a man commits the same crime twice, and is not punished, it seems to him permissible.

— The Talmud

There is more to the diagnostic portion of a sex offender civil commitment than determining whether or not the man has a paraphilia. No current commitment law limits the requisite mental condition to such a disorder, despite the fact that some people have recommended otherwise (Becker & Murphy, 1998). As described in Chapter 1, the possible mental conditions required for commitment only involve (1) a general descriptive phrase that includes a specific predisposition and/or (2) any of a specific set of diagnostic categories, some of which are not paraphilias. This chapter therefore picks up where Chapter 3 left off, discussing diagnostic issues beyond the paraphilias, but still within the context of sex offender civil commitment evaluations.

Nonparaphiliac Diagnoses Common in Sex Offender Civil Commitment Assessments

The Personality Disorders

Personality disorders are one of the most commonly diagnosed mental conditions in cases involving repetitive sexual offending. The basic reason for this is that a personality disorder conceptually describes a maladaptive pattern of behavior (and/or inner experience), and repetitive sexual offending can represent an important portion of such a pattern.

The definition of the personality disorders in the *Diagnostic and Statistical Manual,* 4th edition (*DSM-IV*; American Psychiatric Association, 1994) does not appear to raise as many issues and interpretative problems as were found for the paraphilias. Even so, there are many points to be discussed here.

Criterion Thresholds

The main issue for the personality disorders is determining when thresholds are met for the descriptive criteria, a consideration that is often far from clear. One reason for this situation is because there are varying thresholds for the different criteria even within a single disorder's enumeration.

For instance, within the diagnostic criteria for *antisocial personality disorder*, the clinician needs to demonstrate "evidence of Conduct Disorder . . . with onset before age 15 years" (*DSM-IV*, p. 650). Some clinicians have interpreted this to mean that a full set of diagnostic criteria of *conduct disorder* retrospectively needs to apply to the person being evaluated (now as an adult) before he was 15. This interpretation, however, is far too conservative and does not appear accurate. A clinician only needs to demonstrate that there was *evidence* of the existence of a conduct disorder from before the time the person turned 15, and not that a full conduct disorder condition existed before the subject was 15. The concept here is that the adult's antisocial pattern of "disregard for and violation of the rights of others" started from before he was 15, not just in adulthood.

On the other hand, relative to the criterion of deceitfulness, one documented lie, no matter how heinous, clearly does not constitute demonstration of that feature. Likewise, the criterion of "failure to conform to social norms" cannot be met by one occasion of illegal behavior (as is made clear in the *DSM-IV* where it states "as indicated by repeatedly performing acts that are grounds for arrest"; p. 649).

The manual offers assistance for minimizing the confusion potentially caused by this mixture of criteria thresholds. The underlying definition, or general diagnostic criteria, for a personality disorder describes such a disorder as

> an enduring pattern of inner experience and behavior that deviates markedly from the expectations of the individual's culture . . . manifested in two (or more) of the following areas: (1) cognition . . . (2) affectivity . . . (3) interpersonal functioning . . . (4) impulse control . . . across a broad range of personal and social situations . . . [that] leads to clinically significant distress or impairment in social, occupational, or other important areas of functioning. (p. 633)

This definition can be employed as an overall model for determining when the specific criteria within a personality disorder have been reached.

To use this model, clinicians need to view each criterion enumerated for a personality disorder in terms of whether or not there is evidence that the person demonstrated a "pattern" of the described characteristic through at least two ways of functioning (cognition, affect, etc.) and "across a broad range of personal and social situations." This then becomes not a numerical count per se, but a demonstration that the person exhibits the defined pattern for that attribute.

For instance, if a man is law-abiding, nonaggressive, responsible, honest, and careful in all of his life except with his live-in lover, he may be viewed as a domestic batterer and deceitful lover, but he should not be perceived as meeting the criteria for antisocial personality disorder. Likewise, someone who becomes suicidal only under severely stressful situations and otherwise is well adjusted and emotionally stable should not be viewed as meeting the criteria for *borderline personality disorder.*

Specific Issues for Antisocial Personality Disorder

A very commonly diagnosed personality disorder for incarcerated sex offenders is the antisocial. Even with the use of the above diagnostic application model, there are two situations peculiar to the potential application of this diagnosis to a respondent under the circumstances of a sex offender civil commitment evaluation. The first of these pertains to the circumstance when an offender has shown a very clear behavioral pattern meeting the criteria for antisocial personality disorder during times when he is not in prison, but a very cooperative and compliant set of behaviors while incarcerated. Keeping in mind that some offenders, especially "antisocial" ones, often spend a good deal of their lives in prison because of the repetitively "bad acts" they do in the general community, this comparison of "within prison" and "within community" behaviors can be very striking and about equal in duration. In trying to figure out the appropriateness of applying the label of "antisocial personality disorder" to the man, one can find oneself asking the question, "Which is the real him?"

Of course, that is the wrong question, as the person is all of what he has done in both worlds. The problem with the question posed is that the evaluator is viewing both contexts as equal in their likelihood for eliciting personality disordered traits. That would be the same as seeing someone's likelihood for committing an armed robbery as equally likely (a) on a dark night in a secluded area with a lone stranger versus (b) in broad daylight standing next to a police officer. The likelihood for even a determined armed robber to enact his desired actions under these two different contexts is clearly not the same. The person has not changed between these two situations, only his adaptation to the realities of the situations themselves.

From this perspective, someone's "good" institutional behavior should not be used to discount a pattern of "violating" community behavior. Actions exhibited in the general community should be given more weight as they are a far better measure of the person's behavioral "pattern" that "deviates markedly from the expectations of the individual's culture" (p. 633). Even long periods of incarceration significantly composed of rule-abiding behavior should probably not be viewed as outweighing repetitive "violating" behaviors during short periods of time in the general community.

The second application issue in diagnosing antisocial personality disorder is based in the fact that evaluators often do not get information about the offender's juvenile history. That part of the person's life can be a big blank, despite otherwise excellent records and collateral information. The reason for this varies. Sometimes, the juvenile records are sealed and not available to the evaluator. Sometimes, no one even knows if such a record exists. Sometimes, whatever records may have existed have long ago been destroyed. When a subject's extensive criminal record is recorded to have begun only days after his 18th birthday, the knowledgeable evaluator will typically suspect that there were juvenile offenses as well, but demonstrating the accuracy of what is suspected with documented facts can be near impossible.

This situation can affect the appropriateness of diagnosing antisocial personality disorder. Even when every other criterion is easily demonstrated, the issue of that one piece of evidence of a conduct disorder before age 15 remains. If an evaluator lacks virtually all information from before the person was an adult, then the diagnosis of antisocial personality disorder is not possible, given that the evaluator takes the perspective that diagnosing someone for court-related purposes needs supportive facts for each criterion and not just educated suspicions. This conservative philosophy, recommended here in relation to any aspect of sex offender civil commitment assessments, can best be described as "if you cannot point to it, it does not exist." Without a before-age-15 sign of conduct disorder, antisocial personality disorder cannot be said to exist, at least to a reasonable degree of professional certainty.

This conclusion may seem bizarre under circumstances in which a person has shown a many-decades, lifelong pattern of disregard and violation of the rights of others from his 18th birthday forward. The inappropriateness of diagnosing antisocial personality disorder under such circumstances, however, does not preclude using a different diagnosis that the evaluator can document. Assuming that one can show that a subject has that long-term pattern of antisociality in his adulthood, then one can still diagnose a *personality disorder, not otherwise specified (NOS), with antisocial features*. The only difference between this diagnosis in this situation and the specific antisocial personality disorder is that the NOS form means that the complete set of diagnostic criteria for a specific disorder was not found but that a personality disorder was still found. If the examiner can demonstrate how the general diagnostic criteria for a personality disorder are still met, despite the lack of before-age-18 information, then this alternative diagnosis is quite appropriate.

Sexual Disorder Not Otherwise Specified

Given the selective nature of the population on which sex offender civil commitment evaluations are performed, one may not find it surprising that another somewhat common diagnostic finding in these assessments is *sexual disorder not otherwise specified (NOS)*. The main characteristic of sexual disorder NOS is a "sexual disturbance that does not meet the criteria for any specific Sexual Disorder and is neither a Sexual Dysfunction nor a Paraphilia" (p. 538). Unlike the paraphilias, the central diagnostic determinant is the person's psychological distress about his sexuality, as opposed to his sexual fantasies, urges, and behaviors per se.

The *DSM-IV* lists three examples of conditions that meet criteria for a sexual disorder NOS. One example has to do with marked feelings of inadequacy concerning sexual performance. The second involves distress about repeated sexual encounters involving "a succession of lovers who are experienced by the individual only as things to be used." The third pertains to distress about one's sexual orientation.

Although any of these three examples could be associated with a sex offender's drive toward offending, the second seems the most pertinent. Feelings of inadequacy may underlie an offender's reason for wanting to dominate someone sexually or obtain some type of intimacy through coerced sexual contact. Distress about one's sexual orientation has been used for years (rightly or wrongly) to explain why some men rape—to "prove" their masculinity. To my knowledge, however, the most frequent usage of this diagnosis in civil commitment assessment cases involves the person who seems to be sexual with almost anyone he can make available to himself (at least of a specific gender). When some of these people are under the legal age of consent, or are otherwise unable to give consent (e.g., due to mental deficiency), this condition can represent what drives this person toward repeating sexual crimes.

An exemplary scenario involving this disorder comes from the following case. This 56-year-old man first became involved with the law when he left home at age 11 and was soon picked up for theft. When he was 17, he was sent to a juvenile correctional facility based on his prostituting himself. As a young adult, he had a few more scrapes with the law involving theft and check forgery, the last charge costing him a few years in prison. Starting at age 30, however, he was arrested and convicted four separate times involving three distinct prison terms. The different crimes involved mostly teenage boys, though his last offense involved a young man who was considered "mentally defective." Almost all of his sexual partners and victims were strangers this man had just met earlier in the day. Upon interview, the subject stated that he had "more lovers than there are stars in the sky." He described both prostituting himself when younger and sexual encounters in public bathrooms and similar places multiple times virtually every day. These statements might not have been believed by the interviewer had not this subject also received more than a score of sexual misconduct reports during his incarcerations, all showing similar actions compared with what he reported doing in the community.

The subject described having tried to stop these types of behaviors, both in and out of prison, but found himself virtually incapable when the opportunity for sex presented itself or could be easily created. He described himself as weak. His insight into how he helped such situations to develop was minimal. He did know, however, that consensual sex with adults was legal and that he had gotten himself into legal trouble mostly because of his sexual contacts with teenagers. His stated plan before his most recent crime (involving the mentally deficient adult), therefore, was just to stay away from underage boys. That obviously did not work. His plan at the end of his latest imprisonment was to abstain from sex altogether with "the help of God" and a community-based religious program for ex-inmates. Unfortunately, he had basically failed to follow through with this plan even while incarcerated.

The main overt behavioral sign for this diagnostic condition under the circumstances described is the record of a very numerous and frequent set of sexual encounters largely involving strangers or recent acquaintances. Relationships that are formed in a potentially more lasting manner do not alter the basic pattern of repeated sexual contacts with whomever the subject can make available. The person shows this continual pattern of using other people sexually despite the availability of sex from a potentially ongoing partner. The diagnostic criteria appear to be met if the person experiences distress over what he is doing.

The lack of an official list of criteria may seem problematic. This is similar to any "NOS" diagnosis, however, and should not be thought of any differently.

Impulse Control Disorder Not Otherwise Specified

Impulse control disorder not otherwise specified (NOS) is the last of what can be called even a somewhat common diagnostic category seen in sex offender civil commitment evaluations as driving potential sexual recidivism. The *DSM-IV* describes this condition in the usual "NOS" way. Specifically, this is a "category . . . for disorders of impulse control that do not meet the criteria for any specific Impulse-Control Disorder or for another mental disorder having features involving impulse control described elsewhere in the manual (e.g., Substance Dependence, a Paraphilia)" (p. 621). Basically, this condition pertains to someone who seems unable to control his impulses including, but not solely, the sexual ones.

Besides personality disorders, this disorder is the only condition for a repeat sex offender that (1) is at least somewhat commonly seen as related to driving his sexual offending, but (2) is not of itself a sexual disorder. Instead, the typically relevant pattern here is of someone who shows impulsive actions in multiple life areas including the sexual. He may or may not show a frequency or impersonal attitude similar to the person diagnosed sexual disorder NOS, but many of his sexual actions are clearly without consideration for possible consequences even to himself. In effect, the person fails to modulate the expression of his impulses. The desired stimulus "captures the person" and virtually directly leads to a behavioral or drive release (Joseph Belanger, personal communication, 1999).

A case example will serve to illustrate. This 35-year-old man had been in trouble with the law for shoplifting and fighting, besides sexual contacts with children. He stated a preference for sexual contacts with peer-age women, a report that was substantiated by his history. Even so, he had been convicted on three separate occasions for sexual contacts with children. Each of the criminal acts was opportunistic in nature. He had done little to create any of those situations, but rather simply took advantage of them when they presented themselves. By his own report, he had not given any thought to anything at those times except what he immediately wanted; there were no thoughts about consequences to himself or to the victims. He basically stated that he could not help himself once he realized the opportunity was there. Again, this self-report may not have been believed by the interviewer except for the fact that it was supported by certain prison behavior. An incident had occurred during which the man had been talking with his visitor when another visitor's child walked by. Despite being under active visual scrutiny by a guard, and despite being involved with a visitor of his own, the subject immediately reached out and touched the boy walking by. His recorded comment from the facility incident report was that he could not help himself. Neuropsychological testing showed no abnormalities.

Differentiations Among
Commonly Diagnosed Disorders

Although most evaluators would strongly appreciate having a comprehensive and reliable manual of psychiatric diagnoses that also clearly differentiates one disorder from another, such a manual does not exist. The *DSM* keeps growing in size from update to update, but it is still lacking significantly in certain areas, including relative to the diagnosing of sex offenders.

One of those deficient areas is the differentiating characteristics among commonly diagnosed disorders for sex offenders. The following was therefore written to facilitate clinicians' work in that regard. The subtopics covered are the differentiation between

1. paraphilia and personality disorder,

2. paraphilia and sexual disorder NOS,

3. paraphilia and impulse control disorder NOS, and

4. personality disorder and impulse control disorder NOS.

Of course, none of the following descriptions will serve to differentiate the relevant disorders for all cases. First, there is every reason to believe that a proper diagnosis can involve a combination of any of these disorders. Even when there is only one disorder, the available case-specific details can overlap diagnostic categories and not cleanly differentiate between them. How to handle these most difficult diagnostic calls is the subject of the last topic in this section.

Differentiating Paraphilia From Personality Disorder

If we assume that a respondent has not acknowledged deviant sexual fantasies or urges, then this differentiation must be performed based on documented behavior alone. The behavior of most importance is the person's recorded criminal behavior, at least as a starting point. As described previously, the absolute and relative proportion of sexual offending versus non-sexual offending both seem relevant. If an offender has almost solely done non-sexual offending, which he has shown many times, and his sexual offending has been minimal, then his diagnosis is more likely to be a personality disorder versus a paraphilia. Similarly, a criminal record that is almost solely sexual in nature, involving many sexual crimes and few nonsexual crimes, should lead the evaluator toward a paraphilia diagnosis.

Other factors still matter, however. If the relatively infrequent sexual offending history of an individual shows behavioral consistency relative to clear paraphiliac diagnostic issues, then both a personality disorder and paraphilia diagnoses should be made. For instance, if a very versatile and repetitive criminal also has multiple convictions for child sexual contact, the argument can easily be made that the person is afflicted with both a personality disorder and pedophilia.

The differentiation between antisocial personality disorder (or personality disorder NOS, with antisocial features) and *paraphilia NOS, nonconsent* seems to be one of the most difficult based on behavior alone. Trying to make this differentiation can almost feel like one needs to get inside the offender's head to see if he is paying enough attention to his sexual victims' plight during his assaults. If he shows little attention to his victims, then there is solely a personality disorder. If he shows a lot of attention (during which the perpetrator is also showing arousal), then a paraphilia diagnosis may be considered appropriate.

To diminish this differential diagnostic problem, the recommendation is made to look at two things: (1) the degree to which the person's life beyond the criminal sphere shows signs of a personality disorder (e.g., in interpersonal relationships, employment history, general characteristics of impulsivity) and (2) the list of characteristics of paraphilia NOS, nonconsent enumerated in the last chapter. If the person's life generally shows appropriate behaviors outside of the sexually criminal, and a "significant set" (not clearly defined; sorry) of those characteristics are found, then there seems reason to diagnose the paraphiliac condition, especially if the applicable set does not include only those listed items that are also described as overlapping psychopathy. With an opposite finding, then a lone personality disorder diagnosis seems more appropriate.

There is no suggestion here that all diagnostic situations of this type can be clarified. That clarification is unfortunately not always forthcoming even with careful investigation. For instance, the following list of one person's convictions, starting at age 18, offers enough signs of both diagnoses to make one wonder, but possibly not enough information on which to make the paraphiliac diagnosis with sufficient certainty (at least within the sex offender civil commitment context). Of relevance, the person denied the factual basis for *all* of these charges and was found to be psychopathic based on a Psychopathy Checklist–Revised (PCL–R). Within the following enumeration, convictions known to be sexual in nature are in **bold**:

1. Procuring beer for a minor

2. **Indecent behavior with a child** (detailed information lacking)

3. Operating auto after revocation

4. Operating without a license

5. Disorderly conduct

6. Failure to appear

7. Disorderly conduct

8. Battery

9. Disorderly conduct

10. Battery & Disorderly conduct

11. Public intoxication

12. Disorderly conduct

13. Failure to support

14. Contributing to delinquency of children

15. **Sexual intercourse with a child** (no detailed information available)

16. False swearing

17. Violation of parole

18. Disorderly conduct

19. Battery to police officer & Obstructing an officer

20. Violation of parole

21. Prison escape

22. Interstate transportation of stolen goods

23. Absconding from supervision

24. Transportation of stolen motor vehicle

25. Criminal trespass

26. Carrying a concealed weapon

27. Aggravated battery

28. **Prostitution & First degree sexual assault** (arrest only, then dismissed) (allegedly made some arrangements with a prostitute when he was parked at a truck stop, but then attempted to sexually assault her; reason for no prosecution not clear)

29. **Fourth degree sexual assault** (detailed information not known)

30. **Fourth degree sexual assault** (went to apartment of female friend of his girlfriend, gained admission through a statement about the car she was selling, carried her against her will into her bedroom, was going to force vaginal intercourse but the fact that she was having her period dissuaded him, forced fellatio, ejaculated into her mouth, conviction involved plea bargained charge)

31. Failure to appear

32. **Second degree sexual assault (2 counts)** (involved 14-year-old female on two distinctly different occasions; first time on her birthday, he got her away from others by promise of birthday present, took her into garage, pushed her down on couch, pulled her pants and underpants down, laid on top of her, inserted his penis in her vagina and stated "here is your birthday present" along with a threat about telling anyone, he ejaculated; second occasion he isolated the girl in a room, locked the door, pushed her to the floor, pulled her clothes down to her knees and put his penis in her vagina, making a statement, "You're my Betsy, you're my Betsy" (he used her real name, which is not quoted here), he ejaculated, and he threatened her not to tell her mother)

33. Intimidating a witness

A personality disorder seems strongly indicated from this list of convictions alone, though of course other life areas must be surveyed to ensure the appropriateness of such a diagnosis (including the PCL–R finding of psychopathy). This individual's sexually criminal history has been rather extensive as well, but specific details of a clear pattern seem sketchy, despite this history. The appropriateness of a paraphiliac diagnosis based solely on this information, in addition to the personal disorder, is debatable.

Differentiating Paraphilia From Sexual Disorder NOS

The first differentiating point here is whether or not the subject experiences psychological distress related to his sexuality. This characteristic does not preclude paraphiliacs, but someone denying and showing no overt signs of such distress probably does not meet the criteria for sexual disorder NOS. Documentation of a varied set of sexual partners (both consensual and nonconsensual) tends to diminish the likelihood for certain paraphilias (e.g., pedophilia, when most victims were adults). This is especially true when the documented sexual behaviors do not represent deviant sexual interests (e.g., requesting permission, or discontinuing when asked, vs. repeatedly becoming aroused at nonconsensual interactions). When the sexual victims all appear to be of a single type (e.g., 7- to 10-year-old boys), the likelihood for a paraphilia seems far greater than for a sexual disorder NOS. If virtually all sexual victims were adults, then the diagnosis of sexual disorder NOS is probably not applicable as there is nothing about that condition that specifically leads someone to victimize others, just to seek sexual contact with them.

In any case, an interview of the subject can be helpful if available. People with sexual disorder NOS will tend to acknowledge their sexual frequency and related distress. Rapists who do not have this disorder may be glad to tell you about the many sexual exploits they have had, but they are not distressed in the telling.

Differentiating Paraphilia
From Impulse Control Disorder NOS

The main issue here is the determination of a deviant sexual interest versus a pervasive problem in impulse control beyond solely the sexual realm. In case documentation, one should look for signs of planning the sexual offending including grooming behaviors. These types of behaviors speak against an impulse control disorder as the basis for sexual offending, and more in favor of a diagnosis of paraphilia. Similarly, a record of sexual offending only when the likelihood is for not getting caught indicates that the sexual offending is not driven through an impulse control disorder.

Upon interview, many sex offenders will deny they fantasized in ways similar to their criminal behaviors before enacting them, though the offenders will emphatically state they are in control of themselves and their actions. When an offender states that he lacks control of his actions and that his sexual crimes "just happened" to him, the evaluator can reflect how awfully dangerous this sounds if true. Some offenders will back off from the "It just happens to me, I can't control it" stance when portrayed back to them in this way.

Other offenders will maintain that statement despite the fact that they are facing an involuntary civil commitment. Under such circumstances, the offender's statement might be thought of by some examiners as credible. If so, this type of statement can serve as evidence of an impulse control disorder versus specifically and solely a paraphilia. Of course, the issue of credibility is crucial in this regard, both potentially in terms of deliberate deceitfulness by the offender in his self-report and also in terms of his being so self-unaware as to report a lack of fantasizing and offense planning due to not realizing what he really does in these regards. Typically, information from other than the offender's self-report is needed to substantiate the accuracy of an impulse control disorder diagnosis. Institutional incident reports of the offender's touching stranger children while in the visiting area would be one such example of supporting evidence.

Simple denials of deviant fantasies by the offender should not be viewed as relevant in differentiating a paraphilia from impulse control disorder NOS. These denials are common, especially under the civil commitment evaluation circumstance when offenders are trying to seem as benign as possible, but these denials are not typically to be believed. Virtually all offenders have some degree of relevant sexual thoughts before attacking a victim. The only real question for most sex offenders is how well rehearsed those fantasies are. Spoken denials do not reliably differentiate among diagnostic conditions.

Differentiating Personality Disorder From Impulse Control Disorder NOS

Some personality disorders are defined using the concept of impulsivity as one possible criterion (i.e., antisocial personality disorder, borderline personality disorder). The concept of "impulse control" is in fact listed as one of four possible defined areas of impairment underlying all personality disorders (besides cognition, affectivity, and interpersonal functioning; *DSM-IV*, p. 633). It is easy to see how the differentiation of personality disorders from impulse control disorder NOS can sometimes be a struggle.

There are two key initial issues to explore in the attempt to differentiate these disorders. The first is based in the fact that personality disorders are more pervasively intertwined in the subject's life than just his impulse control. There must also be impairment or distress related to the person's thoughts, feelings, and/or interpersonal functioning. Although problems in impulse control can easily affect one or more of those other life areas, impairment in the other areas related to something beyond impulse control suggests the greater likelihood of a personality disorder.

The second issue to review is whether or not the person shows a pattern of being "captured" by environmental stimuli. The sex offender suffering from impulse control disorder NOS will tend to show spontaneous illegal actions despite a high likelihood for getting caught. Personality disordered offenders may not take the likelihood for negative consequences into sufficient consideration, but they do show at least more regular self-control in keeping with their self-interests.

How to Handle Cases Where the Differentiation Just Seems Impossible

Even the best clinician among us can have difficulties trying to differentiate between two diagnoses when there are strong suggestions of both conditions without clarifying information available. For instance, when a perpetrator has had numerous sexual victims in the 10- to 14-year-old range, is it proper to diagnose him with pedophilia, or paraphilia NOS, sexually attracted to adolescents (hebephilia), or both (assuming no other condition explains these assaultive behaviors)? Although it would be helpful if the offender would offer a full disclosure of his sexual fantasies so we could dissect them for the evidence we need to make such a differentiation, that circumstance is rather rare in civil commitment evaluations. How, then, should we handle the situation of equally descriptive and reasonable diagnoses?

Some clinicians find it necessary, when faced with this apparent dilemma, to "pick one" of the diagnoses, typically whichever appears to be the more conservative or the easier choice. In the example given, the typical choice would be pedophilia over paraphilia NOS because the *DSM* offers specific criteria, and the clinician can still lean on the "guidelines" conceptualization of enumerated diagnoses to overcome the "generally younger than 13" criterion for pedophilia. This procedure is not wrong. At the same time, making a choice under these circumstances, one that feels somewhat arbitrary, is not necessary.

A second unnecessary approach to problems differentiating two equally plausible diagnoses by some clinicians is to diagnose one condition and leave the other as a "rule out" (i.e., R/O). This approach, in effect, is another form of choosing one diagnosis over the other, though the evaluator may feel that at least the second diagnosis is not totally discounted. Such a perspective is fallacious, however, as any "R/O" diagnosis cannot be effectively used to represent the requisite mental condition for commitment. If the evaluator cannot diagnose a disorder with sufficient certainty, that disorder cannot represent the basis for commitment. Hence, this approach does not adequately solve the diagnostician's dilemma of equally reasonable choices.

The third approach, this one being recommended, is to acknowledge the reality of the diagnostic situation in one's final conceptualization of the case. This can be done by the designation of "Condition X versus Condition Y," or "Condition X and/or Condition Y." For the above example, this diagnostic format translates to a final diagnosis of "Pedophilia and/or Paraphilia NOS, Hebephilia."

The advantages of this approach are as follows: (1) It reflects the reality of one's diagnostic assessment as far as the data will allow, (2) it demonstrates to the court that there clearly is a diagnosable condition, and (3) it indicates to the court that there is a remaining technical diagnostic issue that probably does not matter for the legal proceedings. Concerning this last point, the evaluator effectively tells the court that "I know there is a requisite mental condition here and it is represented by either or both of these terms."

For states with "predisposition" toward sexual reoffending as part of the definition of the mental condition required for commitment, the evaluator needs to explain one more point. The statement needs to be made (if true) that either diagnosed condition predisposes the individual to commit sexually violent acts, so the differentiation of the two diagnoses becomes a moot issue for the court. In other words, the evaluator can state (if true) that "no matter which of these two conditions is ultimately thought more appropriate, that condition predisposes the individual to commit sexually violent acts as defined by the relevant statute."

If the statement about predisposition is not true (in the opinion of the evaluator), then this whole approach to diagnostic ambiguity does not work. Most of the time, this "either-or" method for handling diagnostic ambiguity is recommended, as further diagnostic differentiation really only matters to the obsessing clinician anyway. At least in some states (e.g., Iowa, Wisconsin), this approach has been employed by clinicians in maybe a dozen cases (known to me) and invariably (to date) accepted by the courts.

Drawing the Predisposition Nexus

Most states' sex offender civil commitment laws include within their definition of the requisite mental condition a type of psychological impairment phrased something like "that predisposes the person to commit sexually violent acts" (see Chapter 1). In those states, a diagnosis alone is not sufficient. There must also be a statement by the examiner that the diagnosed condition predisposes the person toward committing certain offenses. This concept is typically interpreted as meaning the person's disorder causes him to experience an internal drive toward repeating sexual crimes, analogous to the smoker's urge for a cigarette (even if no longer smoking) or an alcoholic's persistent desire for a drink (even if demonstrating ongoing sobriety). The following is a brief description of how the issue of predisposition can be addressed for each common category of diagnosis.

For Pedophilia

The issue of being predisposed toward sexual crimes based in pedophilia is addressed virtually by definition of the disorder. If one is sexually aroused by children, and presumably has ongoing fantasies or urges in that direction (whether openly acknowledged or not), one is predisposed in the legally relevant way. In the case of pedophilia, evaluators need not make efforts to "individualize" this portion of the assessment beyond the diagnosis itself.

For Paraphilia NOS, Nonconsent

The same is true for paraphilia NOS, nonconsent. By definition of the disorder itself, the person is predisposed to commit sexual acts that are nonconsensual. This perspective alone seems to suffice in meeting the "predisposition" criterion in existing commitment statutes.

For Sexual Sadism

Conceptually, the sexual sadist *usually* is predisposed to commit crimes that meet statutory requirements for commitment. There are some sadists, however, who manage to enact their fantasies with one or more consenting persons and may be satisfied doing so. (This situation is contrary to that of the pedophile where the "partner" cannot legally consent, or the nonconsent paraphiliac who specifically finds partners who do not consent.) On the other hand, sadists who are being reviewed for possible civil commitment have already committed at least one sex crime of relevance, meaning that *those individual* sadists have already had a non-consenting partner. Likewise, for an examiner to know the person meets criteria for sexual sadism, the historical record of offenses typically describes the behavioral enactment of such fantasies and urges. Hence, within the context of these considerations, the conclusion can reasonably be drawn that sexual sadism meets the "predisposition" requirement virtually by definition of the disorder, and certainly for the specific individual being assessed.

For Sexual Disorder NOS

For this disorder, the basis for the diagnosis matters greatly in determining if the condition predisposes the person to commit sexually violent acts. A sexual disorder NOS that is based, for instance, in a person's discontent with his sexual orientation does not often serve as a predisposing condition to sexual assaultiveness. The same diagnosis based in a person's unrestrained sexual contact with virtually anyone available, however, can serve to predispose him toward committing acts with people not able to give legal consent (e.g., children, mentally impaired persons). The issue to be addressed by the examiner is whether or not there is a direct connection between the bases for the diagnosis and the person's sexual offending. Again, the issue of predisposition must be addressed for the individual subject, and not automatically by definition of the disorder.

For Personality Disorders

The relationship of personality disorders and predisposition toward sexual crimes is nowhere near as straightforward as it was for the paraphilias discussed above. Even antisocial personality disorder (where the person suffers an inflexible and persistent pattern of disregard for, and violation of the rights of, others) does not necessarily imply a predisposition toward sexual offending. Some people with a personality disorder, however, are clearly predisposed to commit sex crimes. So how does an evaluator define and describe the difference?

The key issue here is whether or not the examiner can describe the individual subject's personality disorder in terms that include sexual offending (along with nonsexual acts). If all of the person's criminal behavior is sexual in nature, then the existence of a sexual disorder or paraphilia should strongly be considered instead of a personality disorder. If there are almost no sexual misbehaviors in the offender's history, then it can be very difficult and potentially inappropriate to see his personality disorder as predisposing him toward such crimes. Basically, when the person has some degree of repetitive sexual criminality coupled with other types of criminality (and other maladaptive behaviors), one can say that *his* maladaptive pattern predisposes him to sexually violent acts while not being solely defined by such acts. In this last situation, one can conclude that, *for this individual,* his personality disorder predisposes him to commit sexually violent offenses.

For Impulse Control Disorder NOS

The relationship of this diagnosis to "predisposition" is similar to that described above for personality disorders. There is nothing inherent in an impulse control disorder NOS that means the person is driven toward sexual offending. On the other hand, for some individuals, their specific pattern of impulse control disorder NOS shows such a predisposition. Again, evaluators need to clarify this issue for the courts by emphasizing that, for this individual, this disorder causes such a predisposition, based on his specific demonstrated pattern.

The Issue of Substance Abuse/Dependence Disorders

If people listened to sex offenders early in their treatment, or not in treatment at all, the conclusion could easily be made that various substances caused them to do what they did and that without such substances, they would not have done the crimes. On the other hand, after sex offenders have been in treatment for any period of time, those earlier statements are quite regularly found not to contain much truth.

There are various reasons for this. One is that many sex offenders do not readily admit that they had assaultive fantasies or urges before their ingestion of a substance. A second is that some sex offenders use a substance specifically because they already wished to offend, but needed something to help them feel less anxiety about it. They drink, for instance, to disinhibit themselves, to allow themselves to do what they already had desires to do. A third reason is that some offenders never really stop using one or more substances, so the substance use serves as good an excuse as any for them.

For a substance abuse/dependence disorder to serve as a predisposing condition by itself, the substance would need to cause the person to experience sexual fantasies or urges of an illegal nature. Although alcohol, for instance, can increase one's desire for sex, there is no known type of "pathological intoxication" that causes sexual offending. Hence, from my perspective, a substance abuse disorder does not often, if ever—at least by itself—predispose a person specifically to commit sexually violent acts. This, of course, is different from the question of the degree to which a subject's substance use may represent a risk factor for imminent reoffending. There is evidence that this latter perspective is accurate (e.g., Hanson & Harris, 1997), even though substance abuse is not viewed as a lone predisposing condition for sexual reoffending.

Summary Comments

This chapter addressed issues pertaining to diagnoses beyond the paraphilias discussed in Chapter 3, but still relatively commonly made within civil commitment assessments. Of interest, these included disorders mostly defined in terms of dysfunctional behavioral patterns versus disturbances specifically in thought and/or affect. Personality disorders, substance abuse/dependence disorders, and impulse control disorder NOS all represent conditions that can be ego-syntonic and without accompanying negative affect. Of the diagnoses discussed in this chapter, only sexual disorder NOS seems necessarily to involve subjective distress.

These conditions represent behavioral patterns that are not specifically sexual (except for sexual disorder NOS) and not necessarily associated with negative self-attributions. Hence, it may not be surprising that more case-specific determination of the disorder's "predisposing" the individual toward sexual offending needs to be made than was true for the paraphilias. Interestingly, possibly the one type of disorder offenders accept most readily as an explanation of their offending, the substance abuse disorders, is the least likely among the commonly diagnosed disorders to be assessed as specifically predisposing an offender toward sexual recidivism.

CHAPTER 5

Using Risk Assessment Instrumentation

*No question is so difficult to answer as that to which the answer is
obvious.*

— George Bernard Shaw

f one were to sit in on the country's sex offender civil commitment hearings, one
could easily leave those hearings with the impression that the main criterion for
commitment is whether or not the subject was beyond a specified degree of
recidivism risk. Although diagnostic issues can be argued vigorously, the other
clinical criterion is far more commonly the topic of hours and even days of elicited
testimony. Statutorily, both clinical criteria are of equal importance, as both equally
need to be demonstrated by prosecutors for the state for someone to be committed.
From an expert witness' perspective, however, the risk assessment portion of the
evaluation typically comes under far more scrutiny. Explanations for why each step
of a risk assessment was made are required. The fully skilled examiner can offer
those explanations to whatever detail is requested.

This chapter and the next were designed to explicate recommended procedures
for the risk assessment portion of civil commitment evaluations. There are four
main sections in this chapter:

1. The overall risk assessment methodological choice

2. Comparing the accuracy of differing methodologies

3. Selecting what instruments to use

4. Interpreting actuarial instrument results

Through detailed discussions of these topics, support will be shown and concomitant recommendations will be made for a specific structure for the risk assessment under typical civil commitment circumstances.

The Overall Risk Assessment Methodological Choice

There are between four and six different methodological structures for doing a risk assessment, depending on the degree to which one sees the fifth and sixth types as subsumed within the other four. These methodologies are enumerated below, using a combination of the descriptive lists by Hanson (1998b) and Poythress and Hart (1998):

1. Unguided clinical judgment

2. Guided clinical judgment

3. Clinical judgment based on an anamnestic approach

4. Research-guided clinical judgment

5. Clinically adjusted actuarial approach

6. Purely actuarial approach

Unguided clinical judgment refers to the process by which a clinician reviews case materials without any significant a priori list or theory prioritizing the relative importance of the data obtained. Each ultimate judgment made through this process can follow its own unique theory.

Clinicians employing the guided clinical judgment approach start with an a priori set of ideas of what is of importance, but this list is based on the clinician's own ideas and theories without significant concern of their overlap and support from research results. This assessment model, on the one hand, can be viewed as simply a subset of the unguided clinical approach, based on the fundamental lack of research basis to the procedure. On the other hand, there is one effective difference between the two methods. Evaluators using the guided model will at least in theory be more consistent in their assessment procedures across cases than will evaluators using the unguided procedure.

The anamnestic approach is a variant of these first two methods. Clinicians using this approach essentially analyze the subject's life history to surmise the factors of particular importance to the specific subject's historically demonstrated risk, and then examine the degree to which those same conditions still exist. This approach does not necessarily employ research results, but uses the individual's history as guide for what factors appear to be of relevance to his recidivism risk.

These first three approaches do not necessarily rely on any body of professional research, in contrast to the latter three. The fourth methodology enumerated above, the research-guided clinical judgment approach, involves the use of an a priori set of factors to be considered and given weight in the risk assessment, with other considerations typically being given lesser weight. This is the first among those described so far that mandates the employment of a research-supported list of considerations across multiple evaluation cases of a similar nature.

Clinically adjusted actuarial procedures involve the initial employment of one or more actuarial instruments followed by potential adjustments to the actuarial results based on clinically derived considerations. The descriptive title for this methodology does not specify whether or not the adjustments are based on research, so technically they could be inclusive of both. The research bases for such adjustments are discussed in detail later in this chapter.

Finally, the most mechanical process, called the purely actuarial approach, involves the use of actuarial instruments with no adjustments beyond those instruments' results. This is the only model that can be consistently enacted with a simple computer algorithm or basic training of non- or paraprofessionals.

From a theoretical perspective, arguments can be made about the relative strengths and weaknesses of each of these methodologies. The unguided clinical judgment approach, for instance, can be argued as allowing the clinician the greatest flexibility in examining the individualistic and unique characteristics of the subject and his circumstances. From this viewpoint, a priori lists of considerations only constrain a skilled evaluator's ability to apply years of clinical training and fully assess the subject's ever-changing life situation. Similarly, the research-guided procedure structures clinicians into using research-supported considerations while still allowing the examiners flexibility in deciding how much weight to give to any factor in any specific case. The purely actuarial approach ensures that clinicians remain focused on only the set of risk considerations and their relative weights supported by empirical results, avoiding the potential trappings of being swayed by emotionally appealing but nonrelevant considerations.

Theory and arguments aside, the real bottom line is that evaluators should be employing the assessment methodology that has been shown to be the most accurate within the sex offender civil commitment context. This risk assessment ultimately affects if someone loses freedoms for a lengthy period of time, or if the community accepts some degree of risk for future sexual victimization. Both outcomes, in my opinion, represent a high potential cost for inaccuracy. With accuracy in the risk assessment being considered of paramount importance, favorite theories and arguments do not seem as meaningful as the degree to which the procedures have been demonstrated empirically to be accurate. The higher the degree of accuracy empirically demonstrated for a given methodology within this context, the more that procedure should be used by civil commitment evaluators.

There are clinicians who disagree with this stance. They argue that the state of the science is such that either no one can tell which model is most accurate or they simply "know" that what *they* do works best even if there are no data to support their position. Both of these arguments are addressed with the research review that follows, with the conclusion that certain procedures are *clearly* more accurate (on average) than others. People who disagree with the empirical findings that follow would seem to have the burden of proving that either (a) the research described below is not an accurate portrayal of empirical results or (b) their favorite evaluative method is at least as accurate as those described. Simple proclamations about the "best" evaluative accuracy without addressing existing research findings should not be given much credibility, especially within an area as critical as this one.

Comparing the Accuracy of Differing Methodologies

"Clinical Versus Actuarial" Comparisons

Studies involving direct comparisons of different risk assessment methodologies on the same subjects are ideal for determining which methods are superior to the others. Although only a handful of such studies have been conducted specifically involving sex offenders and their recidivism risk, there have been some significant direct comparisons of the different methodologies across a wide variety of subjects and situations.

Two meta-analyses have investigated the relative predictive effectiveness using the same sets of subjects of clinical or subjective judgments (of any of the first three types) with mechanical or actuarial approaches (Grove & Meehl, 1996; Grove, Zald, Lebow, Snitz, & Nelson, 2000). These meta-analyses involved overlapping sets of 136 studies covering more than 50 years of research. The earlier of the two studies (Grove & Meehl, 1996) incorporated any research (within certain parameters) that allowed a comparison of subjective versus mechanical accuracy for predictions of any sort. The latter study (Grove et al., 2000) encompassed only studies where "procedures had to predict human behavior, make psychological or medical diagnoses or prognoses, or assess states and traits (including abnormal behavior and normal personality). Only studies within the realm of psychology and medicine were included" (p. 20).

Both studies came to the same basic conclusion: "Mechanical predictions of human behaviors are equal or superior to clinical prediction for a wide range of circumstances" (Grove et al., 2000, p. 19). The final comment in the Grove et al. article states their findings quite succinctly: "There seem, then, to be no barriers to a general preference for mechanical prediction where an appropriate mechanical algorithm is available" (p. 26).

This last statement was made after investigating whether there were any effects on the general superiority of mechanical predictions from (1) methodological strength of the studies involved, (2) degree of training and experience of the clinicians involved, (3) types of judges (i.e., psychological vs. medical), (4) the relative amount of data available (i.e., same vs. more for the clinician as compared to what the mechanical procedure had available), (5) the types of information available to the clinicians (e.g., psychological test results, trait ratings, behavioral observations), and (6) whether or not clinical interview data were incorporated into the clinician's database. There were no effects on the general superiority of mechanical predictive methods based on any of these considerations, including in regards to the degree of experience of the clinicians involved, except that the use of clinical interview data made the clinicians relatively more *in*accurate than they already were, as compared to the mechanical procedures.

The Grove et al. (2000) study also concluded that mechanical prediction techniques were about 10% more accurate than clinical judgments, outperforming clinical predictions in 33% to 47% of the studies examined (depending on analytic details beyond the need for discussion here), with clinical predictions being superior in only 6% to 16% of the studies. The researchers point out that these represent summary figures and that there was notable variability in the difference in degree of accuracy across the included studies. On some occasions, clinical judgment can be superior to mechanical prediction procedures, though there did not appear from that research to be any consistent situations in which that was true, so no generalization as to when clinical judgment might be the superior method could be made. At the same time, the overall finding was a very clear tendency for mechanical procedures to be at least equal and frequently superior to more subjective procedures.

Based on these two meta-analyses, with the clarity of their results and the variety and volume of studies included, there seems no reason to conclude anything other than mechanical procedures are at least equally if not more accurate and therefore are to be preferred over clinical judgment procedures. This appears to be true even for judgments about which clinicians feel especially confident, not just the "shaky" ones. Garb (1998), for instance, found no correlation between clinicians' confidence in their judgments and the accuracy of those judgments. Likewise, the "well trained" and long experienced clinician should not be viewed as holding superior abilities compared with mechanical procedures in assessing risk (Grove et al., 2000), despite how upsetting that fact may be to those of us who have been "honing our skills" for decades. On average, our judgments are simply not as good as those derived from more mechanical assessment procedures, no matter how sure we feel about ourselves and no matter how long we have been doing such work.

Of course, our ability to use mechanical procedures depends on the degree to which the underlying research for such procedures exists relevant to the type of assessment being done. If very little such research exists (e.g., of recidivism risk factors for adolescent female sex offenders), then mechanical procedures obviously cannot be used.

The Research-Guided Method

The conclusions just drawn address the relative value of unguided clinical, guided clinical, and anamnestic approaches compared with the actuarial approach. To put these findings in context, we can look at Hanson's (1998b) summary about sex offender risk assessment procedures where he stated that there are actually "three plausible approaches" (p. 52) to such evaluations. He listed the (research) guided approach, the clinically adjusted actuarial approach, and the purely actuarial approach as those three, thereby excluding the three more unstructured clinical approaches just mentioned. The comparison of the excluded unstructured clinical approaches to actuarial procedures has just been discussed. The next question is, what do we know about the relative value of the research-guided clinical method, the clinically adjusted actuarial procedure, and the purely actuarial model?

In theory, the research-guided procedure can involve *any* list of risk and protective factors gleaned from empirical results pertaining to a single topic. Variations in the specific content of lists can occur in regards to the same type of risk assessment. This variability can be based on different emphases, different thresholds for inclusion, and/or different subsets of the literature reviewed. In actual practice, empirical tests of the efficacy of the research-guided method have apparently been restricted to formalized risk factor lists.

Currently, the best researched such enumeration is called the HCR-20, a designation that stands for its three subscales (Historical, Clinical, and Risk Management) and for its total of 20 items. This list of 20 items was designed to serve as clinicians' guiding structure in assessing people's risk for committing future violent (not specifically sexual) acts. There have been more than 25 studies on the reliability and validity of this instrument with strong support for its use (Douglas, 1999). Other similarly designed formalized lists of risk factors include (1) the Sexual Violence Risk-20 (SVR-20; Boer, Hart, Kropp, & Webster, 1997), (2) the Spousal Assault Risk Assessment Guide (SARA; Kropp, Hart, Webster, & Eaves, 1999), and (3) the Risk for Sexual Violence Protocol (RSVP; Kropp, 2000), though each has been researched to a far smaller degree than the HCR-20 through the time this book was written.

Research on these tools has typically been performed by having raters assign each risk factor a score of 0, 1, or 2 to reflect the degree to which an item applies in a given case (e.g., Strand, Belfrage, Fransson, & Levander, 1999). A score of 0 means that the attribute was not found in the subject, a score of 2 reflects the assessment that the subject clearly has that attribute, and a score of 1 is somewhere in the middle. The subject's subscale and total scores are computed simply by summing the scores across the appropriate items, resulting in a total score ranging from 0 to 40 for a 20-item instrument, for instance. Subjects' scores are then compared to specified outcomes of relevance (e.g., violent recidivism).

Although this type of data collection is the most common research method for assessing the effectiveness of structured clinical judgments based on these lists, there is a related caveat of importance. Technically, the standardized simple addition of numbers across risk factors does not represent the fully flexible research-guided approach.

One of the potential strengths of the research-guided approach is that evaluators can give different relative weights to the different risk considerations based on the case dynamics. (For example, the presence and intensity of psychopathy can be rated as of very high importance in one case relative to the issue of a history of having been abused as a child, but both could be viewed as equally and proportionately far less relevant in another case where intense pedophiliac interests coupled with a high degree of impulsivity dominate the clinical picture.) By systematically employing a fixed method for rating items and for combining ratings across items, the research may have systematically diminished the variability that evaluators exercising their own clinical weighting might show.

On the other hand, it does not appear correct to argue that research of this type has essentially made actuarial scales from the lists of risk factors. There are important differences between these two methodologies. "Actuarial" means that there is a calculation of statistical risk. In the formalized lists of risk factors, the items are not defined even within empirical studies with specific thresholds for what degree of a factor constitutes is equated to what number, this process being completely left up to the user. For instance, the differing degrees of paraphiliac sexual arousal that constitute scores of 0, 1, or 2 are not defined for the rater. Likewise, even when a numerical scoring system is imposed onto these lists of factors (by the research design), and then summed to derive total figures, those totals are not associated with any a priori statistical interpretation, research based or otherwise. A total score of 20, for example, has no inherent meaning and may be interpreted differently by the same clinician across cases based on the specific characteristics from which those scores of 20 were derived.

Irrelevant of what we title the imposed scoring system, studies conducted concerning the utility of research-guided methodology have shown rather good support for that procedure. Interrater reliability investigations of the HCR-20 have demonstrated positive results (e.g., Dernevik, 1998), though this is not always the case either for certain subscales of the HCR-20 (for the Clinical subscale, Muller-Isberner & Jockel, 1997; Ross, Hart, & Webster, 1998) or other instruments of this same design (e.g., for the SVR-20, Sjöstedt & Långström, in press). Validity explorations have also generally been quite supportive (e.g., for the HCR-20, Grann, Belfrage, & Tengström, 2000; Strand et al., 1999), though again not invariably (e.g., for the SVR-20, Sjöstedt & Långström, in press).

Different types of validity have been investigated. Predictive and postdictive validity studies have been performed, to the degree that sensitivity and specificity of the predictions based on these instruments (using a 0, 1, and 2 per item scoring system) have been estimated (e.g., Strand et al., 1999). Concurrent validity has been investigated as well, using other assessment devices such as the Psychopathy Checklist: Screening Version (PCL:SV; Hart, Cox, & Hare, 1995; e.g., Belfrage, 1998; Douglas, Klassen, Ross, Hart, Webster, & Eaves, 1998) and Violence Risk Appraisal Guide (VRAG; Webster, Harris, Rice, Cormier, & Quinsey, 1994; e.g., Grann et al., 2000; Polvi, Webster, & Hart, 1999) for comparison. In general, there seems good reason to believe that the research-based clinical approach to assessing risk has merit.

The fact that studies testing the research-guided approach rather consistently document statistically significant results does indicate that this assessment procedure is on the better end compared with other clinical procedures reviewed so far. The body of research investigating the research-guided approach serves to emphasize that there are more accurate ways to assess risk than any of the less empirically based procedures.

Compared With the Purely Actuarial Approach

That approach's relative value compared with the purely actuarial, using the same sample of subjects upon which to make this comparison, has been tested only in a small number of studies. In Grann et al. (2000), the H subscale of the HCR-20 performed as well as the VRAG. Of statistical importance, that study employed estimates for several VRAG items along with omitting (baselining) two items, and thereby diminished the VRAG's potential effectiveness. The VRAG was found superior to the complete HCR-20 by Polvi (1999). On the other hand, Nicholls, Vincent, Whittemore, and Ogloff (1999) found the HCR-20 to be incrementally superior to the VRAG with a forensic sample in predicting inpatient verbal and physical violence.

Various studies showing incremental validity of the HCR-20 over the PCL:SV (e.g., Belfrage, Fransson, & Strand, 2000; Douglas, Ogloff, Nicholls, & Grant, 1999; Strand et al., 1999) are mentioned here but are not considered relevant in the comparison of the research-guided and actuarial approaches. There were two reasons for this omission.

First, the PCL:SV, although actuarial in its design in the same way as most psychological tests, is not a risk assessment instrument per se. The PCL:SV assesses a certain personality structure, not specifically someone's likelihood for violence. The fact that the PCL:SV tends to correlate with violent recidivism is good reason for inclusion of that consideration in the HCR-20, but describing the PCL:SV as *the* independent actuarial measurement of violence likelihood against which the HCR-20 is compared seems improper. Even more important than the first reason, the HCR-20 includes an item "Psychopathy" in which the use of a Psychopathy Checklist is a recommended scoring consideration. The PCL:SV, HCR-20 comparison studies therefore more represent investigations of the incremental value of the HCR-20 compared with one of its own items, rather than a comparison to an independent actuarial instrument.

The two completed studies of the SVR-20 found less supportive results than have been found for the HCR-20. In one of those two studies, the SVR-20 was found to be

1. essentially equal to the VRAG, Sex Offender Risk Appraisal Guide (SORAG; Quinsey, Harris, Rice, & Cormier, 1998), and Rapid Risk Assessment for Sex Offender Recidivism (RRASOR; Hanson, 1997) when it came to assessments of violent recidivism and simple correlations to sexual violence, but

2. lacking compared to the RRASOR (though not the other instruments) within the context of sexual recidivism when more general violence was statistically scaled out (Dempster, 1999).

In the other study (Sjöstedt & Långström, in press), the SVR-20 failed to find support for sexual violence postdictive validity, whereas the RRASOR was strongly supported in that same study.

Overall, of the four studies reviewed, one (Nicholls et al., 1999) indicated that the research-guided approach was superior to the purely actuarial model. On the other hand, this study used an actuarial instrument (the VRAG) within a context beyond which it was designed (i.e., an average maximum time period of only about 3 years, whereas the VRAG was designed for assessing risk over at least a 7-year period). The proper interpretation of this result is therefore not clear. Attempts at replication of this result over different time periods (more in keeping with the actuarial instrument's supportive research) would clarify the issue of when these different procedures may be of more or less relative value.

With only three other comparison studies, a strong conclusion about the relative value of these different methodologies cannot be made. The indication from these three is that the actuarial process is at least as good as the research-guided method, and sometimes better. To come to that conclusion, however, one has to discount the meaningfulness of the Nicholls et al. (1999) study. Instead, a different, more inclusive conclusion may be appropriate:

> There is a bandwidth-fidelity tradeoff.... First, the [Simon Fraser University] structured professional guidelines are intended to assess risk, defined broadly to include the nature, severity, imminence, frequency, and likelihood of violence. In contrast, existing actuarials focus only on nature (to a limited extent) and likelihood. Second, the content is general with no fixed and explicit combinatoric algorithm—that is, there is no attempt to "optimize" the guidelines a priori for a specific assessment context. So, in sum, structured guidelines are broad-bandwidth, likely to be only moderately useful but in many situations, whereas actuarials are high fidelity, likely to be very useful but in only a few situations. (Stephen Hart, personal communication, December 2000)

In other words, where an actuarial instrument is found to be on target to the specific context of the desired risk assessment, and the risk assessment is concerned only with the nature and likelihood for certain behaviors (for certain types of people), the actuarials are probably to be preferred over the structured lists of risk factors. When there is no actuarial instrument on target or sufficiently inclusive to that which one is trying to assess, the research-guided approach can serve well.

Of great importance, the sex offender civil commitment evaluation context seems to represent the situation in which "high fidelity" actuarial instruments work well. The type of risk to be assessed solely involves nature and likelihood considerations. The types of subjects being evaluated are usually representative of the people upon whom the actuarial instruments have been researched (though there are important and notable exceptions, such as juvenile and female sex offenders, being assessed for possible commitments). Hence, there appears to be reason to conclude that actuarial instruments are supported for use over the research-guided clinical approach under sex offender civil commitment situations when the subject of the assessment is considered sufficiently similar to the research samples.

One other consideration also happens to fall in favor of the actuarial methodology versus the research-guided within the context of civil commitment assessments. For the civil commitment evaluator, the question is not whether or not the subject will reoffend, but whether or not the individual's risk for reoffending is beyond a specified legal threshold (e.g., more likely than not). As accurate as the research-guided approach may be, the actuarial methodology more lends itself to addressing this question. Results from actuarial instruments come in terms of risk percentages, whereas the research-guided approach leaves the evaluator to make a guess whether or not the subject's specific set of risk factors is sufficient or not to represent more than the risk threshold for commitment.

Compared With the Clinically Adjusted Actuarial Approach

Direct comparisons between the research-guided approach and the clinically adjusted actuarial method appear to be lacking. Hence, the relative value of these two approaches is only known to date through extrapolation from the research described above (contrasting the research-guided and purely actuarial approach) in conjunction with that in the next section concerning comparisons of the purely actuarial to the clinically adjusted procedure.

The Clinically Adjusted Actuarial Procedure

The concept behind the clinically adjusted actuarial procedure is to employ actuarial instrumentation as the foundation for the risk assessment, and then to go beyond the instruments in a less structured way under at least some circumstances. Given the apparent relative accuracy of the actuarial methodology (within at least certain circumstances) described above, the question arises as to the rationale for adding clinical considerations to actuarial findings. The danger is that such additional considerations may serve only to lessen rather than increase the overall risk assessment accuracy (Quinsey et al., 1998). Despite this concern, there is at least one conceptual reason for using this methodology over the purely actuarial: The *current* actuarial instruments are believed not to be comprehensive in the inclusion of significant items. (If and when the day comes that an actuarial instrument is developed, specific to the risk of concern, that is fully comprehensive of all risk and protective factors known and thought to exist, this conceptual argument for the clinically adjusted actuarial model goes away. Until that day, however, this argument will apply.) Clinicians need to look beyond the current set of instrument results to ensure that no obvious reconsideration of actuarial findings is needed. The accuracy of this argument is testable by research comparing pure actuarial instrument results with those same results with added "clinical adjustments."

To date, there are not many such studies. Given that the actuarial instruments specifically designed for use with sex offenders and their reoffense risk are themselves rather new, this relative deficit is not surprising. "Second stage" research (i.e., beyond the first stage of simply testing instruments' reliability and validity) has only recently occurred.

Eight examples of such research involving sex offenders were found (Allam, 2000; Beech, Erikson, Friendship, & Ditchfield, 2001; Hanson & Harris, 1997; Haynes, Yates, Nicholaichuk, Gu, & Bolton, 2000, written up by Nicholaichuk & Yates, in press; McGrath, Cumming, Livingston, & Hoke, 2001; Quinsey, Coleman, Jones, & Altrows, 1997; Thornton, 2000b, as written up in Thornton, in press; and Wong, Flahr, et al., 2000; based on Wong & Gordon, 1999). All of these studies explored the potential predictive utility of dynamic (changeable) considerations beyond the effectiveness of static actuarial instruments. Interestingly, all of these studies supported the clinically adjusted actuarial process, though under specific circumstances that need to be remembered.

The details of what these pieces of research said concerning when to "clinically adjust" is discussed in Chapter 7. For the sake of drawing conclusions from the above about the relative value of this approach, a few summary statements are offered here. First, there are not a lot of studies testing the utility of the clinically adjusted actuarial methodology. Those that exist consistently support its effectiveness beyond current actuarial instruments, but sometimes only with selective factors. Replications of existing results, as well as further clarification of which dynamic factors are of importance and under what circumstances, would be most useful to the field.

The Purely Actuarial Method

Based on the Grove and Meehl (1996) and Grove et al. (2000) meta-analytic findings involving comparisons of mechanical versus clinical predictive accuracy, there is strong reason to believe that a process with explicitly defined factors and rules for combining those factors into a single assessment outcome is equal or superior to more subjective procedures. As reflected above, this degree of confidence in the purely actuarial model has led researchers often to employ an actuarial result as the model against which other methodologies are tested.

Two overlapping problems present themselves in implementing the purely actuarial model, however, at least within the sex offender civil commitment evaluation context. The first of these is that there are no actuarial instruments designed to assess people's (1) lifetime sexual recidivism likelihood, (2) lifetime violent recidivism likelihood, or (3) anything else over the course of complete lifetimes.

Similarly, no instrument exists that is known to assess true reoffending risk (sexual or otherwise), as opposed to reconviction or rearrest likelihood. In other words, the commitment laws require assessments involving parameters for which no purely mechanical procedure exists. Given what we know about the effect of altering base rates on predictive accuracy (see Chapter 5) and that there is reason to believe that lifetime reoffending base rates are different from what the existing actuarial instruments assess, the conclusion is drawn that the actuarial instruments do not do a complete job in assessing what is required of civil commitment evaluators.

The same conclusion can be drawn after reviewing the second problem. As was documented in the prior section, existing actuarial instruments do not yet include enough of the relevant considerations to maximum our predictive effectiveness. That is why the Sex Offender Needs Assessment Rating scale (SONAR; developed by Hanson and Harris) could be developed beyond the RRASOR, and the Violence Risk Scale–Sex Offender (VRS–SO; Wong & Gordon, 1999; Wong, Flahr, et al., 2000) could be developed beyond the Static-99. Described another way, the preponderance of existing actuarial instruments employ mostly or solely static (historical) factors and few if any dynamic factors. Ultimately, there is every reason why actuarial instruments can be developed incorporating both static and dynamic factors of relevance, but until all empirically supported (and sufficiently statistically independent) factors are included in one instrument, then a reason for a clinical adjustment will still exist. Presumably, as research continues and more of the statistically useful dynamic and static variables are incorporated into actuarial instrumentation, the lack of inclusiveness of the instruments will become less of a concern.

Neither of these shortcomings indicates that the use of existing actuarial risk assessment instruments is inappropriate within the civil commitment context. Evaluators simply need to keep these issues in mind when using the current set of instruments. In doing so, most evaluators will therefore typically decide to employ some degree of clinical adjusting beyond whatever the instruments indicate, if for no other reason than to extrapolate beyond fixed time periods and official outcome measures to lifetime reoffense estimates.

Recommended Procedures Within Sex Offender Civil Commitment Evaluations

Based on the above findings, coupled with the proposed national standards described in Chapter 2, the use of actuarial risk assessment instruments within sex offender civil commitment evaluations seems ethically mandated to the extent that such instruments both (1) are meaningfully related to the assessment of long-term sexual recidivism likelihood and (2) appear applicable to the individual subject. In using actuarial instruments within the civil commitment context, one still needs to consider both base rate effects and potentially meaningful clinical adjustments as part of the overall assessment. In other words, the recommendation here is specifically not for the use of a purely actuarial procedure, for the two reasons stated just above. Under circumstances where no actuarial instrument exists (e.g., when assessing a female sex offender), or the application of existing actuarial instrumentation seems to be too much of an extrapolation from existing research (e.g., when assessing a younger juvenile), then the research-guided clinical approach becomes the clear recommendation.

These recommendations may sound as if there are clear distinctions among the different procedures in how they are actually practiced. This is not as true as may first appear. Evaluators using a research-guided approach involving an instrument such as the SVR-20 often score the items (0, 1, or 2) and add up the scores as part of their way of using the instrument, despite the fact that this type of procedure is not recommended in the manuals for these instruments. By using this type of addition across items, the evaluators have effectively weighted each factor equally to one another, a weighting system that is not dissimilar to those found on the Static-99 (where all but one item in each is scored with the same metric, 0 or 1). Likewise, evaluators employing the actuarial instruments sometimes make clinical adjustments based on considerations not specifically shown to be meaningfully useful beyond what the instruments assess (e.g., a diagnosis of pedophilia as indicating greater risk than the RRASOR assesses, an issue to be explicated in Chapter 7), and do this with only a subjectively determined relative weighting being applied (more in keeping with the authentic research-guided approach).

In terms of how evaluators actually use these systems, the practical difference between the research-guided approach and the clinically adjusted actuarial approach may be more a difference in degree than kind. Theoretically, one differentiating consideration is the degree to which factor "weights" are specified by the procedure versus imposed by the evaluator. A second is the degree to which factors with completely unspecified weights are considered in determining the overall assessment result.

This situation does not change the results from research to date, however. Specifically within the longer-term (i.e., 10-15 years) sex offender sexual recidivism context (defined by existing civil commitment laws), actuarial instruments show significant accuracy that seems equal to or beyond what existing research-guided approaches have shown. To the extent that research on the clinically adjusted actuarial approach exists, there is reason to believe that this methodology offers selective promise of improving risk assessment accuracy beyond the current set of actuarial instruments. Hence, the above recommendations remain despite the lack of significant practical difference in how evaluators sometimes implement these procedures.

Selecting What Instruments to Use

As in any assessment procedure, an evaluator needs to select the instrumentation most helpful for the task at hand. In this section, no final recommendations will be made about the specific tools civil commitment evaluators should use. The reason for this is that such recommendations would only reflect current research results, and obviously ignore empirical findings from after the publication date of this book. Instruments can be updated, combined, improved on, or in some way altered over time, with new instruments being developed that statistically surpass the old. Therefore, recommendations herein concern meaningful procedures for how evaluators might determine which instruments to use in their assessment work, and to do so in keeping with professional ethics (e.g., American Educational Research Association et al., 1999).

Even in the rather short history of sex offender risk assessment instruments, there has been a slew of scales developed about which someone has claimed utility. In one recent attempt to develop a comprehensive list of such devices, I found 25 such instruments (mostly actuarial, but also including some research-guided structures) only to learn of 2 more soon afterward (Doren, 1999a, 1999b).

The first thing that an evaluator must do, therefore, is to assess the empirical soundness, appropriateness, and utility of each instrument potentially to be selected for use. Issues to be addressed here include the following:

1. Statistical demonstration of reliability and validity

2. Degree of concordance between what the instrument was designed to measure and the legally defined task

3. Reasonableness of applying the instrument to the type of case being assessed (i.e., the scale's generalizability to the individual subject)

4. Availability of information required to employ the instrument

5. Availability of interpretative information

All five of these considerations are measured in "matter of degree" rather than "it's there or it's not" terms, irrelevant of the instrument being scrutinized. Issues such as reliability, validity, degree of concordance, and generalizability are grounded in statistical findings, but have no clear thresholds for what is "good enough." Likewise, the availability of information can be lacking to some degree and still be considered sufficient under various circumstances.

Even without definitive thresholds in this regard, selecting one's choice of assessment instruments can be well guided by concentrating on the above considerations. For instance, an evaluator can significantly narrow the choices from among all current risk assessment instruments using the following criteria, each representing an operationalization of a characteristic above:

1. It was designed for use with sexual (and potentially also non-sexually violent) offenders.

2. It was designed to assess sexual (and potentially also non-sexually violent) recidivism likelihood.

3. It has been tested for its interrater reliability at least twice, always with support.

4. It has been tested for its predictive/postdictive and/or concurrent validity at least four times beyond the developmental process, again with support (given that there are instruments from which to choose—for more rare types of offenders and therefore few instruments from which to choose, this threshold may be relaxed).

5. The empirically demonstrated degree of predictive utility is acceptable.

6. The subject to whom the evaluator is going to apply the instrument is similar in basic characteristics to the study samples.

7. The information needed for using the instrument is likely to be available for the case(s) upon which the instrument is to be applied.

This list, although not incredibly stringent in its requirements for the frequency at which an instrument's statistical properties have been studied, actually narrows the scope of an evaluator's selection to the following instruments (in alphabetical order) among all that exist as of the writing of this book:

1. Historical, Clinical, Risk Management-20 (HCR-20; Webster, Douglas, Eaves, & Hart, 1997)

2. Minnesota Sex Offender Screening Tool–Revised (MnSOST–R; Epperson et al., 1999)

3. Rapid Risk Assessment for Sex Offense Recidivism (RRASOR; Hanson, 1997)

4. Sex Offender Risk Appraisal Guide (SORAG; Quinsey et al., 1998)

5. Static-99 (Hanson & Thornton, 2000)

6. Violence Risk Appraisal Guide (VRAG; Webster et al., 1994)

There are clearly other instruments used regularly in certain places. The Sex Offender Risk Assessment (SORA; Atkinson, Kropp, Laws, & Hart, 1996) is a research-guided clinical judgment instrument that has been regularly used in British Columbia, Canada, by community supervising agents. The Iowa Department of Corrections (DOC) has systematically used the (New York) Sex Offender Registry Risk Assessment Scale (Hopper, 1998) as an actuarial tool within its screening for civil commitment referrals. Likewise, the Registrant Risk Assessment Scale (RRAS; Ferguson, Eidelson, & Witt, 1999) has been regularly employed as an actuarial risk assessment tool within the New Jersey DOC for the same purpose. Commonality of use, however, does not necessarily mean the above selection criteria will be met, and in fact, often does not. None of the instruments mentioned in this paragraph meet the empirical study thresholds enumerated above. The first two, in fact, have never been put to any empirical test to my best knowledge.

To emphasize the caveat that commonality of use even among some sex offender civil commitment evaluators should not serve as the guide for selection of risk assessment instrumentation, there is another important example. Sets of evaluators (in the states of Florida and Washington) have consistently employed the SVR-20 (Boer et al., 1997) as part of their sex offender civil commitment examinations. That instrument has been empirically tested only three times (Dempster, 1999; Sjöstedt & Långström, in press; with the third study, a master's thesis in the United Kingdom first being finalized as this book was written, according to Stephen Hart, personal communication, December 2000). Support for its interrater reliability was significantly lacking in the one known study directly investigating that consideration (Sjöstedt & Långström, in press). Empirical support for the instrument's postdictive validity was mixed. The Sjöstedt and Långström study did not support such validity (while supporting the validity of other instruments). The Dempster research showed the instrument had more utility for a general violence risk assessment than specifically one pertaining to the sexual violence of importance within the sex offender civil commitment realm, though a simple correlation between SVR-20 scores and within 5-year reconviction sexual recidivism was found. Overall, these findings do not demonstrate strong support for the use of the SVR-20 within the civil commitment context. A better selection consideration than the fact that other people are using the instrument needs to be used.

Getting back to the six instruments currently found to meet the listed illustrative selection criteria, these six can again be divided according to their designed purpose. Half of the instruments were designed to assess the risk of general violence (i.e., HCR-20, SORAG, and VRAG) inclusive of sexual offending, and half were designed more specifically for assessing the likelihood for sexual recidivism (i.e., MnSOST–R, RRASOR, and Static-99). Given that existing sex offender civil commitment criteria are uniformly inclusive of only sexual reoffense risk and not the risk for general violence, these latter three instruments would appear more applicable for use in civil commitment evaluations than the other instruments whose utility is more tangential within this context. (There is some research suggesting that the VRAG, for instance, assesses the risk specifically for sexual violence beyond chance [Harris, Rice, Quinsey, Lalumière, Boer, & Lang, 2001], but the lack of interpretative risk categories specific to this type of recidivism makes the use of this instrument problematic for this purpose.) The fact that the former three instruments are also actuarial in nature means that a potential issue of meeting proposed national standards is also addressed by the employment of at least one of them.

With this caveat in mind, a short digression will be made concerning the general description and to document the empirical support (to date) of the six instruments. The remaining portion of the chapter will concentrate on the three tools most applicable within civil commitment evaluations. The process of interpreting each of these latter instruments both individually and when multiply employed is described.

Empirical Support for the Instruments Currently Selected

The HCR-20

Description. The most frequently empirically investigated instrument among the six (at the time this was written) was the HCR-20, this also being the only research-guided, nonactuarial instrument in the set. This enumeration of 20 risk considerations includes 10 that are historical, 5 that are more clinical in nature, and 5 representing risk management concerns. All of the published research, and much of the unpublished work concerning this instrument, has used a numerical scheme for scoring the items (0, 1, or 2) and overall total rating (0-40). The reader should remain aware that this is not the method the HCR-20 was designed for during clinical application (Webster et al., 1997), but this scoring procedure does make various statistical analyses possible.

Interrater reliability. There have been at least eight direct studies of the interrater reliability of the HCR-20 specifically within forensic psychiatric and correctional populations. (The designation of "direct" tests of interrater reliability is made to point out that all tests of an instrument's validity are also indirect tests of its interrater reliability. Validity cannot consistently be shown without implied interrater reliability, with the relationship between the two actually being statistical in nature. Hence, all validity studies should be counted as tests of interrater reliability as well.) The results from direct tests have varied to some degree, but only within the small range generally found acceptable except when the Clinical subscale has been studied alone:

1. Belfrage (1998): Interrater reliability (IRR) for total scores = .81

2. Dernevik (1998): IRR ranged from .76 to .96

3. Douglas et al. (1998): Interclass correlation (ICC) = .81

4. Muller-Isberner and Jockel (1997): Mean kappa for Historical items = .89; mean kappa for Clinical items = .49

5. Strand and Belfrage (1999): Kendall's tau-b = .67

6. Strand et al. (1999): Kendall's tau-b = .69

7. Douglas and Webster (1999): IRR (for Historical + Clinical totals) = .80

8. Dunbar (1999): IRR = .88-.94

Interrater reliability for the Historical items of the HCR-20 has regularly been found to be in the acceptable to very acceptable range. Overall HCR-20 scores show a similar degree of interrater consistency. The items within the Clinical subsection appear to be more problematic in this regard, though one could argue that the deliberately dynamic nature of these items (e.g., "negative attitudes," "active symptoms of Major Mental Illness") might lead one to expect lower reliability figures even by the same rater at different times.

Validity. Validity indices are similarly supportive to the meaningfulness of this enumeration of risk factors within forensic and correctional populations. Correlations with the type of violent outcome being assessed have ranged from .31 (Nicholls et al., 1999) to as high as .63 (Dunbar, 1999). Receiver operating characteristic (ROC, or area under the curve, AUC) findings are of similar relative (and significant) magnitude, ranging from .66 (Grann et al., 2000) to .80 (Strand et al., 1999). No less than 13 studies of the HCR-20's validity specifically with these populations are documented within a wonderful annotated bibliography prepared by Kevin Douglas. This bibliography can be found online at www.sfu.ca, where more than 25 studies are described concerning this instrument.

Utility within civil commitment assessments. The strengths of the HCR-20 within the civil commitment evaluation context are that examiners are free to give weight to each factor as they believe fits each case, and to do so with an instrument that shows a high degree of interrater reliability and predictive validity. The downside to using this instrument within this context is that it was designed and tested as a measure of general violence likelihood, not specifically sexual violence. In fact, no empirical test for the instrument's relationship with sexual recidivism has been conducted. The instrument, by its very nature as a simple enumeration of risk factors, also does not offer guidance as to when someone's risk is beyond any specified threshold, such as "more likely than not."

The VRAG

Description. The VRAG comes in a close second to the HCR-20 in the amount of investigative research performed to date. Like the HCR-20, the VRAG was designed to assess the violence risk in previously convicted violent offenders, not specifically the sexual violence potential for sex offenders. Unlike the HCR-20, this instrument (and each of the rest) was clearly designed to be actuarial in use and interpretation.

The VRAG includes 12 items. The first item is the score from the psychological test called the Psychopathy Checklist–Revised (PCL–R). Remaining items largely pertain to different aspects and patterns of "acting out" and criminal behaviors: (1) elementary school maladjustment, (2) diagnosed personality disorder, (3) age at index offense, (4) lived with parents until at least age 16, (5) failure on prior conditional release, (6) criminal history score for nonviolent offenses (based on a rating system for nonviolent offenses), (7) marital status, (8) diagnosis of schizophrenia, (9) degree of victim injury in index offense, (10) history of alcohol abuse, and (11) victim gender in index offense. The process of scoring these items is described

TABLE 5.1. Interpretation of Violence Risk Appraisal Guide (VRAG) Scores Relative to Probability of Violent Recidivism

VRAG Score	7 years	10 years
Less than −21	.00	.08
−21 through −15	.08	.10
−14 through −8	.12	.24
−7 through −1	.17	.31
0 through +6	.35	.48
+7 through +13	.44	.58
+14 through +20	.55	.64
+21 through +27	.76	.82
+28 or higher	1.00	1.00

SOURCE: From *Violent Offenders: Appraising and Managing Risk,* by V. L. Quinsey, G. T. Harris, M. E. Rice, and C. A. Cormier, 1998, Washington, DC: American Psychological Association. Copyright © 1998 by the American Psychological Association. Reprinted with permission.

in both Quinsey et al. (1998) and Webster et al. (1994), with the first listed source being more detailed in this regard.

Total scores on the VRAG ultimately involve a 55-point range, but the interpretation of VRAG scores is actually done by using nine score categories, as shown in Table 5.1, taken from Quinsey et al. (1998).

Once an individual's VRAG score is obtained, the evaluator uses the information in Table 5.1 to see what percentage of people falling into the same range of scores recidivated within the designated time period postincarceration (either 7 years or 10 years). Of great importance, these percentages refer to recidivism defined as at least rearrested for a new violent (interpersonal) offense. These percentages do not directly translate to sexual reoffending risk.

Interrater reliability. There have been two direct tests of the VRAG's interrater reliability to date (excluding interrater reliability research involving just the PCL–R, the psychological test incorporated into the VRAG as its first and primary item). Harris, Rice, and Quinsey (1993) documented an average interrater correlation across the 12 variables of .90, with a mean kappa (again across all 12 variables) of .83. Barbaree, Seto, Langton, and Peacock (2001) also documented an interrater reliability of .90. All of these findings are within the highly acceptable range.

Validity. There have been at least 21 different studies investigating the validity of the VRAG, 20 of which involved either forensic or correctional samples. Of those 20, at least 19 supported the validity of the instrument (e.g., Loza & Dhaliwal, 1997; Rice & Harris, in press) with the remaining study (Douglas, Hart, Dempster, & Lyon, 1999) having used approximations for some of the VRAG variables and hence potentially diminished the veracity of that validity test. Correlations with violent recidivism (beyond short-term institutional behavior) have been in the .42 to .45 range (e.g., Hilton, Harris, & Rice, 2001; Hilton & Simmons, 2001). ROC statistics for studies pertaining to violent recidivism have ranged from .70 (Glover,

Nicholson, Hemmati, Bernfield, & Quinsey, in press) to .80 (Rice & Harris, in press) when two studies that involved approximations of VRAG variables are excluded. These statistics all clearly support the validity of the VRAG relative to violent recidivism through existing empirical explorations.

Within the civil commitment context, however, the real issue is the degree to which the VRAG is a valid assessment device concerning specifically sexual recidivism. Studies have been consistently supportive in that area as well (e.g., Barbaree et al., 2001; Dempster, 1999; Rice & Harris, 1999), but the correlations and ROC statistics are also regularly smaller in relation to sexual recidivism compared with violent recidivism.

Utility within civil commitment assessments. The main strengths of the VRAG within this context are that it represents a well-researched and well-supported actuarial instrument with a relatively high degree of generalizability for what it measures. The main problem in applying this instrument to the civil commitment context is that the interpretative data are based on recidivism as measured by general interpersonal violence as opposed specifically to sexual violence. In other words, despite statistically significant correlations between the VRAG and sexual violence, the interpretation of VRAG scale scores is problematic when applied specifically in the sexual violence risk evaluation.

The SORAG

Description. The SORAG may best be considered a variation of the VRAG designed specifically for sex offenders. Unlike what some evaluators have been heard to say, the SORAG was *not* designed to assess the risk for sexual violence per se. The instrument was developed for the same purpose as the VRAG, to assess the likelihood for general violence. Just as with the VRAG, research results have shown SORAG results to be correlated with sexual recidivism, but not to the same extent as the instrument correlates with violent recidivism more in general (e.g., Dempster, 1999).

The two instruments are very highly correlated (i.e., r = .93; Rice & Harris, 1999), an empirical result that should come as no surprise once one realizes that the instruments share 10 of their 12 or 14 items (for the VRAG and SORAG, respectively), with another item involving significant overlap (i.e., the VRAG's "female victim in index offense" vs. the SORAG's "history of sex offenses solely against girls under 14"). The one item on the VRAG not on the SORAG is the "degree of victim injury in index offense." The SORAG's three unique items involve (1) penile plethysmographic (PPG) results, (2) criminal history score for violent offenses (similar in structure to the nonviolent offending score on both instruments), and (3) number of previous convictions for hands-on sexual offenses. The process of scoring these items is described in Quinsey et al. (1998).

Just like the VRAG, the SORAG has the potential for a very wide range of scores (i.e., a range of 76 possible scores), but its interpretation is based on nine score categories. These are enumerated in Table 5.2, a table taken from Quinsey et al. (1998). These listed percentages, like the VRAG's in Table 5.1, represent the findings from groups of people scoring in the listed ranges who were at least

TABLE 5.2.   Interpretation of Sex Offender Risk Appraisal Guide (SORAG)
Scores Relative to Probability of Violent Recidivism

SORAG Score	7 years	SORAG Score	10 years
Less than −9	.00	Less than −10	.08
−9 to −4	.08	−10 to −5	.10
−3 to +2	.12	−4 to +1	.24
+3 to +8	.17	+2 to +7	.31
+9 to +14	.35	+8 to +13	.48
+15 to +19	.44	+14 to +19	.58
+20 to +24	.55	+20 to +25	.64
+25 to +30	.76	+26 to +31	.82
+31 or higher	1.00	+32 or higher	1.00

SOURCE: From *Violent Offenders: Appraising and Managing Risk,* by
V. L. Quinsey, G. T. Harris, M. E. Rice, and C. A. Cormier, 1998, Washington, DC:
American Psychological Association. Copyright © 1998 by the American Psychological
Association. Reprinted with permission.

rearrested for a new violent (interpersonal) offense during either a 7-year or
10-year postincarceration period.

Interrater reliability. With the very significant degree of overlap between the VRAG
and SORAG, similarly supportive findings for the SORAG's interrater reliability
and validity should come as no surprise. Rice and Harris (1999) found an interrater
reliability coefficient of .90 for the SORAG. Barbaree et al. (2001) documented a
coefficient of .92. Bélanger and Earls (in press) obtained 94.7% agreement between
two raters when each reviewed the same 23 files. These figures are very much in
keeping with the excellent interrater results discovered for the VRAG.

Validity. There have been at least eight studies of the SORAG's validity (separate
from the VRAG), seven of which supported that validity relative to violent recidivism (Doren, 2000). The exception was Firestone, Bradford, Greenberg, Nunes, and
Broom (1999), with one potential reason for that failing being that the sample used
was clearly a very low risk group involving a very restricted range of SORAG scores.
A variable's restricted range of scores statistically limits the degree to which that
variable can correlate with any other variable, such that a failure to find a significant relationship may solely reflect the restricted range effect. Among the studies
found supportive, correlations with violent recidivism have ranged from .43 (Rice &
Harris, in press) to .53 (unpublished data from the study by Hanson & Thornton,
2000), with ROCs ranging from .67 (Rice & Harris, in press) to .82 (Bélanger &
Earls, in press). Again, these results strongly suggest very good reliability and validity for this instrument in terms of assessing risk for violent recidivism. Just as with
the VRAG, the SORAG's correlations and ROCs specifically with sexual recidivism
have consistently been smaller than with violent recidivism, though still of statistical significance (e.g., Dempster, 1999).

Utility within civil commitment assessments. Basically, the same statements can be
made in this section about the SORAG as were made pertaining to the VRAG. The

instrument has found consistent and significant support for its interrater reliability and validity, but it loses something in the translation from a general violence risk assessment to a sexual violence risk assessment, and does so to a degree not quantified by the risk percentages available for score interpretation.

The RRASOR

Description. This section begins the summary of empirical results for the three instruments that were designed specifically to assess sexual recidivism likelihood. The RRASOR is the first to be covered. This scale, actuarial in design, is by far the shortest of all of the instruments meeting the selection criteria delineated above. There are only four items to the RRASOR, covering the topics of prior sex offenses, offender age, having sexually victimized a male, and having sexually victimized outside the offender's family.

A detailed description of the research development of the RRASOR can be found at www.sgc.gc.ca/EPub/corr/e199704/e199704.htm. Although there was a series of drafts of coding rules for the RRASOR items, the finalized scoring key for the RRASOR can actually be found within the rules for scoring the Static-99, at www.sgc.gc.ca/EPub/Corr/eCodingRules/eCodingRules.htm. Rules governing items numbered 1, 6, 8, and 9 on the Static-99 represent the complete set of coding rules for the RRASOR items.

RRASOR scale scores range from 0 (at the lower-risk end) to 6. A score of 6 is very rare, with literally no one with that score found in the developmental sample involving nearly 2,600 people. I have seen or heard of only four such people in the evaluation work I have done or supervised. The interpretation of scale scores is based in Table 5.3, from Hanson (1997).

Unlike the VRAG and SORAG, the RRASOR is interpreted per score, not from derived score categories. The percentages in Table 5.3 represent the proportion of people with the listed RRASOR score that were found to have recidivated with a new sexual offense within the specified time frames postincarceration. The recidivism measure employed by Hanson (1997) varied due to his use of multiple, different databases from different researchers. About half of the studies used a reconviction measure, whereas the other half also included rearrest for a new sexual offense, besides for using reconviction. Apparently, the proportion of "rearrest without reconviction" recidivist cases in the total sample used to derive the RRASOR was rather small, however, such that it is reasonable to interpret the figures in Table 5.3 as basically representing reconviction percentages.

Interrater reliability. The RRASOR's interrater reliability has been empirically investigated three times to date. Sjöstedt and Långström (in press) found an interclass correlation of .91 and a mean kappa of .87 based on 15 cases each scored by two raters. A separate study by those same researchers (Sjöstedt & Långström, 2001) obtained the very high mean kappa of .91 (across three items, excluding the use of a computerized process to score the RRASOR's first item). Barbaree et al. (2001) found the astounding interrater reliability coefficient of .94. These figures are all clearly supportive to a conclusion of high interrater reliability for the RRASOR.

TABLE 5.3. Interpretation of Rapid Risk Assessment for Sex Offender
Recidivism (RRASOR) Scores

RRASOR Score	Recidivism Rates Adjusted for Time Periods	
	5 years	10 years
0	4.4	6.5
1	7.6	11.2
2	14.2	21.1
3	24.8	36.9
4	32.7	48.6
5	49.8	73.1
6	(no data, as no one in either the normative or validation samples scored this)	

SOURCE: Hanson (1997).

Validity. There have been at least 17 studies relevant to the RRASOR's validity with
forensic and correctional populations (Doren, 2000). Sixteen of those investigations have clearly been supportive (e.g., Barbaree et al., 2001). The results from a
17th study (Epperson et al., 1999) can be read as supportive or as nonsupportive,
depending on the details one wishes to emphasize.[1] Empirical support for the
instrument's validity has been found in seven countries: Canada (e.g., Barbaree
et al., 2001), England (Hanson, 1997), Ireland (Quackenbush, 2000), New Zealand
(Hudson, Wales, Bakker, & Ward, in press), Sweden (Sjöstedt & Långström, in
press), United States (McGrath et al., 2001) and Wales (Hanson, 1997) and various
U.S. states: California (Hanson, 1997), Ohio (Konicek, 2000), Vermont (McGrath
et al., 2001), and Wisconsin (Roberts, Doren, & Thornton, in press), as well as
potentially Minnesota (as described above in the study by Epperson et al., 1999).

Correlations with sexual recidivism (not simply general violence) have ranged
from .13 (from the restricted sampling by Epperson et al., 1999) to .58 (Jan
Looman, personal communication, December 2000, from a study conducted in
1998), with (statistically significant) correlational results varying rather evenly
across this range (e.g., at $r = .25$, Smiley, McHattie, & Mulloy, 1998; at .38, McGrath
et al., 2001; at .48, Dempster, 1999). Less variable (probably due to being relatively
unaffected by the differing recidivism base rates across the studies) are the results
from ROC analyses. Most of the ROCs have been above .70, with a range from .59
(Harris et al., 2001) to .77 (Dempster, 1999).

Utility within civil commitment assessments. The RRASOR's interrater reliability and
predictive/postdictive validity seem well supported. The context for this support is
specifically sexual recidivism, typically measured in the various studies by sex
offense reconvictions. The sexual nature of the instrument's outcome measure
makes this instrument particularly useful for civil commitment evaluators. The relative ease of use of this instrument can be viewed as both a strength and a weakness. With only four items to score, evaluators have few areas in which to gather
relevant information. By the same token, the fact that only four factors are
addressed directly leaves the greatest potential for not being sufficiently comprehensive in covering other relevant considerations.

The Static-99

Description. The Static-99 is effectively a "second generation" actuarial instrument in that it incorporated the RRASOR along with other items from a commonly used (in the United Kingdom) though rarely tested instrument, the Structured Actuarial Clinical Judgment–Minimum (SACJ–Min; Grubin, 1998). The reader is referred to the article by Hanson and Thornton (2000) for a description of the research development of this scale.

Beyond the RRASOR's four items, the other items on the Static-99 include (1) number of sentencing occasions (5+ vs. 4 or less), (2) conviction for noncontact sexual offense (yes or no), (3) conviction for nonsexual violent offense at same time as index sexual offense (yes or no), (4) conviction for nonsexual violent offense prior to index sexual offense (yes or no), (5) any stranger victim to sexual offense (yes or no), and (6) ever lived with lover for two consecutive years (no or yes). Those additional six items are all scored either 1 or 0 (respectively, in the order listed parenthetically per item above), so the variability per item beyond the RRASOR is minimal. The coding rules for scoring the Static-99 can be found at www.sgc.gc.ca/Epub/Corr/eCodingRules/eCodingRules.htm. With six additional items beyond the RRASOR, the potential total score range went from 7 points (the RRASOR's 0-6) to 13 points (the Static-99's 0-12), close to a doubling of possible outcomes. I have never heard of anyone scoring either 11 or 12 on the Static-99, however, with only a handful of 10s over the past two years of applied work with this instrument.

The interpretation of the Static-99 is mostly based per score, though the highest risk category is represented by the range of scores 6+, as enumerated in Table 5.4. The score range 6-12 was collapsed into one risk category due both to relatively small numbers of people with these higher scores and the fact the recidivism rates within this range did not differ significantly. (One can compare the people scoring exactly a 6 who showed recidivism rates of 37%, 44%, and 51% with the 6+ rates in Table 5.4 to see there is little apparent risk difference above that threshold.)

The recidivism rates in Table 5.4 essentially represent reconviction rates for the groups of people with the listed score over the postincarceration time periods designated.

Interrater reliability. There have been three direct tests of the Static-99's interrater reliability to date, two of these being from research that also investigated the RRASOR. Those two (Barbaree et al., 2001, and Sjöstedt & Långström, 2001) clearly supported the Static-99's reliability, with an interrater reliability coefficient of .90 and a mean kappa of about .90, respectively. The third study, Wong, Flahr, et al. (2000), employed three raters and 33 sex offender cases. One rater assessed all 33 cases, and the other two raters split the cases evenly between them, such that all 33 cases were scored by two of the raters. Overall, the interrater reliability correlation coefficient was .81 ($p < .01$).

An interesting point was noticed by the researchers in addition to this overall finding, however. When just the "longer term" treatment sample was employed in this study, the correlation coefficient went up to .94. An interpretation offered by one of the research coordinators was that the latter cases represented situations in

TABLE 5.4.   Interpretation of Static-99 Scores

Static-99 Score	Recidivism Rates Adjusted for Time Periods		
	5 years	10 years	15 years
0	5.0	11.0	13.0
1	6.0	7.0	7.0
2	9.0	13.0	16.0
3	12.0	14.0	19.0
4	26.0	31.0	36.0
5	33.0	38.0	40.0
6+	39.0	45.0	52.0

SOURCE: www.sgc.gc.ca/epub/corr/e199902/e199902.htm, by R. Karl Hanson.

which "those who had been in treatment longer tended to be more forthcoming in volunteering information" (Witte Treena, personal communication, September 2000), suggesting that reliability and retrieval of information may have been easier with the longer-term treatment participants. Either way, of course, the Static-99's interrater reliability has been consistently supported through direct empirical tests.

Validity. At least 15 studies of the Static-99's validity within correctional and forensic populations have been conducted to date (Doren, 2000). Amazingly, *all* of those were clearly supportive to the validity of this instrument relative to sexual recidivism.

Specifically, the ROC findings for the Static-99 relative to sexual recidivism range from .62 (Harris et al., 2001) to .89 (Thornton, in press). Interestingly, *all* of these results were equal to or higher than those found in the developmental (Hanson & Thornton, 2000) samples except one, the Harris et al. results! It is unusual that replications of research results find stronger relationships between variables than did the original work, certainly as compared to the far more frequently obtained shrinkage in statistical relationships upon retesting. Correlational findings have shown this same unusual resistance to the typical trend, with the original developmental research showing a correlation with sexual recidivism of .33, whereas McGrath et al. (2001), for instance, documented a correlation of .35.

As with the RRASOR, support for the validity of the Static-99 comes from various countries: Canada (Barbaree et al., 2001), England (Beech et al., 2001), Ireland (Quackenbush, 2000), Sweden (Sjöstedt & Långström, 2001), United States (see below), and Wales (Hanson & Thornton, 2000) and U.S. states: California (Schiller & Watnik, 2001), Texas (Poole, Liedecke, & Marbibi, 2000), Vermont (McGrath et al., 2001), and Wisconsin (Roberts et al., in press). Overall, clear support for the instrument's predictive/postdictive validity exists.

Utility within civil commitment assessments. The Static-99 may represent the most comprehensive actuarial risk assessment instrument currently available that both is specific to sexual recidivism likelihood and has been frequently researched with very consistently supportive findings. It actually does not clearly lead the list in any one of these categories (with the VRAG and RRASOR having been more frequently studied; the MnSOST–R is inclusive of more items, and the RRASOR has arguably been as consistently supported for its interrater reliability and validity). In combination, however, the Static-99 can be argued to be the current leader in what may be thought of as the best single instrument for use within the context of a sex offender civil commitment evaluation.

At the same time, it is not clear that it adds a significant utility beyond the RRASOR. Conceptually, some of the "added" items on the Static-99 had already been found not to be of significant use beyond the RRASOR items during the original RRASOR research (i.e., the items of stranger victim and marital status; Hanson, 1997). Adding them back into an actuarial instrument has the potential of increasing someone's assessed risk (i.e., by increasing their scale score) without actually doing so using a meaningful measurement of additional risk. From an empirical perspective, I have also found that neither instrument appears to be better than the other when it comes to assessing the people specifically in the high-risk ranges, the area of greatest concern to civil commitment evaluators (Doren, 2001b). A recommendation for how to deal with this finding will be addressed later in this chapter.

The MnSOST–R

Description. The last of the instruments meeting the criteria for potential selection enumerated above is the MnSOST–R. Like the Static-99, this is also a "second generation" scale, though not quite in the same way as the Static-99 was built upon the RRASOR. The MnSOST–R borrowed a good deal from a prior actuarial scale, the Minnesota Sex Offender Screening Tool (MnSOST; Epperson, Kaul, & Huot, 1995), but did not comprehensively incorporate that prior instrument. Twelve of the items overlap the two instruments if one ignores changes in the relative scoring systems. The MnSOST–R has an additional 4 items beyond these 12, whereas the MnSOST has an additional 9 and was actually the longer instrument.

The 16 MnSOST–R items are (1) number of sex-related convictions, (2) length of sexual offending history, (3) having been under supervision when committing a charged sexual offense, (4) having committed a charged sexual offense in a public place, (5) having used force within any charged sexual offense, (6) having done multiple acts on a single victim within a charged sexual offense, (7) number of victim age groups for charged sexual offenses, (8) history of victimizing 13- to 15-year-old within any charged sexual offense, (9) stranger victim within charged sexual offense, (10) evidence of adolescent antisocial behavior by offender, (11) history of drug or alcohol abuse, (12) employment history, (13) discipline history while incarcerated, (14) chemical dependency treatment while incarcerated or on release, (15) sex offender treatment while incarcerated or on release, and (16) age of offender. A description of the research development of the MnSOST–R and of its coding rules can be found at http://www.psychology.iastate.edu/faculty/homepage.htm.

The MnSOST–R was devised specifically to assess the rearrest risk for a new hands-on sexual offense within a specified time period. The postincarceration period that seemed most effective was 6 years. Unlike the RRASOR, and more in keeping with the VRAG, the interpretation of MnSOST–R scores is done by score categories and not by individual scores. See Table 5.5 for the per score category percentages for interpretation.

TABLE 5.5.   Interpretation of Minnesota Sex Offender Screening
Tool–Revised (MnSOST–R) Scores (in percentages)

Score Range	Estimated Recidivism Base Rate	Associated Recidivism Rate
3 and below	35	16
	21	8
	15	6
4 to 7	35	45
	21	29
	15	22
8 and above	35	70
	21	54
	15	44
13 and above	35	88
	21	78
	15	70

SOURCE: Epperson et al. (1999).

There is one unique characteristic of the MnSOST–R compared with the other risk assessment instruments previously discussed. The reader can see on Table 5.5 that there are three separate recidivism figures for each of the four score categories. Those three figures are always preceded on that table with an "estimated recidivism base rate," being 35%, 21%, or 15%. These estimated rates reflect the underlying total sample recidivism rate from which the recidivism rate per score category was derived. For instance, if one were to use a sample with a 35% recidivism base rate, then a MnSOST–R score of less than 3 (the lowest risk category) would be associated with about a 16% six-year sexual rearrest rate. If the base rate in the sample were assumed or found to be different, however, for instance closer to 21%, then the associated recidivism risk for people in the same score category of "3 or below" would only be 8%.

In other words, the interpretation of the degree of recidivism risk represented by any of the four score categories is dependent on the assumed sexual recidivism base rate underlying the analysis. Given that the actual sexual rearrest rate for the populations from which the developmental and cross-validating research samples were drawn was about 21%, assuming that underlying rate for interpreting MnSOST–R scores seems most appropriate. A counterperspective, however, is that because the civil commitment assessment is typically looking at an individual's sexual reoffense risk over a period potentially much longer than 6 years, the higher assumed base rate of 35% offers a more meaningful estimate of the relevant risk (Douglas Epperson, personal communication, 2000). The problem with that latter perspective is that the MnSOST–R, as a risk assessment tool, still only considers risk factors related to the first 6 years postincarceration and really does not directly assess longer-term recidivism risk no matter what base rate is assumed correct. It seems more correct to use the MnSOST–R to formulate an accurate 6-year risk estimate (using the 21% figures), and then acknowledge any extrapolation beyond the 6-year hands-on sexual rearrest measure is based on considerations beyond the MnSOST–R itself.

Interrater reliability. The MnSOST–R has been researched the least among the six being explored in this chapter. Two studies have been performed concerning the instrument's interrater reliability (Barbaree et al., 2001; Epperson et al., 1999). The interclass correlation (ICC) obtained in both investigations was .80. This figure is certainly acceptable, but is somewhat lower than what was found for the other scales reviewed. There are two good possible reasons why this is true. Foremost is that the Epperson et al. (1999) study ultimately employed 10 raters (after 1 rater ignorant as to how to find file material was eliminated) in computing the ICC, as opposed to the more typical 2 raters. This extra degree of variability both explains some of the difference in figures found and allows the results to be even more confidently applied to raters beyond the study.

The other reason is that the MnSOST–R items less frequently involve the two-level (yea-nay) scoring system common to the other scales. At least 5 of the 16 MnSOST–R items involve three or four possible scoring levels, suggesting that per item interrater agreement may not be as easily obtained as with a dichotomous scoring system.

Validity. To date, there have been only three attempted replications of the MnSOST–R's predictive validity (Barbaree et al., 2001; Epperson, Kaul, & Huot, 2000; Schiller & Watnik, 2001). The latter two studies clearly supported the earlier research results, with the Schiller and Watnik study being more exploratory in nature. Barbaree et al., however, did not. One could argue that a trend was found in the right direction (the degree of significance approached significance; $p = .10$), but no obvious reason for the technically failed replication seems available. The Schiller and Watnik study was most notable for its sample size (about 1,400 subjects, in contrast to the Epperson et al. original developmental much smaller sample size of 256) coupled with a clear sampling selection bias toward lower-risk offenders (i.e., virtually everyone with three or more felony convictions during his lifetime, for any type of offending, was excluded from the sample). The fact that the MnSOST–R scores showed a statistically significant relationship to sexual recidivism with this sample suggests some degree of robustness in that relationship.

In addition to predictive validity tests, there have been three empirical demonstrations of concurrent validity of the scale (Doren & Roberts, 1998; Fanning, Zimmel, Jaskulske, & Curran, 1999; Quackenbush, 2000). (Concurrent validity means that the "test" has been found to relate to measures of similar constructs as it should, and not to relate to dissimilar constructs, also as it should.) All of these studies supported the concurrent validity of the instrument as a measure of sexual recidivism likelihood.

Arguably, an evaluator could additionally borrow from the MnSOST predictive validation research to investigate the degree to which the MnSOST–R predictive validity is supported (in the same way reference was made to the RRASOR research for the Static-99). Two studies have been conducted concerning the predictive validity of the MnSOST (Fischer, 2000; Hanlon, Larson, & Zacher, 1999), with neither of these serving impressively in support of the MnSOST–R. The first involved a minor adaptation of the MnSOST, so it was not strictly a test of that instrument but of an adaptation of that instrument. The Hanlon et al. (1999) study involved a sample of only about 50 people, so although statistical significance was found (which is impressive given the small sample size), the small number of people involved makes generalizability more of a question.

Utility within civil commitment assessments. Putting all of this together, the inter-rater reliability of the MnSOST–R has to date been supported. The predictive validity of the instrument has not been as well tested, nor uniformly as well supported as was found for the other instruments reviewed above. (One contrary finding, the Barbaree et al., 2001, study, stands out here relative to the small number of supportive findings, in contrast to the rare nonsupportive findings for all of the previously reviewed instruments where a far greater number of supportive findings were discovered.) Even so, the (above arbitrarily selected) minimal criteria for possible selection as a tool for use within the sex offender civil commitment evaluation realm appear to have been met. Whether or not these criteria are in keeping with any individual evaluator's perspective is up to that individual and the options available.

Strengths of the MnSOST–R within the civil commitment assessment arena include the fact that it is more inclusive than the other scales by using more items. Even more important, the MnSOST–R is the only actuarial scale among those reviewed that incorporates the individual's participation and potential completion of any treatment (actually assessing both sex offender treatment and chemical dependency treatment participation). The MnSOST–R is also the only scale among those that directly assess sexual recidivism risk (i.e., the RRASOR, Static-99, and MnSOST–R) that allows for someone's risk to be assessed as below average (i.e., scored in the negative direction, which the MnSOST–R does both for most individual items and for the scale overall).

The relative weaknesses of the MnSOST–R within the civil commitment context actually stem from the same things that relate to its strengths. The fact that there are more items to score, and more than just two levels within most items, makes for a more difficult scoring process than occurs with scales as short or binary as the RRASOR and Static-99. Likewise, the scoring of the items related to treatment participation can become problematic when one realizes that the treatment programming and experience of an individual subject may not be sufficiently similar in important ways to the type of programming that served as the basis for the scoring system on these items in the MnSOST–R (from the Minnesota DOC). Areas of potential relevance in this regard include (1) the completion rate of the people going through the treatment program (because the MnSOST–R assesses higher risk to people who are terminated from a treatment program), with the Minnesota DOC programs having shown about an 80% completion rate for those entering the program; and (2) that the treatment involved about a year or more of programming, and not just something like a short-term didactic group (Stephen Huot, personal communication, 2000).

Due to that last consideration, some people use the MnSOST–R by only employing the first 12 items on the scale (sometimes referred to as the static portion of the MnSOST–R), thereby eliminating the treatment-related items. Interpretive risk percentages are available for just this set of items (at the same Web site listed above), with the highest risk category for the total score from these items being 10+. If an evaluator has difficulty applying the MnSOST–R to specific subjects solely because of the treatment-related items, then using just the static portion of the MnSOST–R is recommended instead.

A final consideration in using the MnSOST–R is that research has indicated that it does not work well, and should not be used, with people whose sexual convictions involved solely incestuous contact, unless that contact involved penetration of the victim and/or the offense clearly involved a "brutal" physical attack. The fact is that relatively few purely incest offenders are found to represent high enough risk to be referred or supported for civil commitment across the country as it is. In cases where such offenders are being reviewed, however, evaluators should not employ the MnSOST–R as part of those assessments.

Caveats to Using Any of the Actuarial Risk Assessment Instruments

Concerning the Use of Coding Rules

Mental health clinicians are not typically familiar nor are they initially comfortable with using actuarial instruments. There is a tendency to want to "interpret" one or more items because of what we "know" is "really" being measured when case specifics do not directly show the actuarial outcome we expected. We tend to want to go beyond the strict coding rules in computing someone's actuarial score, so the score "makes more sense" to us.

The fact is that if we really knew what we were measuring, we would not be using variables that clearly serve as a proxy for something else. For example, a high number of prior sexual convictions obviously does not *directly cause* an offender to recidivate more than a low number of prior convictions does. The higher number simply serves for us as a useful substitute for something more directly related (such as strength of drive for the illegal type of sexual contact, to make one of many possible conjectures). Because we do not truly know what we are ultimately measuring with current actuarial instrumentation, all we can know is the degree to which the instruments "work" (i.e., are supported empirically). To keep them working, we must apply the research-based coding rules as they exist, not as we may wish them to be in any given case. Any clinical "interpretation" of the items for the purpose of scoring a subject through "reinterpreted" coding rules is to be avoided. Clinical adjustments of actuarial results to estimate a subject's overall risk can be fine, but clinically adjusting the actual scale scoring rules is not.

In addition, the evaluator needs to be aware that the coding rules for different instruments can use the same words in different ways. What counts as a charge for the RRASOR and Static-99, for instance, includes certain types of parole revocations. The term *charge* in the coding rules for the MnSOST–R, however, does not. The recommendation is strongly made that evaluators download the scoring rules for each instrument they use, and become quite familiar with the rules before using the instrument.

Concerning Error Rates

All of the actuarial risk percentages listed in Tables 5.1 through 5.5 represent findings from a specific set of samples. As with any sampling process, there is always some degree of potential variability due to the sampling process, meaning that if the same study were done using a different sample there would be some, albeit potentially only slight, degree of difference in the overall findings just because of the difference in sample used. Evaluators should be aware of the degree to which this type of variability (usually called sampling error) can affect the interpretation of an actuarial scale score.

The statistic that estimates this type of error is the confidence interval (CI). Within the context of actuarial risk assessments, the CI basically offers an estimate of how variable the risk percentages associated with each scale score (or score category) might be if the sampling process were replicated over and over. Generally (though not fully accurately) speaking, the CI is a "plus or minus" figure to attach to the risk estimates enumerated in Tables 5.1 through 5.5.

The computation of the relevant CIs involves two main considerations: (1) the degree to which the actuarial instrument's risk percentage is closer to 50% or closer to one of the extremes (0% or 100%) and (2) the total sample size from which the specific risk percentage was computed. Extremely low- or extremely high-risk estimates from the actuarial instruments will tend to be associated with far smaller plus-or-minus figures (i.e., CIs) than risk estimates that are near 50%. The larger the number of people sampled for computing the recidivism percentage for a given scale score (or score category), the smaller will be the corresponding CI.

Tables 5.6 through 5.9 offer CIs for each of the actuarial scales described in this chapter (except for the SORAG, that instrument's CIs not being listed separately because they were very similar to the VRAG's except somewhat larger across the board due to smaller samples having been studied). These numbers were computed and presented by me (Doren, 2000) based on different samples for each instrument.

The reader should *not* think of these as exact figures in some absolute sense, for two reasons. The computation results represented in Tables 5.6 through 5.9 were based on the specified set of samples. The addition of other samples to any of these composite samples would very likely make at least small changes in the computed numbers. More important, there is an assumption underlying the computation of these statistics that is probably not accurate (i.e., that a sufficiently comprehensive sampling of the domain of relevant risk-related characteristics is represented by each instrument's set of items). The improper assumption was made to facilitate the computation of CI estimates. Based on these considerations, evaluators should think of these figures as estimates that assist in determining how confident we can be that a certain actuarial score represents a risk that falls below or above the legal threshold for commitment (before any extrapolation to lifetime reoffending or for any other reason).

All of the results in the CI tables represent information related to what are called 95% confidence intervals. The choice of a 95% CI, versus some other percentage, is by convention. The interpretative wording that goes along with the figures in Tables 5.6 through 5.9 is something like the following, using RRASOR = 4 over 10 years for

TABLE 5.6.   Confidence Intervals for the Violence Risk Appraisal Guide
(VRAG)

Score Category	7 years	10 years
1 (lowest bin)	0.0 +/– 0.0	9.1 +/– 17.0
2	8.5 +/– 6.5	9.9 +/– 6.9
3	11.8 +/– 6.3	23.8 +/– 8.3
4	17.9 +/– 6.9	30.6 +/– 8.6
5	33.0 +/– 8.3	48.3 +/– 9.1
6	40.4 +/– 9.0	58.3 +/– 9.9
7	52.3 +/– 10.6	63.5 +/– 11.0
8	62.9 +/– 16.0	82.8 +/– 13.7
9	100.0 +/– 0.0	100.0 +/– 0.0

SOURCE: Based on a total of two data sets from Webster, Harris, Rice, Cormier, and
Quinsey (1994), and Sjöstedt and Långström (in press). Thanks to Grant Harris, Marnie
Rice, Gabrielle Sjöstedt, and Niklas Långström for permission to use their data.

TABLE 5.7.   Confidence Intervals for the Rapid Risk Assessment for Sex
Offender Recidivism (RRASOR)

Score Category	5 years	10 years
0	4.4 +/– 1.9	6.5 +/– 2.1
1	7.6 +/– 1.9	11.2 +/– 2.2
2	14.2 +/– 2.5	21.1 +/– 2.9
3	24.8 +/– 4.5	36.9 +/– 5.2
4	32.7 +/– 7.5	48.6 +/– 8.3
5	49.8 +/– 12.4	73.1 +/– 12.1
6	(no data are available for this score)	

SOURCE: Based on a total of three data sets from, and with thanks to the primary
authors of, Beech, Erikson, Friendship, and Ditchfield (2001), Hanson and Thornton
(2000), and Nicholaichuk, Templeman, and Gu (1999).

TABLE 5.8.   Confidence Intervals for the Static-99

Score Category	5 years	10 years	15 years
0	5.0 +/– 3.9	11.0 +/– 6.0	13.0 +/– 6.4
1	6.0 +/– 3.7	7.0 +/– 4.2	7.0 +/– 4.2
2	9.0 +/– 3.9	13.0 +/– 4.6	16.0 +/– 5.1
3	12.0 +/– 4.4	14.0 +/– 4.8	19.0 +/– 5.4
4	26.0 +/– 6.1	31.0 +/– 6.6	36.0 +/– 6.8
5	33.0 +/– 9.1	38.0 +/– 9.5	40.0 +/– 9.6
6+	39.0 +/– 5.8	45.0 +/– 6.2	52.0 +/– 8.6

SOURCE: Based on a total of six data sets from, and with thanks to the primary
authors of, Beech, Erikson, Friendship, and Ditchfield (2001), Epperson et al. (1999),
Hanson and Thornton (2000), Nicholaichuk, Templeman, and Gu (1999), and Sjöstedt
and Långström (2000, in press).

TABLE 5.9. Confidence Intervals for the Minnesota Sex Offender Screening Tool–Revised (MnSOST–R)

Score Category	6 years
3 or lower	14.0 +/– 5.1
4 through 7	39.0 +/– 10.4
8 through 12	59.0 +/– 12.3
8 or higher	62.0 +/– 10.3
13 or higher	70.0 +/– 18.3

SOURCE: Based on the 35% base rate figures from, and with thanks to the primary author of, Epperson et al. (1999). Confidence intervals (CIs) based on a lower assumed base rate, such as 21%, would affect the computed CIs in a nonlinear way. The CIs would grow smaller as the anchoring risk percentage moves way from 50%. For example, movement of the risk percentage from 52% to 29% would decrease the size of the CI, whereas a movement from 70% to 45% would increase the size of the CI.

the example: A score of 4 on the RRASOR is associated with a group of people who showed a sexual reconviction rate of 48.6%, give or take about 8.4%.

Actually, from a technically statistical perspective, this illustrative statement is not fully accurate. The risk estimate of 48.6% does not really represent the center point of the CI. Theoretically, one first needs to take the degree of interrater reliability of the scale into consideration (which was not found to be perfection for any of the scales), a process that moves the center point very slightly (for scales with these high degrees of reliability) toward the score distribution mean.

For example, the developmental samples for the RRASOR showed a score distribution mean of 1.77 (Hanson, 1997). In practice, with interrater reliability figures as high as were found for the RRASOR (and all of the instruments reviewed), there is little to be gained by recomputing each new CI center point compared just to using the 95% CI range as described in the paragraph above. For a RRASOR score of 4, for instance, the ultimately different center point for the 95% CI range, instead of 48.6%, is about 47%, a difference of less than 2%. (Lower scores on the RRASOR all show even smaller changes in their 95% CI center point.) This would make the technically accurate description of the 95% CI for a RRASOR score of 4 to be 47% plus or minus about 8.4%.

We all should know that none of the actuarial risk percentages and CI figures is so perfect that the relatively small change in center point to the CI should make all the difference in our deciding if a specific subject's risk is higher or lower than the commitment threshold. All of these figures help us to know what general range of risk each actuarial score represents, not some exact percentage range with an exact boundary on each end.

Choosing One Versus Multiple Risk Assessment Instruments

During an assessment, an evaluator first needs to determine the potential risk assessment instruments of choice. Then there is a second basic question to be addressed: Should one choose the single "best" instrument, or use a set of instruments from among the qualified candidates? This is a complicated question to answer, such that the pros and cons of each approach are explicated below.

From a purely statistical perspective, the idea of doing a comparison of the statistical strengths and weaknesses among the three or six potential instruments, with the purpose of finding the "best" scale, has merit. Examiners could review

1. the interrater reliability results,

2. numbers and proportions of replicated validity studies (concentrating on predictive/postdictive validity, because this is more directly pertinent to the civil commitment context than concurrent validity results),

3. the degree to which the instruments were tested on samples similar in attributes to the subject of the current evaluation, and

4. the degree to which the instruments' outcome measures are in keeping with the relevant statutory definition of sexual violence.

With some estimation of the relative importance of these different attributes, a single instrument may stand out as "better" than the others from which one is choosing.

This process of "single instrument selection" has positive and negative attributes. A strongly positive characteristic is that the evaluator can rightfully state in court, if necessary, that the selected instrument was considered the best available for the immediate purpose and here are all the reasons as to how that conclusion came to be made.

This same strength could, at least in theory, lead to evaluators changing their single-instrument selection over time, either as further research results become available and/or as the evaluator changes jurisdictions in which the assessments are being conducted. Explanations in court testimony for why the evaluator changes assessment procedures over time would become necessary, at least in response to cross-examination looking to discredit the evaluator's procedures in a given case. Then again, the process of updating procedures and needing to explain changes over time should occur whether or not one chooses to use one or more risk assessment instruments. The only evaluator who stays with one fixed selection of assessment procedures over time is one who ignores newer research results, this being true in any applied scientific endeavor: medical, psychological, or otherwise.

The potentially negative side to picking the single "best" instrument is that the resultant assessment ignores the theoretical possibility that there are different etiological pathways affecting a subject's recidivism risk. To explain this concept, a metaphor may serve well. When you wish to check on the degree to which there is risk to your health, you can get yourself evaluated by going to a physician for a checkup. In doing that "risk assessment," the physician needs to check your multiple bodily systems to conduct a proper examination. If a checkup covered only your cardiac health, a life-threatening condition such as emphysema could be missed. Likewise, if only your pulmonary system were investigated, a malignant brain tumor might not be discovered. By evaluating only one bodily system, the physician could draw conclusions about the overall risk to your health, but those conclusions would be based on significantly incomplete information. Only by checking all known bodily systems can the physician meaningfully make conclusions about current risks to your health.

The same may very well be true within the assessment of sex offender recidivism risk. There may be different systems (or theoretical dimensions, or etiological pathways, whatever phrase seems most meaningful) related to a sex offender's risk for sexually reoffending. If evaluators assess only one dimension, conclusions of high risk may still be accurate (in keeping with the somatic metaphor involving finding cancer in the one system investigated), but a conclusion of low or moderate risk might be in serious error (like having an undiscovered malignant brain tumor in a person who was found to have a healthy heart).

A single instrument, at least as currently designed, cannot simultaneously assess multiple dimensions across the full range of risk possibilities well. For instance, let us assume that there are two functionally independent dimensions to be investigated (i.e., metaphorically, the cardiac and pulmonary). If one instrument is employed to assess both simultaneously, then the following outcomes are possible:

1. Each dimension was really at low risk; the instrument shows low risk.

2. Each dimension was really at high risk; the instrument shows high risk.

3. One dimension was really at high risk and the other was really at low risk; the instrument shows a middle/moderate degree of risk (effectively by averaging the two dimensional measures).

4. Each dimension was really at moderate risk; the instrument shows moderate risk.

Outcomes 1 and 2 do not represent a problem for interpretation. The issue is in differentiating Outcome 3 from 4. A "moderate" risk finding may disguise a really high risk overall by summing (or averaging) results across dimensions. Current risk assessment instrumentation, both of the research-guided and actuarial styles, do not differentiate and keep independent any subcomponents of the risk assessment based on theoretically different dimensions. They all effectively allow for, and may even mandate, the interpretation of only the complete sum of scores found applicable to the individual subject.

All of this discussion might be intellectually interesting but quite irrelevant if there were no evidence for multiple dimensions underlying the routes to sexual recidivism. Such evidence exists, however, with some clear consistency in the dimensions being uncovered.

Doren and Roberts (1998; later written up in Roberts et al., in press) investigated the interrelationships among RRASOR, Static-99, MnSOST, MnSOST–R, VRAG, and PCL–R along with sex offenders' types of psychiatric diagnoses, known victims' age categories, and known victims' genders. The results strongly indicated the existence of two dimensions that were apparently relatively independent of one another. The simple descriptions those researchers gave to the two dimensions were "deviant sexual interests" and "antisocial/violent personality characteristics." Put a different way, there was suggestion of at least two underlying drives toward sexual recidivism: (1) diagnosable and illegal sexual desires and (2) a general propensity toward interpersonal violence, without a diagnosable sexual disorder, where that violence included but was not specific to sexual offending. The sample employed in this study, however, consisted of offenders already screened as representing a high-risk group, such that these results could be interpreted as simply reflecting biases in the earlier screening process.

On the other hand, the results from the Hanson and Bussière (1998) meta-analysis (of risk factors for sex offender recidivism) support the Doren and Roberts findings. This meta-analysis found support for the statistical relationship with sexual recidivism of various factors falling under the rubrics of "sexual deviance" and "criminal lifestyle," with nonsignificant relationships found involving "psychological maladjustment" and "negative clinical presentation" variables. Factors under the heading of "sexual deviance" included diagnostic findings such as deviant sexual interests as well as prior sexual offending. "Criminal lifestyle" included factors such as antisocial personality disorder and prior offending (of any type, including nonsexual). These results seem to support both of the dimensions found by Doren and Roberts, and likewise seem to exclude certain other clinical considerations. This study did not address whether or not these two sets of variables were statistically independent, however.

That issue has been addressed by David Thornton. He conducted a series of factor analytic investigations (described in Roberts et al., in press) that, in summary, was supportive to both the idea of multiple underlying dimensions and the independence of those dimensions. Findings suggested the presence of three underlying clusters of risk factors. The first two have been described by the researcher as "general criminality" and "sexual deviance," very much in keeping with the research described above. (The third factor was labeled "detachment" and was represented by under-25-years-old, never married males who victimized strangers.)

Support for two or three underlying pathways for sexual offending was also found by Hudson, Ward, and McCormack (1999). Initially investigating eight possible pathways to sexual offending, those researchers discovered that about 73% of their sample fell into three main groups. About one third of the sample showed a "pathway . . . primarily characterized by positive affect, explicit decision making with respect to the sexual activity involved, and a commitment to continue to behave in a similar manner" (p. 793), a pattern that was about equally shown by child molesters and rapists in this study. This description seems to overlap the aforementioned sexual deviance/illegal sexual interest dimension. The next largest pathway, comprising about one quarter of the sample (19% of the child molesters, but 50% of the rapists), showed an absence of both positive affect and explicit planning specific to sexual offending, though such plans were made more "implicitly." (Examples of implicit planning were "I decided to smash her place up, was angry, and decided to have sex with her when I found her home" and "wanted her to feel as unhappy as he did"; p. 789.) The sexual offending for these perpetrators was apparently more in reaction to their "negative" affect than some explicit desire for sexual arousal of a deviant type. In other words, these offenders did not show signs of paraphiliac interests, but instead demonstrated the self-focus coupled with disregard of and violence toward others characteristic of the antisocial/violent dimension. The final major pathway, involving about 16% of the sample (with no proportional difference between child molesters and rapists), appeared to be a variant on the second one, with the major difference being that there was clear sexual planning (including grooming) by the perpetrator once he entered into the negative mood state. This third pathway can be viewed as representing an independent dimension compared with the first two, or simply representative of the combination of both of their attributes. Interestingly, the remaining five minor pathways were all found to pertain only to child molesters, as all the rapists in the study fell into one of the three major groupings.

Finally, Ray Knight (1999) presented a "unified theory of sexual coercion" in which two (and only two) main types of drives toward sexual offending were described. The first he called "sexual drive/promiscuity," being composed of attributes such as "short-term mating strategy," "preference for partner variety and casual sex," and "higher sexual drive, preoccupation and compulsivity" (p. 14). The other type of drive was termed "negative (or hyper) masculinity," covering attributes such as "hostility towards women," "accept violence towards women as appropriate," "defensive, hypersensitive, and hostile orientation," and "gratification from dominating" (p. 15). These dimensions largely stemmed from earlier typological research by Knight and his colleague Robert Prentky (e.g., Knight, 1998; Prentky & Knight, 1991). As the reader can see, Knight's research-based theory of sexual offending significantly overlaps with the other empirically determined dimensions described above.

This evidence for multiple underlying dimensions potentially driving sexual reoffending represents the main relative weakness to using only the "best" single risk assessment instrument in a sex offender civil commitment evaluation. Concomitantly, this multiple etiological perspective is the foundation for the strongest reason for selecting more than one instrument for simultaneous use (though, quite significantly, only if the instruments appear to be tapping different dimensions). To the extent that multiple assessment instruments serve to assess all relevant recidivism etiological dimensions, an assessment procedure using multiple instruments will clearly be at least as good if not superior to the single-instrument approach.

The downside to the use of multiple instruments is twofold: (1) The evaluator needs to know to what extent each instrument assesses the different "pathways for risk" (i.e., etiological dimensions), and (2) the process of interpreting "mixed" results is clearly more complicated than interpreting any single-instrument outcome alone. These considerations are not insignificant. Based on the empirical and theoretical support for more than one type of drive toward sexual recidivism coupled with our ethical responsibility to do as accurate an evaluation as we can, however, the recommendation is made that sex offender civil commitment assessments investigate subjects' risk for all known risk dimensions. This suggests, despite the added difficulties, that at least two relatively independent risk assessment instruments should typically be used (one to assess each theorized risk pathway), assuming their applicability to the case in the first place.

Interpreting Actuarial Instrument Results

Single-Instrument Interpretation

Single actuarial instrument result interpretation is rather straightforward. When using one scale, the subject is scored according to the coding rules, and the total scale score comes with an attached percentage likelihood for specified type of sexual offending within a specified time period postincarceration. For instance, on the Static-99, a score of 6 or higher falls into the category with associated risk described as 52% likelihood for being reconvicted of a new sexual offense within 15 years postincarceration.

Errors in single-instrument interpretation tend to be of three types, assuming the application is to a proper subject and there were no rating errors by the examiner. The first error involves how evaluators describe a score's associated risk percentage application to the specific subject. The proper application is that the subject's score falls into the category that research has shown to be associated with $X\%$ likelihood for sexual reconviction within Y years after incarceration (with a statement about error rates being ignored, but just for the moment). The common error is an improper shorthand: the subject's score means that he is $X\%$ likely to be reconvicted of a new sexual offense within Y years after his incarceration. These are not the same statements. The first statement represents a statistical finding. The latter type of statement involves various additional assumptions, and it should simply be avoided.

The second type of error in interpretation is in forgetting that there are sampling variations underlying all research involving these scales. This is a statistical type of error that can be approximated through the use of confidence intervals (i.e., the same type of description of error described by the media from public polls, that is, a "give or take $X\%$" qualifier). The exact numbers are not so important in this discussion of evaluator errors, just the idea that the general degree that sampling variability should not be forgotten in actuarial scale score interpretation. Even if an evaluator were not clear about the confidence interval surrounding a risk estimate percentage, describing the concept of "give or take some error in estimation" after the above paragraph's proper statement seems warranted.

The third kind of error occurs when the evaluator ignores the qualifiers to what has been assessed. Such an error is of the type "the associated sexual recidivism risk is $X\%$" when the proper statement would be closer to "the associated risk for being reconvicted for a new sexual offense within Y years after incarceration is $X\%$." The improper interpretative description ignores the differences between lifetime sexual reoffense rates and official recapture rates from shorter time periods, along with all other base rate effects described in Chapter 6.

When these three types of errors are avoided, single risk assessment instrument results become a meaningful segment of an overall risk evaluation. As stated above, however, the potential multidimensionality of sex offender recidivism risk is not best addressed through any current single scale.

Multiple-Instrument Interpretation

The most accurate multiple-instrument interpretation requires prior knowledge of the degree to which different scales assess each of the multiple etiological dimensions. There are empirical suggestions to assist evaluators in that regard, though direct predictive/postdictive tests specifically of combinations of instrument results (vs. of comparative single results from a group of scales) are minimal in number.

The Instrument-Dimension Relationship

The clearest findings to date documenting how the main risk assessment instruments work in combination are those from Doren and Roberts (1998) and Roberts et al. (in press). Both studies involved the actuarial MnSOST, MnSOST–R, RRASOR, Static-99, and VRAG scales along with the PCL–R, diagnostic information, and different aspects of victim information, all with a highly selected, presumably high-risk sample. (Of statistical importance, the vast majority of the sample was not selected based on actuarial instrument results, so this is not a confounding consideration.) Two main correlational clusters of information were discovered. The first involved

1. the RRASOR,

2. the diagnosed presence of a paraphilia (vs. not),

3. children victims versus adolescent or adult victims, and

4. ever having had a boy victim (vs. all female).

The second correlational cluster included

1. the MnSOST, MnSOST–R, Static-99, VRAG, the PCL–R;

2. the diagnosed presence of a personality disorder (quite commonly being antisocial personality disorder or personality disorder not otherwise specified, with antisocial features);

3. adult and/or adolescent victims both without children victims; and

4. no male victim (despite "male victim" being an item scored in the higher-risk direction on two of the actuarial scales within this correlational clustering, the Static-99 and VRAG, the latter if the boy victim was in the index offense).

If we dissect these findings by concentrating on the two-dimensional model described above, we find that the RRASOR tended to correlate with the sexual deviance dimension, whereas the other actuarial instruments tended to correlate with the general violence dimension.

This result may appear surprising in that one might have thought that the Static-99 would demonstrate the same dimensional correlations as the RRASOR given that the latter is totally included in the former. The researchers investigated this issue and found that the sum of the six non-RRASOR items on the Static-99 had a particularly strong correlation with the PCL–R and VRAG, with lesser though still clearly significant correlations with the other items in that cluster. Apparently, the six non-RRASOR items were sufficient to make the overall Static-99 scale function differently from the RRASOR it contains, at least in that high-risk sample.

Additional support for a difference between the RRASOR and the Static-99 in what they assess comes from my reanalysis (Doren, 2001b) of the long-term recidivism data underlying the development of the Static-99. When looking at the combination of three long-term recidivism databases (i.e., with an average of 16.6 years follow-up), I found that both the RRASOR and Static-99 were effectively independent of one another specifically when assessing high risk, with their relative overall predictive accuracy being statistically equal. Statistical independence yet equal effectiveness suggests that these two scales assess different aspects of what ultimately leads to sexual recidivism.

Quackenbush (2000), who clearly used a far lower risk sample than did Doren and Roberts (1998), documented an intercorrelational matrix that also supported the latter researchers' findings. The results from the Quackenbush study showed the MnSOST–R and Static-99 to be *very* highly correlated (i.e., $r = .70$, $n = 204$ for this correlation), whereas the RRASOR was found to function differently from the MnSOST–R, SORAG, Static-99, and the newly developed Irish Sex Offender Risk Tool (ISORT) in assessing sexual recidivism risk.

Finally, there is supportive evidence that the RRASOR assesses risk within the sexual deviance dimension from Haynes et al. (2000) (also in Nicholaichuk & Yates, in press). In that study, the simple finding of PPG sexual deviance added nothing to the statistical accuracy of the RRASOR in predicting sexual recidivism, despite the earlier finding from the Hanson and Bussière (1998) meta-analysis that PPG-measured deviance was the highest single correlate with sexual recidivism. In other words, the RRASOR already addressed and included this predictive relationship, statistically speaking, without requiring subjects to go through the PPG physiological assessment procedure.

Collectively, these studies do not offer the final word concerning how the actuarial instruments assess different recidivism drives, but the studies do offer important guidance based in their apparent result consistency. Given a two-dimensional model for sexual recidivism etiology and our current choices of sufficiently tested and validated risk assessment instruments, the following conclusion seems warranted: The RRASOR is more useful in assessing the sexual deviance risk dimension, and the MnSOST–R and Static-99 are better suited for evaluating risk along the violent/antisocial pathway for sexual recidivism. Hence, the recommendation is made that sex offender civil commitment evaluators employ both the RRASOR (or other instruments found in the future to share the above same attribute) and at least one of the instruments that appears to assess the other risk dimension (e.g., Static-99, MnSOST–R), to be as accurate as possible.

Interpreting Multiple-Scale Results

Using the physical checkup metaphor, of assessing different body systems to evaluate overall health, the proper multiple-instrument interpretation is not difficult to comprehend. For the sake of discussion, let us concentrate solely on actuarial instrument results, though this is by no means the recommended overall evaluation procedure.

Just as with one's health, if the risk in one bodily system is high, then one's overall health risk is high even if every other bodily system is doing fine. Obviously, high-risk findings from multiple directions is a particularly bad sign, but the only proper low-risk conclusion stems from a finding of low risk across all systems.

From that perspective, a high-risk finding on the RRASOR (or other instruments documented in the future to assess the sexual deviance dimension at least as well) indicates high risk overall, irrelevant of the other actuarial instrument results (which assess the one or more other etiological dimensions). Likewise, high risk indicated on the Static-99 or MnSOST–R (or similar tool) indicates high sexual recidivism risk exists even if the RRASOR outcome is low or moderate. If both sets of instruments are high, then again a high risk exists. If instruments assessing both dimensions suggest low risk, then the overall risk is low.

There is one last possibility. An evaluator can use both the Static-99 and the MnSOST–R to assess the same dimension, with the idea that consistency across multiple measures of the same construct increases our confidence in the results. In using both, however, there is the possibility that these two instruments will not always indicate the same degree of recidivism risk stemming from that single dimension. In that case, the evaluator is left either to look for other signs of risk related to this same dimension, to clarify the mixed actuarial result, or to pick the result from the actuarial instrument more research supported. Other signs on this dimension appear to include a diagnosed personality disorder, a high score on the PCL–R, a sexual assault pattern of victimizing adults and not solely children, and no diagnosed paraphilia.

Putting these theoretical relationships into practical terms, archetypal descriptions of people high in risk for each dimension can be offered. The "high sexual deviancy dimension, low violent/antisocial dimension" person is the strongly paraphiliac individual who continues to act illegally on his sexual deviancy despite otherwise being a rule-abiding citizen with a steady job and stable background. The epitome of the "high violent/antisocial dimension, low sexual deviancy dimension" individual is someone who is rather psychopathic, sees violence as an appropriate means for getting what he wants, does not have much use for social mores and expectations, tends to take what he wants from others, and often has a criminal record including but significantly beyond the purely sexual. The reader should note that these depictions of classic types of individuals representing different pathways toward high risk were not made in victim characteristic terms such as "child molester" or "rapist," though some degree of relationship is expected between such characteristics and the risk dimensions. Rapists can be assessed as high risk on the sexual deviancy dimension, and child molesters can basically be psychopathic individuals who obtain sexual gratification from children simply because of availability or ease at doing so.

The caveat was suggested above that using purely the actuarial instruments to assess the different dimensions was not recommended and was used solely for the sake of simplifying the discussion. Actually recommended is that examiners concentrate on assessing the two dimensions as fully and as accurately as possible, and not just concentrate on the proper interpretation of multiple actuarial scales. If the recommended clinically adjusted actuarial assessment methodology is being employed, then all clinical adjustments should be viewed in light of the two-dimensional theory as well. Chapter 7 offers instructional information in this regard.

Summary Comments

This chapter covered four main topics: (1) the overall risk assessment methodological choice, (2) comparing the accuracy of differing methodologies, (3) selecting what instruments to use, and (4) interpreting actuarial instrument results. When at least one relevant actuarial risk assessment instrument is available, the recommended evaluation methodology within the civil commitment context is the clinically adjusted actuarial model. Certain current actuarial instruments were found that met enumerated standards, with three such instruments being specific to sexual recidivism risk assessments: the RRASOR, Static-99, and MnSOST–R.

Caveats to the way in which actuarial instruments are used and interpreted were described. Printed for the first time were confidence interval statistics for the described scales, to be used in keeping with one of the interpretative caveats.

The exploration of different paradigms to interpret actuarial results led to the recommendation that a multiple risk pathway model be used. This is in contrast to alternatives such as "the single best instrument" approach and the approach that uses multiple instruments specifically to find consistency across (virtually) all instruments used, though there are rationales supportive to those approaches as well.

Note

1. The sample involved virtually no incest offenders, so the range of RRASOR scores was restricted because the relationship of the perpetrator to the victim is one of the RRASOR's four items. The resultant nonsignificant correlation of the RRASOR with sexual recidivism could therefore be interpreted as reflecting this statistical limitation. That interpretation was supported by those same researchers (Douglas Epperson, personal communication, 2000). To address this statistical problem, a follow-up to the original finding was conducted where the researchers altered the relevant one item on the RRASOR from "extrafamilial versus incest" victim to "stranger versus non-stranger" victim. The latter variable is a correlate of the original, but the new variable was not artificially limited by the sample selection. When this "altered RRASOR" was tested, the correlation with sexual recidivism was found highly significant ($p < .001$).

CHAPTER 6

Recidivism Base Rates

Statistics: A group of numbers looking for an argument.

— Gerald F. Lieberman

What is a "recidivism base rate," and why should I care about such a thing when doing a civil commitment evaluation? This chapter addresses underlying issues to the risk assessment portion of the civil commitment evaluation that are sometimes neglected or poorly understood—issues that actually matter a great deal toward both the conclusions we draw about a subject's recidivism risk and the degree of confidence we have surrounding that conclusion. Those issues fall under the rubric of base rates.

A base rate is simply the proportion of a designated population sharing a certain characteristic. The base rate within the U.S. human population of female members is reportedly just over half. The proportion of days in which it rains within a calendar year in some desert areas is near zero. The base rate for criminal sexual recidivism for previously convicted sex offenders is the concept of relevance within the risk assessment portion of sex offender civil commitment evaluations.

This chapter will discuss what we know about sexual recidivism base rates and how that knowledge can affect our civil commitment risk assessments. Although some evaluators may not regularly think of recidivism base rate information as of direct concern during a risk assessment, the information in this chapter should be found to indicate otherwise. There are two types of information covered in this chapter: what we know about base rates and why it matters.

What Do We Know About the Sexual Recidivism Base Rate?

The question is frequently asked regarding how many or what proportion of sex offenders recidivate or reoffend. Contrary to an underlying assumption, there are actually various sexual recidivism base rates for sex offenders. Any single answer depends on qualifying parameters. These various qualifiers are needed before any meaningful answer can be given.

The Qualifiers

To begin, there is no such thing as *the* sexual recidivism base rate. Even very accurately measured recidivism base rates vary within the same population over different time periods (e.g., Prentky, Lee, Knight, & Cerce, 1997; Soothill & Gibbens, 1978). The proportion of recidivists in a given sample must either stay the same or increase as the follow-up time expands, with increasing rates being absolutely common across at least the first 10 years or so (Doren, 1998). The follow-up time is one of the crucial variables affecting the proper answer to this section heading's question. Given the context of this discussion is the civil commitment evaluation, and all current commitment laws do not specify a time limitation on the risk being assessed, the following discussion will assume that offenders' remaining lifetime is the most appropriate time frame within the commitment context.

Three other factors are also of potential importance to the figuring of recidivism base rates: (1) the method by which one defines an offender as a sexual recidivist, (2) what acts are included in that measurement process, and (3) the type of sex offender. Each of these is addressed below.

Quantifying Recidivism

If researchers could directly measure which sex offenders actually commit a new sexual offense, they would. The problem, of course, is that we do not have any direct way of knowing which offenders repeat such crimes even within a specified follow-up time period because not all of them are caught and, certainly, not all of them self-report (Groth, Longo, & McFadin, 1982). Proxy measures (i.e., operational estimations) must therefore be used for all research purporting to reflect actual recidivism. By definition, all proxy measures are not as exact as the underlying true variable of interest, in this case true recidivism counts, but they are used because there is currently nothing better.

The most common research method for operationalizing "sexual recidivism" is by counting the number of sample members who were reconvicted for a new sexual offense. For instance, in reviewing 61 data sets from six different countries, Hanson and Bussière (1998) found that 84% of them employed reconviction rates at least as one of the measures of sexual recidivism. Sexual rearrests came in second place, with 54% of the studies employing that type of proxy measure (obviously, with many studies inclusive of both). Self-reports and parole violations rounded out the rest of the methods (at 25% and 16%, respectively), with 44% of the studies using multiple indices.

Recidivism base rates differ quite significantly among these types of proxy measures, even given specified follow-up time periods. Doren (1998), for instance, found that rearrest rates seemed to coincide with about a 27% to 47% increase over reconviction rates for the same samples and time frames. Since that review, Doren (2001a) documented that the Song and Lieb (1995) study showed a 50% increase of the same type, a finding interpreted as in keeping with the earlier results.

Offender self-reports are known to differ greatly depending on the context in which those reports are made. Polygraph-solicited self-reports are quite regularly much higher in their acknowledgment of occurrence (and frequency) of recidivism than under other circumstances (e.g., Ahlmeyer, English, & Simons, 1998). Under nonpolygraph circumstances, offender self-reports are often lower even than their reconviction rates. Under the polygraph, however, their reported crimes are far greater than their history of having been rearrested, no less reconvicted.

Parole violations may most reflect jurisdictional practices that vary from locale to locale. In some places (e.g., Minnesota), it is a rare event for someone to have a parole revoked for a sexual behavioral reason without a new charge being filed (Douglas Epperson, personal communication, 1999). This differs from Wisconsin, again by way of example, where the filing of new charges may not occur given that the person is "going back to prison anyway." In addition, people can have new charges filed against them without their parole being revoked. Sometimes, there appears to be an attitude among the prosecutors and supervising agents (possibly with good reason) that if the person is reconvicted for a new sexual offense while on parole, and there is little time left on that parole, then the process of revoking the parole may be a waste of time and energy (i.e., the revocation is viewed as serving no purpose). Under those circumstances, the person is allowed to discharge his parole even though he was reconvicted of a new offense. The substantive reason(s) why someone may have his parole revoked can vary as well, with some people being revoked based on a new sexual crime whereas others for simply not following nonsexual rules of their community supervision. Hence, numbers associated with the use of "parole violations" as the proxy measure for sexual recidivism may be particularly difficult to interpret.

The interpretation of *any* of the proxy measures involves one aspect often forgotten or not understood. Direct and cross-examiners, for instance, will often suggest that the evaluator's using reconvictions as a proxy measure assumes that everyone convicted was actually guilty of the crime. This argument is frequently emphasized when the proxy is rearrest. The fact is that no such assumption has been, or need be, made.

As described in Doren (2001a), the real point to the use of any of the above operationalizations for sexual recidivism is that they can be employed without assuming the criminal justice system was fully accurate in deriving the outcome being counted. Counting a (sexual) reconviction (or rearrest) as demonstrative of sexual recidivism only means that the researcher assumes that the subject did at least one sexual offense sometime between the beginning of the study time period and the time the offender was reconvicted (or rearrested). The researcher may be absolutely accurate in counting recidivists without assuming that the crime for which each person was reconvicted (or rearrested) was perpetrated by the offender.

The one and only real assumption being made when using a proxy measure for reoffending is that each counted recidivist did at least one new sexual offense (at least one act of reoffending) for which he may or may not have ever been caught. In other words, although it may be that one or more people were labeled as recidivists due to false allegations, if those people actually did reoffend at other times for which they were not rearrested/reconvicted, then those people would still be labeled accurately as recidivists despite the official record stemming from false allegations. This perspective on the assumption being made applies, in fact, both to the recidivism figures attached to base rate estimates and, separately, to the interpretation of any given subject's historical (i.e., prior) charges and convictions.

Defining Recidivism (Beyond Time Frames)

What exactly constitutes a sexual offense for counting recidivism events? The answer may seem obvious, but only until one sits down with multiple case records and applies one's implicit definition.

The fact is that different studies employ different definitions of recidivism. Some use basically any type of criminal sexual behavior (e.g., Hanson, 1997), whereas others use a more limited definition, such as one that necessitates physical contact between the offender and the victim to be included (e.g., Epperson et al., 1999). Obviously, the more inclusive is the definition, the higher is the recidivism base rate, and vice versa.

This issue matters during the evaluator's application of research findings within · the context of civil commitment assessments. If the research relied on used a different definition of sexual recidivism than the relevant statute's definition of sexually violent acts, then the evaluator needs to take that difference into consideration. For instance, the process of using research findings stemming from an "all inclusive" definition in a state where sexually violent acts are almost solely defined in terms of physical contact offenses may overestimate statutorily relevant recidivism outcomes (e.g., using the Rapid Risk Assessment for Sex Offender Recidivism [RRASOR] in Wisconsin).

On the other hand, research findings based on only physical contact recidivism may underestimate recidivism likelihood when applied in states where noncontact sexual offenses can count (e.g., using the Minnesota Sex Offender Screening Tool–Revised [MnSOST–R] in Iowa). Neither of these base rate differences is clearly substantial, but evaluators should be aware of this issue nevertheless.

The Type of Offender

Do incest offenders, extrafamilial child molesters, rapists, and exhibitionists all demonstrate the same recidivism base rates, or do they differ in consistent and predictable ways? Once we put aside the issues of time frames, types of proxy measures, and the specific definitions of recidivism employed, there is still the issue of the type of sex offender that *may* affect the recidivism base rate. A perspective that gets bantered about by both sides during commitment hearings is the effect of the specific type of offender in determining what recidivism rate should be applied to (i.e., expected of) him. Evaluators need to be ready to address questions and arguments of this type, both to keep the courts informed of scientific reality versus either attorney's confusion or obfuscation and to ensure the perception of credibility in the evaluator's knowledge. The answer to this question is currently partly known and partly debated.

What is clearly known is that incest offenders are consistently found to have lower sexual recidivism rates than the other listed types of offenders (e.g., Hanson & Bussière, 1998). This finding seems to hold beyond the short run into long-term outcomes. For instance, David Thornton (personal communication, September 2000) studied all of the released sex offenders from United Kingdom prisons from the year 1979 for 16 to 19 years (the time varying based on the outcome data source). About 14% of the incest offenders were sexually reconvicted over the extended time period (i.e., 8 of 56). This percentage was lower than that for both the extrafamilial child molesters and rapists from the same population (the rates for the latter two subject groups from this study being described below). There are many possible reasons for incest offenders showing lower sexual recidivism rates than the other mentioned types of offenders, including (1) the lowered rate reflects the true reoffense rate differences, (2) the perpetrators' family members are particularly unlikely to report further offending, and (3) the offenders lose access to their most recent victims (due to incarceration, or other reasons for separation from their family) and must wait until the next generation of family members becomes available (e.g., a granddaughter to replace the victimized daughter) coupled with the fact that our research studies are not typically carried out that long. No matter the reason, however, the fact is that empirical findings consistently show incest offenders to show lower recidivism rates than extrafamilial child molesters and rapists.

The relative and absolute base rates for extrafamilial child molesters (defined as ever having a child victim outside the perpetrator's family, even if other crimes were incestuous) and rapists (defined as having adult victims) are more debated. Janus and Meehl (1997) reviewed literature with the conclusion that both of these groups fall into the range of 20% to 45% lifetime sexual recidivism, with no specified difference between rapists and the child molesters. In 1998, I employed a different review method with the conclusion that rapists' and extrafamilial child molesters' lifetime sexual recidivism rates are more like 39% and 52%, respectively. Hanson (1998a) expressed the perspective that the range 30% to 40% is most accurate for lifetime recidivism (which he later changed to an upper limit of 45% in a deposition), with no difference between the two offender groups. Weighing into this discussion is the research results mentioned above from Thornton, as those findings were not available previous to any of the above stated perspectives. The 16- to 19-year *reconviction* rates for rapists and extrafamilial child molesters were 36% (i.e., 65 of 180) and 26.5% (i.e., 63 of 238), respectively.

These actual "hard body" reconviction counts (vs. results from survival analyses) clearly indicate that the lower end of the Janus and Meehl estimated range (of 20%-45%) is too low. Arguably, so is Hanson's (of 30%), unless one assumes that over lengthy time periods such as these a reconviction rate is a very accurate proxy for the actual reoffense rate, that is, that virtually everyone who sexually offends during the score of years after incarceration eventually gets caught and convicted for at least one such sexual crime. That would be the only way in which Thornton's sample average reconviction rate (30.6% for the combination of rapists and extrafamilial child molesters, 29.3% if incest offenders are added into the computation) could be read as supportive to a 30% approximation for lifetime sexual reoffending.

Thornton's data also do not support my 1998 conclusion that extrafamilial child molesters seem to have higher long-term recidivism rates than do rapists. In fact, the rapists in Thornton's sample sexually recidivated (as measured by reconviction) at a higher rate than did the extrafamilial child molesters (chi-square = 4.08, $df = 1$, $p < .05$). This result is opposite that derived from survival analyses by Prentky et al. (1997) over similar follow-up time periods, though the two complete sample average reconviction rates did not differ from one another. It could be that Janus and Meehl (1997) and Hanson (1998a) are correct insofar as they say there is no lifetime recidivism rate difference between extrafamilial child molesters and rapists.

Less appears to be known about the long-term recidivism rates for exhibitionists, a class of sex offenders relevant for commitment purposes in only some states. During relatively short time periods, there is reason to believe that exhibitionists are on the high end of sexual recidivism rates compared with other sex offenders (e.g., Hanson & Bussière, 1998). Long-term studies of this group, however, seem to be lacking. The only long-term recidivism data found by me was from the same Thornton 16- to 19-year follow-up study mentioned above. The working definition of this type of offender had the following characteristics in that database: (1) They had been convicted of a noncontact sexual offense, (2) they were incarcerated for that or a subsequent contact sexual offense, and (3) then released from a United Kingdom prison in 1979. Of that set of sex offenders, 59% of them (i.e., 32 of 54) were later reconvicted for a new sexual offense (Thornton, personal communication, December 2000). This percentage, though obviously based on a small sample, suggests that the long-term sexual recidivism rate for exhibitionists might be higher, maybe even significantly higher than comparable figures from other types of sex offenders.

The main point of this discussion is *not* an ultimate determination of "the" lifetime sexual recidivism rate for certain sex offenders. There are too many potential parameters still not specified. For instance, it seems to matter whether or not the offenders completed treatment, were released to community supervision versus not, and how long they were under such supervision. In addition, the fact that some considerations are potentially changeable over time (such as the charging and plea bargaining practices even within the same jurisdiction) makes a single number to be of questionable accuracy. The numbers above, instead, represent the coalescing of different viewpoints into a relatively small and therefore meaningful range.

Most important, these numbers all suggest that lifetime sexual recidivism by previously convicted sex offenders is not a statistically "rare event." As described below, the fact that long-term recidivism statistics approach 50% versus 0% means that the potential accuracy in predicting sexual recidivism statistically approaches being optimally possible.

Taking Base Rates Into Consideration in the Evaluation

One of the significant faults clinicians regularly show in making assessments of risk of almost any type is failing to consider the effects of different base rates (Grove, Zald, Lebow, Snitz, & Nelson, 2000). Within sex offender civil commitment evaluations, there are four times during which such considerations need to occur.

Why Base Rates Matter

As described above, there are various qualifiers to the question of sex offender recidivism rates that make all the difference in determining whether the base rate is near 50% (analogous to females among the U.S. population), represents a very rare event (analogous to desert rain), or is somewhere in between. Two main considerations determine which among these three descriptive ranges most likely applies to a case being evaluated.

The Rare Versus Common Event

The first of these reasons is that the base rate affects the degree to which any assessment methodology can accurately differentiate between recidivists and non-recidivists. Statistically, the more rare an event is, the more difficult it is to predict those situations in which it will occur without also including many cases in the same prediction where the event would not actually occur. Put in terms of sexual recidivism predictions, the more rare is the sexual recidivism being predicted, the more likely the predictions will include nonrecidivists in the predicted recidivist category. Predictions trying to distinguish the occurrence of rare events from the far more common are notoriously high in their inaccurate inclusion of the common events in the set where the rare one is predicted, an error that is largely statistically determined rather than reflective of "bad" assessment techniques per se.

By way of illustration, one can think of what it would be like to try to predict when and where a tornado will next strike in Kansas. Although Kansas has more than its share of tornadoes, the fact is that the chance of a tornado striking any specific town or city in Kansas within a given year is remote. If we try to predict what is going to happen within the next year within all of Kansas, we can be quite confident that a tornado will hit somewhere, but we will very likely show a great deal of error to the extent we try to predict (the rare events of) in which towns a tornado will strike, and within far shorter time frames than one year. The more rare the event we are trying to predict, the more likely we will show substantial error in that prediction.

This type of error is called the false positive rate, with the described situation reflecting a high false positive rate. The danger within the civil commitment realm for this type of error is that, to the extent this circumstance is deemed to exist, far too many people would be referred/recommended for commitment who would not sexually recidivate if they had simply been released to the community.

On the other hand, where the sexual recidivism base rate hovers somewhere much closer to 50%, the ability to minimize this type of error (and other types of error) exists, even if our assessment technology has not changed as compared to the previous example. In effect, our evaluation methodology is of maximum *predictive* utility, from a statistical perspective, when employed within a near 50% base rate situation. Knowing a reasonable approximation of the underlying sexual recidivism base rate, therefore, tells evaluators something about the statistical limitations of the predictive accuracy of the methods being employed, at least relative to other base rate circumstances of application.

Differences in Sampling Base Rates

The second, and even more important, reason that base rates matter is to under-stand when and how to apply specific risk assessment instrumentation to a given case. If the instrument was developed and replicated using people representing one general range of base rates, and the subject is best described as being a member of a group with a significantly different recidivism base rate, then there can be prob-lems in the application of the instrument to that case. Scale scores can, of course, still be derived because the required information is likely available for the subject, but the interpretation of the score may be far more inaccurate for this subject than is true more generally. For instance, if

1. an instrument has been tested on samples with a sexual recidivism base rate of about 35% (temporarily leaving off the descriptors of follow-up time and type of recidivism measurement typically needed to give meaning to such a figure, just to avoid complicating the described point), and

2. the subject to whom one wishes to apply the instrument is best perceived as being a member of a group that typically shows a 20% (of the same type of) recidivism rate, then

3. the recidivism rate associated with this subject's score on this instrument will be too high to some degree.

To explain by way of analogy, loggers wishing to clear a specified acreage of trees within the week will obtain different fruits from their labors depending on the den-sity (i.e., base rate) of trees within the area available. If the specified acreage has a high density of trees within its boundary, then the loggers will reap far more logs than if the acreage contains a low density. In both cases, the measure of what will be logged is the same acreage, but the outcome varies significantly.

When the assessment situation appears to involve this circumstance, the evaluator needs to (1) find more applicable interpretative figures for this instrument, (2) con-ceptually lower the estimated recidivism rate associated with the subject's score, or (3) use a different instrument. To be clear, this same process also applies in reverse. Whenever an examiner applies an assessment tool that was tested using recidivism base rates lower than those assumed for the category of offenders inclusive of an evaluation subject, the recidivism rate associated with the subject's score should be thought of as needing to be increased for purposes of greater accuracy.

The current single best example of the need to consider sample base rates in using interpretive recidivism risk figures occurs with the use of the MnSOST–R (Epperson et al., 1999). The derivation research employed a sampling process that ultimately resulted in a recidivism base rate (for rearrest for a physical contact sexual offense within 6 years postincarceration) of 35%. Most unselected incarcerated sex offender populations do not show this kind of rearrest rate within 6 years of release, however. More typical is a substantially lower rate, around 20%. (This approximate figure is supported by the actual sexual recidivism rate of 18% from the complete set of released sex offenders from the Minnesota Department of Corrections [DOC] for the same year as the test sample was drawn; by the 22% figure from the Minnesota DOC replication sample from the following year [Epperson, Kaul, & Huot, 2000]; and from the findings of Prentky et al., 1997.)

The primary researcher of this instrument, Douglas Epperson, being aware of the base rate issue and its potential effect on the score interpretations, formulated interpretive risk percentages per score category for each of three assumed base rates, including the original 35% and a figure of 21% that very closely approximates the unselected finding. The effect of differences in base rates for the MnSOST–R can be viewed in Table 5.5, in the previous chapter.

As the reader can see, as the estimated recidivism base rates decrease per score range category, the associated risk percentages also decrease, though not in linear proportion. The instrument scores do not change as the reader traverses different estimated base rates, but the interpretation of the instrument scores can change substantially. This is exemplary of one reason why evaluators need to be cognizant of what recidivism base rate they are assuming for the instruments and offender category in which the subject appears to fall. This type of table, however, can facilitate the meaningful application of a risk assessment instrument within a variety of different circumstances, differing in their underlying estimated recidivism base rates.

There is another, quite regular occurrence within the sex offender civil commitment evaluation where relative presumed base rates matter greatly. To explain, let us start with the RRASOR (Hanson, 1997). The published data assist in the evaluator's interpretation of RRASOR scale scores through about a 10-year postincarceration period, and basically with the use of reconviction as the recidivism outcome measure. To date, no sex offender civil commitment statute puts a time limit on the recidivism risk to be assessed or states that the person needs to be caught, prosecuted, and convicted following a sexually violent act. Hence, there is reason to perceive the RRASOR (and other similar instruments) as not being comprehensive in covering the time period and potentially the relevant type of recidivism risk to be assessed under the commitment evaluation circumstance.

Put another way, if

1. one draws the conclusion from existing research, or even makes the assumption, that sex offender first-time recidivism (as measured by first-time sexual reconvictions) continues to go up at all beyond a 10-year postrelease period, and/or if

2. one concludes or assumes that the set of people reconvicted within a 10-year period does not include all of the sexual recidivists (beyond the number of totally innocent of all new sexual wrongdoing but inaccurately reconvicted), then

3. there is reason to see the sexual recidivism base rate applicable within a "lifetime sexual reoffense" context as higher than that employed by the RRASOR (or any other instrument for which the same type of argument is made).

Only if one assumes that 10-year sexual reconviction base rates are about equal to lifetime sexual reoffense rates for the same offender population would the effect of this argument not apply. There are few, if any, serious sexual recidivism researchers who make this latter argument. The debate seems only to concern the extent that 10-year reconviction figures underestimate the true lifetime sexual recidivism rate. The current relative limits to that debate appear to be portrayed by Karl Hanson (1998a), who voices about a "5%, maybe 10%" increase to reach the true recidivism rate, and David Thornton (2000a), who espouses a 3-time multiplier from existing risk percentages attached to risk instrument scores to arrive at the proper estimate. In my humble opinion, the true rate is likely to fall between these two extremes, probably closer to the 25-year postrelease survival curve data summarized by Prentky et al. (1997; see Table 6.1).

For instance, based on these data, one might extrapolate from a 10- or 15-year reconviction rate to a 25-year re-charge rate (similar but not exactly the same as a rearrest rate) for either a rapist or extrafamilial child molester, with the assumption that rearrest rates are ultimately closer to true reoffense rates than are reconviction. This type of extrapolation can be summarized as either involving an increase in recidivism rate estimate of at least 19% (vs. 5%-10%) or involving a multiplier for these specific time frames and recidivism proxy measures that is closer to 2 than 3. If one restricts the extrapolation just to the time periods involved (i.e., moving from 10-year to 25-year rates), and leaves the type of recidivism as reconviction, the relative figures are about 8% to 18%, or a 1.5 to 1.8 multiplier. Either way, these numbers fall in between Hanson's and Thornton's estimates.

No matter which formula one finds most realistic for extrapolating beyond existing risk assessment instruments' longest time frames and their measures of recidivism, the main message should be clear. As one expands the relevant recidivism base rate beyond the researched limits of risk assessment instrumentation, one needs to assume a corresponding increase in the actual recidivism risk assessed by each scale.

For Which Sex Offenders Do Base Rates Matter?

The answer is, all of them. The above points are general statistical principles, not principles specific only to certain sex offenders.

Shorter- Versus Longer-Term Assessments

As described above, long-term sexual recidivism base rates were found to be in the range where meaningfully accurate differentiating predictions can potentially

TABLE 6.1. Cumulative Failure Rates for Sexual Offenses Over Nine Time Gates

Disposition	1 yr	2 yr	3 yr	4 yr	5 yr	10 yr	15 yr	20 yr	25 yr
				Rate at a Given Time Gate					
Rapists									
Charge	.09	.12	.15	.17	.19	.26	.31	.36	.39
Conviction	.04	.06	.08	.09	.11	.16	.20	.23	.24
Prison[a]	.04	.06	.07	.08	.10	.14	.17	.19	.19
Child molesters									
Charge	.06	.10	.14	.17	.19	.30	.39	.46	.52
Conviction	.04	.07	.10	.12	.14	.23	.31	.37	.41
Prison	.04	.07	.09	.11	.13	.21	.28	.33	.37

SOURCE: From "Recidivism Rates Among Child Molesters and Rapists: A Methodological Analysis," by R. A. Prentky, A. F. S. Lee, R. A. Knight, and D. Cerce, 1997, *Law and Human Behavior, 21*(6), 635-659. Reprinted with permission of Kluwer Academic/Plenum.
a. Prison refers to people who were both reconvicted and imprisoned.

be made between recidivists and nonrecidivists. This works out well for civil commitment evaluators assessing long-term recidivism risk.

At the same time, however, there are occasions when civil commitment evaluators are asked about a shorter-term degree of risk represented by a sex offender. These questions can ultimately represent a base rate-inflicted problem. There are two main circumstances under which this situation can occur: (1) questioning in the courtroom and (2) in application to certain commitment cases.

Courtroom questioning can be along the lines of "what is the likelihood that my client will sexually recidivate during the next year?" or "what is the likelihood this patient will recidivate during the next 2 years if I put him under community supervision?" (The latter type of questioning typically occurs by a court trying to determine the least restrictive alternative for a committed individual.) Once the follow-up time frame is considerably shortened from the lifetime view, the concomitant base rate also clearly becomes lessened. This means that the underlying base rate about which the evaluator is essentially being questioned has become more restrictive in statistically allowing good accuracy in individual predictions.

The other circumstance involves the commitment subject for whom one has reason to believe his remaining life span is relatively short. This can be true based on his being elderly or being seriously physically ill.

An evaluator's method for addressing the above questions and situations may be straightforward. If the person has shown a deviant sexual arousal pattern and a high degree of psychopathy (both as defined in keeping either with Rice & Harris, 1997, or Harris, Rice, Quinsey, Lalumière, Boer, & Lang, 2001), then the survival curves from those studies can be used to assist in a meaningful answer. This specific type of sex offender seems to have a very high risk even within short-term periods (i.e., less than 5 years), such that the applicable base rate still allows for a reasonable assessment.

Under more typical circumstances, evaluators may be tempted to answer that we collectively know less about the short-term prediction of recidivism than of longer-term predictions, though this is not really true. There are far more studies of shorter-term sexual recidivism than of very long-term (e.g., Doren, 1998; Hanson & Bussière, 1998), both in terms of recidivism rates and of predictive factors. The fact is, we currently know more about shorter-term recidivism than we do longer-term recidivism.

The real problem with the questions being asked is that they put the evaluator into the position of making an assessment within the context of "rare event" base rates—base rates that are far closer to zero than they are to 50%. The shorter the time frame being asked about, the greater the degree to which this is true. Evaluators need to remember that the shorter the time frame being addressed, the more the examiner should respond by stating that the question cannot be answered with reasonable *predictive* accuracy, at least in terms of our ability to differentiate future recidivists from future nonrecidivists. Contrary to the general perspective that our short-term predictions are better than our long-term predictions (e.g., Wettstein, 1992), within the context of civil commitment assessments, the effect of the ever-increasing recidivism base rates makes us potentially more accurate in the long run and of questionable differentiating accuracy in the very short run. This consideration means that examiners should maintain their long-term focus within civil commitment assessments, for the sake of statistically optimizing the accuracy of their evaluation.

Risk Assessment Instrumentation Selection

A second application of base rate considerations is in the choice of risk assessment instrumentation to be employed. An instrument developed solely using probationers and people who have only been alleged but never even been charged with a sex crime (e.g., Irish Sex Offender Risk Tool [ISORT]; Quackenbush, 2000) will reflect interpretative statistics formulated on significantly lower base rates than is typical for the at least once imprisoned sex offender (e.g., Doren, 1998). This difference makes the interpretation of the improperly employed instrument problematic at best. The evaluator will know that the instrument underestimates recidivism likelihood within the higher base rate context (see discussion on the MnSOST–R above), but by how much will be unknown. Comparing the underlying recidivism base rate for an instrument before its selection with the estimated base rate for the population from which a subject comes saves the evaluator this interpretative problem. Ultimately, evaluators should avoid using an instrument developed and tested on significantly different base rates from the type of person being assessed, and thereby avoid the interpretive problem described.

Cases "Beyond the Actuarial Scheme"

After the most representative risk assessment instruments are selected for use, evaluators can find that specific characteristics of a subject suggest that he may be significantly atypical compared with the general sex offender population from which he came. Relevant differences may be demographic (e.g., age), physical capability (e.g., a relevant physical disability, such as quadriplegia), diagnostic (e.g., sexual sadism, or certain brain injuries), or any of a variety of other characteristics. This difference may or may not actually be relevant. After all, if one delineates enough differentiating characteristics in describing a subject, all subjects will look "atypical" compared with the general sex offender population from which they came.

The real issue is not just that a person appears atypical in some way, but that both of two features apply to the defined difference:

1. The characteristic has a known or essentially obvious relationship with sexual recidivism potential.

2. The degree to which the subject is different in possessing this characteristic (either by having it or by not having it) is very clearly significant compared with the general distribution of this characteristic in the instrument's researched samples.

The concept being addressed here has been described as being "beyond the actuarial scheme." This means that the attribute is beyond the things studied through the actuarial instrument research in either quantity and/or quality. To the extent that no. 1 and no. 2 above are collectively *both* true, there is reason to believe that the recidivism base rates underlying the instrument may not be representative of the sex offender being evaluated. This difference can affect the interpretation of risk assessment instruments through either under- or overestimation of recidivism risk.

Some examples of being beyond the actuarial scheme are obvious and can serve to illustrate the point. If a subject has a clearly terminal disease with a minimal likelihood for living more than a few months, and his physical condition significantly interferes both with his access to potential victims (e.g., children) and his ability to interact with them physically, then an evaluator might easily decide that this individual is beyond the actuarial scheme for existing sexual recidivism risk assessment instruments. His risk is clearly much lower than the typical, based on factors rather unique to him as compared to researched samples.

Of course, the simple fact that a person's characteristics are beyond the actuarial scheme does not necessarily mean that the person's risk is lower than that estimated by a risk instrument. Someone who already repetitively offended as a quadriplegic might not be assessed as having lowered risk because of his quadriplegia. A very elderly man may not be thought of as too decrepit, or having too low a libido, if his last recorded offense occurred at age 91. In these cases, it might be argued that the characteristics leading to their being found beyond the actuarial scheme do not significantly alter the assessed risk from an actuarial instrument.

There are the cases that represent higher risk than estimated by the actuarials, however. In some cases, evaluation subjects make it clear during their interview that they have every intention or expectation of recidivating when they are released from incarceration and even describe plans for how they will accomplish this. There have been few reported cases of people about to leave prison making such clear statements, suggesting that these select cases are way beyond the typical. (In David Thornton's population of 1979 Her Majesty's Prison Service-released sex offenders, three people were recorded to have made statements such as this before their release, out of about 550 sex offenders being released [Thornton, 2000a], demonstrating the rarity of the event. For the record, those 3 people all recidivated upon prison release.) This factor, of course, suggests increased risk, as opposed to the previous example involving a decreased risk. Being beyond the actuarial scheme does not imply specifically either an increase or decrease of risk, just that there is an acknowledged atypical consideration involving the proper base rate in which to conceptualize the case.

One caveat needs to be emphasized here. There is a human tendency to be emotionally affected by descriptions of (1) particularly onerous crimes and (2) numbers that appear elevated compared with what we usually encounter. At the same time, examiners have the obligation to be as objective as possible in their evaluations. When assessing if some attribute is beyond the actuarial scheme, great care should be used. Our emotional reactions to what we read should not enter into the assessment. We should remain cognizant that research suggests that more offenders are considered high risk through clinical assessments than by the actuarials alone, possibly because emotional reactions are factored into the former but not the latter types of assessments (e.g., Nicholaichuk, Templeman, & Gu, 1999).

For something truly to be beyond the actuarial scheme, it needs to be beyond the set of information incorporated into the development of the instrument and beyond the common attributes of the research samples, not simply beyond what we feel is tolerable. Quite typically, instrument developers have included data concerning number of victims, degree of force, degree of injury to victims, and many other factors in the research underlying the instrument's development. If those factors were not ultimately included on the instrument, then the reason was typically because those data did *not* add anything to the instrument's effectiveness as compared to the included items. Hence, if a subject used a significant degree of force to subdue his victims, this consideration, although emotionally upsetting to read in its details, should not typically be viewed as beyond the actuarial scheme.

Likewise, if a twice-convicted subject has stated during sex offender treatment that he really has 20 victims, this should not be thought of as a reason for adjusting his risk upward. (Such treatment disclosures may actually be signs of treatment involvement, a sign of potential lowered risk.) Statistically, his apparently high number of victims was essentially accounted for in the other factors included on most risk assessment inventories, most particularly by his two convictions. This is not to say that two convictions should be directly translated to mean that such offenders have 20 victims, only that the number of acknowledged victims does not regularly add information increasing our accuracy in assessing risk beyond the type of data already included in the instruments. A subject would need to have a very large number of victims to be considered beyond the actuarial scheme, and not simply a number that seems emotionally quite disturbing. Although prosecutors can attempt to make the individual sound worse than Jack the Ripper by emphasizing how many victims the person has acknowledged, evaluators should avoid assessing additional risk where it is empirically known that no extra risk exists.

Deciding when something is both beyond the actuarial scheme and that the characteristic adds useful information beyond what the actuarials assess can be problematic. A description of such things is delineated in Chapter 7.

Extrapolating Beyond Risk Assessment Instrument Parameters

The final situation to be discussed concerning how base rates need to be incorporated into civil commitment evaluations is after actuarial risk assessment instruments have been employed. That is when examiners need to extrapolate from existing recidivism risk percentages from the instruments (involving time-defined criminal justice determinations) to the lifetime sexual reoffense figures demanded by the statutes. The use of actuarial instrumentation within the civil commitment context helps anchor evaluators in assessing subjects' risk, but these tools do not necessarily directly inform about the statutorily defined risk no matter how valid and accurate the instruments may be.

This extrapolation is actually of a one-directional nature. To explain, consider that the degree of recidivism, from the perspective solely of base rates, cannot go down over time or through the expansion from more restrictive (e.g., reconviction) to less restrictive (i.e., reoffending) measures of recidivism. Once a person meets the criteria to be counted as a recidivist, he will remain so throughout the remainder of any study no matter how long it goes. Relative risk figures therefore minimally remain the same over time, though virtually all research supports the idea that new, first-time recidivism rates continue to increase beyond the time periods of the current actuarial instruments (e.g., Hanson, Steffy, & Gauthier, 1993). This finding reflects changing base rates over increasing amounts of time.

The effect of these increasing base rates is that an actuarial instrument assesses an individual within the context of one type of base rate when the individual is being viewed ultimately (by an evaluator) from another one (from a longer time period and reflective of true reoffending, not just reconvictions). As described above, when one assesses differences in base rates between the subject's properly defined classification of sex offenders and the measurement tool one is employing, that difference must be taken into account. How that accounting is best done is debatable, however.

In some situations, it does not matter much. If the subject already clearly shows a "beyond commitment threshold" degree of likelihood for being reconvicted of a new relevant sexual offense within 10 years, for instance, then the extrapolation beyond reconviction and beyond 10 years only increases the support for that finding. Trying to assess a reasonable estimate of the degree of this extrapolation becomes an intellectual exercise, but not a meaningful one for assessing if the person's risk is beyond the legal threshold.

Far more problematic is the extrapolation in the other direction, when the person's actuarially assessed risk is below the commitment threshold, especially if not by much. How much risk one should add to reflect the difference in base rates (i.e., to extrapolate beyond the fixed time period and restrictive measurement of recidivism) is not clear. As stated earlier in the chapter, Hanson (1998a) and Thornton (2000a) have derived very different conclusions from existing research (i.e., as low as 5% to as high as using a 3-times multiplier). The Prentky et al. (1997) survival curves offer a third, more intermediary alternative. The bottom line is that research is not clear about how to perform this extrapolation, or whether (as described above) there should be different extrapolations for different types of sex offenders.

Given this lack of clarity, the recommendation is made that evaluators use caution, have a well-defined rationale for whatever they do in this regard, and communicate the limits to our current knowledge no matter what perspective is chosen.

Summary Comments

This chapter explored the issues related to the recidivism base rates of certain sex offenders. Although no single figure was promoted as *the* answer to the commonly asked question of what is *the* recidivism rate of sex offenders, all supported long-term estimates were found to be in a range meaningful for predictive purposes. Next described were issues and recommendations for how the issue of base rates should be factored into civil commitment assessment procedures. The greatest degree of caution was recommended as concerns labeling cases as beyond the actuarial scheme and thereby allowing for potentially significant clinical adjustments to actuarial risk estimates. The issue of clinical adjustments in general will be discussed in detail in Chapter 7.

Clinical Adjustments

*The fact that an opinion has been widely held is no evidence what-
ever that it is not utterly absurd.*

— Bertrand Russell, *Marriage and Morals*

This chapter is designed to describe what we know about the process of clinically
adjusting actuarial findings and how to conduct those adjustments. Conceptually, this chapter exists essentially because of the perspective that the currently best method for evaluating a sex offender's recidivism risk is the clinically
adjusted actuarial model (though the information herein could also be used in a
research-guided approach to a risk assessment).

The idea that such a chapter should exist is quite commonly though not univer-
sally accepted. Quinsey, Harris, Rice, and Cormier (1998) have argued for clinicians
to employ a purely actuarial approach, a methodology that by definition excludes
clinical adjustments under all but extreme circumstances. Grove and Meehl (1996)
and Grove, Zald, Lebow, Snitz, and Nelson (2000) have emphatically made the
point that "mechanical" procedures should be employed for virtually any type of
prediction, a view that could be read as excluding clinical adjustments. Despite the
empirical underpinnings to these opinions, there does not seem to be anyone else
in the violence (including sexual violence) field arguing for the purely actuarial
methodology.

The point of departure between what those listed researchers argue and what
most evaluators practice is the apparent fact that there has yet to be developed a
"mechanical" procedure that is sufficiently inclusive of risk and protective considerations known to be of importance in the civil commitment risk assessment. Without
a sufficiently comprehensive mechanical procedure available, evaluators seem to be
left with adding clinical judgments where the actuarial instruments leave off.

With that perspective in mind, this chapter was written with the underlying assumption that actuarial instruments have already been applied to the evaluation case, as the concept of clinically adjusting research-guided clinical judgments has little practical meaning. The topics to be covered include the following:

1. Defining proper adjustments

2. The theoretical basis for clinical adjustments

3. Adjustments based on risk factors

4. Adjustments based on protective factors

5. Assessing beyond the actuarial scheme

6. Evaluator bias

Defining Proper Adjustments

The most common problem based in the concept of clinical adjustments to actuarial instrument results is that too many evaluators make "clinical adjustments" as if anything they think important is cause for an adjustment, irrelevant of research considerations. The "clinically adjusted actuarial approach" label serves those evaluators as an improper rationale for supplanting actuarial information with the evaluators' clinical judgment (both guided and unguided). Discounting actuarial findings and substituting clinical judgment is *not* the clinically adjusted actuarial approach, but simply the clinical judgment wolf in sheep's clothing.

A couple of actual descriptions of this incorrect way of implementing the clinically adjusted actuarial approach follow. (The sources were deliberately not cited so as not to point fingers so publicly.)

1. A very long prosaic description of the individual's history, with a delineation of factors the writer thought were related to risk (some research supported, some not), after which the writer had a paragraph listing actuarial scale scores for the subject, which were never interpreted or mentioned again in the final assessment

2. An acknowledgment of high actuarial scores but these were discounted in favor of the subject's interview statements essentially saying that he would not commit another sex crime (despite a very long list of them and similar "promises" in the past), this being from a clinician who regularly finds reason to discount the actuarial results

The first example is of the type "clinical judgment + actuarial results = clinically adjusted actuarial methodology" even if the actuarials are not really employed. In this case, the evaluator really never considered the actuarial information one way or another, but simply listed the actuarial results in the evaluation report because the recipient of the report basically had mandated that the clinically adjusted actuarial procedure be used. Obviously, simply putting actuarial information into a report does not make the evaluation actuarially grounded. The examiner must seriously consider that information.

The second type of misuse of this procedure involves a more active process of discounting the actuarial results. Although this can be appropriate from time to time (e.g., with a female sex offender), to do so on a regular basis in favor of clinical information means the evaluator is basically not using that information at all.

Both of the above represent clinical judgment procedures, pure and simple. The fact that actuarial results are "viewed" during the clinician's examination is not sufficient to constitute a clinically adjusted actuarial methodology. Likewise, there is no "adjustment" to the actuarials being made that is different from a more straightforward clinical judgment methodology. The actuarial results should never be employed as an apparent "afterthought" compared to the rest of the assessment, or referenced and then discounted in a way that could have been known in an a priori way.

The true clinical adjustments being discussed in this chapter are with the provisos that (1) actuarial risk assessment instruments were first found applicable to the evaluation subject, (2) actuarial results were obtained, and (3) these results served as the ongoing foundation for anything else considered (i.e., both risk and protective factors, the latter being considerations that indicate lowered risk). If other situations apply, then the information found in this chapter may not be applicable.

The Theoretical Basis for Clinical Adjustments

As the above provisos suggest, the discussion herein follows directly from that of the last chapter. Based on the same rationale and empirical support explicated in Chapter 6, the multiple dimensionality theory of sexual recidivism is viewed as highly important in deciding how to structure one's process of clinically adjusting actuarial findings. Conceptually, for instance, if an offender shows high actuarial risk in the antisocial/violent dimension, then protective factors *related to this type of sexual offending* need to be found to make an overall assessment other than high risk. Finding that the subject does not show sexual deviance on a penile plethysmograph (PPG) should tell the evaluator nothing in this regard. On the other hand, the treatment-based lowering of PPG-measured deviance may be of importance for someone whose risk stems mostly from the sexual deviancy pathway.

In other words, the evaluator needs to know that the clinical consideration is related to the subject's specific type of sexual offending risk. In the treatment world, we know this obvious fact. We do not expect someone's likelihood for physical problems stemming from diabetes to go down if we treat the person's cholesterol level, even though both can be assessed through blood tests. Alterations to actuarial risk assessments need to be soundly connected to the understood or at least theorized etiology of that risk.

Adjustments Based on Risk Factors

There appear to be three types of occasions in which clinical adjustments to actuarial results can be appropriate, at least considering what is known empirically through the time this book was written:

1. When research has demonstrated the information to add incrementally to the actuarial instruments' predictive (or postdictive) accuracy

2. When the information (or set of case characteristics) is clearly "beyond the actuarial scheme"

3. When there is a rare characteristic in the case for which there is also an "obvious" degree of associated risk or protection even if never researched

Beyond these considerations, there may not be good reason to adjust any actuarial finding. Evaluators should always look for the existence of one of these, but there can easily be cases where none apply.

The existing research results of the first type, demonstrating an incremental utility for predictive accuracy beyond applied actuarials, currently comes from eight pieces of research: (1) Allam (2000); (2) Beech, Erikson, Friendship, and Ditchfield (2001); (3) Hanson and Harris (1997); (4) Haynes, Yates, Nicholaichuk, Gu, and Bolton (2000; also written up by Nicholaichuk & Yates, in press); (5) McGrath, Cumming, Livingston, and Hoke (2001); (6) Quinsey, Coleman, Jones, and Altrows (1997); (7) Thornton (in press); and (8) Wong, Flahr, et al. (2000; also Wong, Olver, Wilde, Nicholaichuk, & Gordon, 2000). Beyond these studies, there does not yet appear to be empirical information about what factors specifically demonstrate incremental predictive validity beyond actuarial instruments.

In general, sex offender treatment compliance/completion/benefit is a replicated protective consideration beyond actuarial risk, having been studied in various ways in six of these eight studies (Allam, Beech et al., Hanson & Harris, McGrath et al., Thornton, and Wong, Flahr, et al.). (This relationship may not exist with the Minnesota Sex Offender Screening Tool–Revised [MnSOST–R], as that instrument already includes the consideration of treatment completion.) This general finding is reassuring to those of us who worry that static actuarial findings will represent a person's risk no matter what he might do to change himself.

The most straightforward piece of research in this regard, and also the most pertinent to sex offender civil commitment evaluations, was conducted by McGrath et al. (2001). That study investigated the effectiveness of a specific prison treatment program for sex offenders (in the Vermont Department of Corrections). The research design involved controlling separately for each of two actuarial scores, the Rapid Risk Assessment for Sex Offender Recidivism (RRASOR) and the Static-99 (Hanson & Thornton, 2000), in the comparison of people who entered the treatment program and people who did not. The follow-up (postincarceration) time period was an average of 5 years, a period that begins to have meaning within the sex offender civil commitment realm.

In keeping with usual validity findings (summarized in the next section), both instruments' sets of scores were found predictive of sexual recidivism irrelevant of whether the subjects came from the treatment or nontreatment groups. Of relevance to this investigation of the clinically adjusted actuarial model, the completion of the treatment program, versus noncompletion of that program (either through never entering or through premature termination), showed a statistically significant relationship with sexual recidivism (by lowering it) beyond what the actuarial instruments did alone. This finding was despite the fact that each of the two instruments statistically showed predictive effectiveness without taking the treatment programming result into consideration; that is, there was incremental improvement in the predictive accuracy beyond the actuarial instrument results.

A study of a similar type to McGrath et al. (2001) was completed by Wong, Olver, et al. (2000), though the outcome recidivism measure employed was generic violent recidivism. In that study, Wong, Olver, et al. tested the Violence Risk Scale–Sex Offender (VRS–SO) with a sample of subjects who had gone through a sex offender treatment program (in a Canadian correctional treatment facility). The VRS–SO is composed of the historically based actuarial instrument the Static-99 and 20 dynamic considerations each reflecting pre- and posttreatment assessments. The follow-up period was 4 years. The Static-99 alone was again found validated for its relationship with violent recidivism within a sample of sex offenders, but the dynamic treatment-related variables again were found to add to the overall predictive accuracy. The measurement of treatment participation and benefit in this study was clearly different from the more categorical quantification in the McGrath et al. investigation, but the two studies' results complement one another.

Beech et al.'s (2001) results were similar to Wong, Olver, et al.'s (2000), in that dynamic considerations (related to treatment benefit) showed predictive utility beyond the effectiveness of an actuarial instrument. The dynamic factors used here consisted of certain psychometrically determined measures of deviance (vs. normality; based on earlier findings from Beech, 1998, and Beech, Fisher, & Beckett, 1999) and corresponding changes following treatment programming. The Static-99 was the actuarial instrument employed. These psychometrically determined dynamic considerations showed incremental predictive utility beyond the already effective Static-99.

Jayne Allam's (2000) results were similar to Beech et al.'s (2001), in that the same psychometrically determined dynamic considerations (related to treatment benefit) showed predictive utility beyond the effectiveness of a currently existing actuarial instrument. In Allam's research, however, the instrument of choice was the Structured Actuarial Clinical Judgement scale (SACJ; Grubin, 1998), not the Static-99, suggesting that the specific actuarial instrument may not be so much of relevance in finding that certain dynamic treatment-related considerations are of additional predictive utility to currently employed static variables. (To be clear, as stated above, all of these variables, both dynamic and static, could be built into one actuarial instrument. The point is that most *current* actuarial instruments do not include considerations such as treatment participation and completion. Hence, there is support being found for using the clinically adjusted actuarial model with the current set of instruments.) Generalizability from this study alone, however, is hampered by the fact that the number of subjects in any category was exceedingly small, ranging toward zero, though the length of follow-up was the same as Wong, Olver, et al.'s (i.e., 4 years).

David Thornton (in press) effectively expanded on the Beech et al. (2001) and Allam (2000) studies by including one additional type of dynamic treatment-related consideration. He used the Static-99 as his actuarial instrument of choice. The same positive findings described above resulted, using a 3-year follow-up period. The sample size in this study was larger than that employed for the other two studies.

Before we are too comforted, however, we need to realize that all of these studies involved shorter follow-up time periods than are typically relevant within the civil commitment evaluation context. The time periods ranged from 1 to 5 years among the six studies. It is only by untested extrapolation, and hope, that we assume the protective effects of treatment completion continue beyond the first 5 years postin-carceration. For a subject who is in his 20s, and who does not continue his partici-pation in "maintenance" treatment programming on a long-term basis, this hope may be misplaced. Hanson, Steffy, and Gauthier (1993), for instance, found that treated child molesters initially showed reduced recidivism rates compared with untreated child molesters but that the difference in recidivism rates dissipated through the first 10 years postincarceration. Starting around Year 10, and continuing thereafter, there was no overall recidivism rate difference between the groups. The protective effect of treatment had apparently worn off. Probably of importance, the treated individuals in that study did not have scheduled follow-up treatment in the community. This may be a very important consideration (Gordon & Packard, 1998).

In addition, research has indicated that not all even well-designed sex offender treatment works (e.g., Hall, 1995; Marques, 1999). Simply adjusting someone's actuarially assessed risk downward because he has completed treatment may not be appropriate without some reason to believe that the program lowers recidivism rates in general. Finally, as mentioned above, one of the current actuarial instru-ments, the MnSOST–R, already considers treatment completion. (This is notably within the context of a program with a high completion rate, with applications to programs with far lower completion rates being problematic. In that latter situa-tion, evaluators often use just the first 12, or static, items from that scale.) If that instrument is employed with the inclusion of the treatment items (numbers 14 and 15), then it seems quite inappropriate to use treatment completion as a reason for clinical adjustment to this instrument's results.

Besides the general protective factor of treatment completion/benefit, all eight of these studies offer information concerning risk factors of incremental utility beyond an actuarial instrument. The risk factors found useful in this way are delineated below:

1. From the Allam (2000) investigation, dynamic considerations (in combi-nation) were found useful through a clustering of psychometric data to assess "deviance" (vs. normalcy) of a psychological nature. The constructs of importance included emotional loneliness, self-esteem, how upset the person gets with other people's upset, social responding, admission and denial of

deviant sexual interests, victim empathy, and cognitive distortions related to children and sexuality, as well as a social desirability measure.

2. From the Beech et al. (2001) study, the same types of dynamic considerations from psychometrically determined deviancy found by Allam were supported.

3. From the Hanson and Harris (1997) study came considerations in five different dynamic categories:

    a. Intimacy deficits (i.e., degree of stable romantic relationship with appropriate partner, constructive long-term friendships)

    b. Negative peer influences (i.e., degree to which significant people are positive and negative influences in the offender's life)

    c. Attitudes tolerant of sexual assault (i.e., degree to which sexual assault is justified/excused vs. viewed as always wrong)

    d. Emotional/sexual self-regulation (i.e., degree to which negative mood or stress leads to sexual fantasizing and/or high-risk behavior)

    e. General self-regulation (i.e., degree to which person cooperates with supervision and/or treatment, willing to sacrifice personally to avoid high-risk situations)

4. From the Haynes et al. (2000) research, there was demonstrated importance of the degree to which a person who has shown deviant interests on a PPG can (or at least is willing to) suppress that response when instructed to do so.[1]

5. From the McGrath et al. (2001) investigation comes support for whether or not the person completes a prison treatment program before prison release, where noncompletion includes either never starting the program or not completing it for any reason once begun.

6. From the Quinsey et al. (1997) study (for an outcome that overlapped sexual recidivism, but was mostly different from that, and likewise did not typically involve sex offenders), there were seven dynamic categories of apparent importance (all from the Problem Identification Checklist, an instrument described in the Quinsey et al. publication):

    a. Inappropriate/procriminal social behaviors (i.e., consisting of the total sum from the following 18 items: impulsivity; insulting, teasing, and obnoxious verbal behaviors; lack of consideration of others; unconventional attitudes; criminal attitudes; shallow affect, superficiality; tension; medication noncompliance; problems with housekeeping or cooking; poor self-care and personal hygiene; substance abuse; physical self-abuse; suggestible and easily led; problems with money management; sexual misbehaviors; firestarting; criminal associates; inappropriate dependency)

    b. Mood problems (i.e., consisting of the following 7 items: excitement, anxiety, mania, anger, blunted affect, depression, guilt feelings)

    c. Social withdrawal (i.e., consisting of the following 9 items: poor use of leisure time, unpopular, social withdrawal, inactivity, excessive shyness, refusal to participate in nonmedical therapy, preoccupation with staying in the institution, poor assertion, lack of family support)

    d. Dynamic antisociality (i.e., consisting of the following 10 items: complains about staff, shows no remorse for crime, takes no responsibility for own behavior, ignores or passes over previous violent acts, has more antisocial attitudes and values, shows no empathy or concern for others, has unrealistic discharge plans, psychiatric symptoms are not in remission, has made threats aimed at specific victims, has same delusion as that involved in index offense)

    e. Psychiatric symptoms (i.e., consisting of the following 7 items: disordered thought content, reports command hallucinations, has not acquired new vocational skills, eating or sleeping difficulty, appearance/dress, helplessness and/or despair, considered escape risk by staff)

    f. Poor compliance (i.e., consisting of the following 3 items: escape or escape attempt, exhibits few positive coping skills, poor compliance with rules)

    g. Medication compliance/dysphoria (i.e., consisting of the following 3 items: poor compliance with medication, anxiety/anger/frustration, no support from family or friends). (This complete list was from Table 2 of Quinsey et al., pp. 801-802.)

7. From the Thornton (in press) research, a combination of the following dynamic considerations was suggested as useful:

    a. Attitudes supportive of sexual offending (i.e., degree to which the person continues to demonstrate such attitudes)

    b. Socioaffective functioning (i.e., degree to which the person continues to show problems with rumination of anger, feeling grieved by others, self-derogation, emotional loneliness, emotional intimacy with children, rehearsal of negative emotions)

    c. Self-regulation (i.e., degree to which the person continues to act impulsively and without consideration for relapse prevention plan)

8. From the Wong, Olver, et al. (2000) study, the 20 dynamic factors found useful in a pre- and posttreatment fashion included the following:

    a. Violent/criminal lifestyle variables (i.e., Violent Lifestyle, Criminal Personality, Criminal Peers, Interpersonal Aggression, Violence During Institutionalization, Weapon Use, Substance Abuse, Violence Cycle)

    b. Cognitive variables (i.e., Criminal Attitudes, Work Ethic, Insight into the Cause of Violence, Mental Disorder, Cognitive Distortion)

c. Affective variables (i.e., Emotional Control, Impulsivity)

d. Interpersonal variables (i.e., Stability of Relationships with Significant Others, Community Support)

e. Risk management variables (i.e., Released Back to High-Risk Situations, Compliance with Community Supervision, Security Level of Anticipated Release Institution)

The actuarial instruments beyond which these results were found included the RRASOR, SACJ, Static-99, and Violence Risk Appraisal Guide (VRAG), with the RRASOR and Static-99 each being employed four times across these pieces of research (the SACJ and VRAG were each employed once). Hence, consistency across pieces of research may be interpretable as meaningful beyond the additive utility to the single instrument employed in a single study.

There are probably multiple ways to make sense of the above findings as a group. One such summary of the above enumeration of dynamic considerations found incrementally useful beyond the actuarial instruments is the following:

1. Current attitudes supportive of, or at least not protective against, (sexual) offending

2. Chronic negative mood, especially if a main coping mechanism is sexual fantasy

3. Lack of emotional connection to others, such as shown through emotional loneliness, lack of empathy and/or remorse, lack of family and/or other community support, social withdrawal

4. Acting in ways contrary to (or ignorant of) a relapse prevention plan, including both generally impulsive acts and behaviors that demonstrate a lack of concern for increasing one's situational risk

This formulation certainly does not represent the only possible summary from the above research findings, but it does suggest an important point. Suggested is that all four life spheres may have some predictive relevance beyond the current set of actuarial instruments. Included in the above are components of a cognitive nature (i.e., attitudes), an emotional consideration (i.e., negative mood and the manner by which the person copes with it), concerns with the person's interpersonal connection, and the more purely behavioral realm.

On the other hand, there are many caveats to understanding that summary properly. First of all, not everything that falls in *any* single life sphere has been found useful beyond actuarial instrumentation results. Quinsey et al., for instance, found no support for "psychotic" symptoms such as "unusual thought content, hallucinatory behavior, conceptual disorganization . . . inappropriate suspicion, [and] grandiosity" (p. 801) beyond the VRAG. Except possibly for the Hanson and Harris study, the concept of "negative mood" relates more to a chronic condition than it does a temporary state, with the concomitant high-risk coping style clearly being of a longer- versus shorter-term nature. The same is true for the type of emotional connection the individual has with other people, with simple temporary situational considerations not included in the chronic nature that was studied. Overall, evaluators are cautioned about extrapolating much beyond the empirical findings above, at least until further research results become available.

The second caveat, possibly even more important than the first, is that almost all of the research findings were related to relatively short-term recidivism. Only the Quinsey et al. study employed a lengthy follow-up time frame (up to 15 years), with all of the others falling between 1 and 5 years. As described above when discussing the additive predictive utility of treatment completion, the actual long-term utility of dynamic factors useful in relatively "short term" predictions is an open, as yet untested question. There is a reasonable argument that dynamic factors, by their very nature as changeable, may not be of much use for long-term assessments of risk even if useful in the shorter term. Long-term risk assessments may be most accurate through the continued reliance on stable life patterns of the individual, despite the fact that changeable characteristics increase prediction accuracy in the earlier years of that long-term period. Besides the Hanson et al. (1993) findings mentioned above (where positive treatment effect diminished and disappeared by the tenth year after incarceration), the Wong, Olver, et al. (2000) study also found that violence predictions using dynamic considerations were particularly effective at Year 2, but already showed decreased utility by Years 3 and 4 (as measured by receiver operating characteristics, or ROCs).

A third caveat stems from the fact that (virtually) all of the above types of data are dynamic (though oftentimes stable) in nature. There is nothing from any of these studies that looked at whether—no less was suggestive that—purely static, historical information of *any* type should be viewed as indicative of added risk beyond that which is already assessed by existing actuarial risk assessment instruments. "Common sense" static considerations of risk such as the number of prior victims, severity of injuries caused to victims, diversity of victim types, and the like have *not been shown* as incrementally useful in estimating recidivism risk beyond current actuarial instrument results.

This does not mean that there are no important static variables yet to be discovered. In fact, some of the considerations in Chapter 6 that were described as "beyond the actuarial scheme" may eventually be researched and found of great relevance. Possible examples of additional risk that come to mind include (1) an offender's number of victims being greater than a very high number, (2) the presence of sexual sadism, and (3) the offender's having killed one or more victims.

Fourth, this compilation was not driven by any specific theory, as none of the underlying studies employed a coherent theory in exploring which variables to investigate. If one attempts to apply the two-dimensional sexual recidivism model to the above four types of relevant dynamic factors, the considerations of attitudes, negative mood, interpersonal lack of connection, and behavioral signs of risk do not readily differentiate between the two dimensions; that is, all four factor types might be viewed as applying equally well to either or both pathways (sexual deviance and antisocial/violent character traits). Maybe that is the true state of affairs in this area—the same dynamic factors influence both types of recidivism etiologies. On the other hand, Hudson, Ward, and McCormack's (1999) research documented different sexual offending patterns with each suggesting differing degrees of influence of emotional and attitudinal considerations. Maybe, it is simply our lack of sophisticated knowledge in the application of dynamic variables within risk assessments that is the issue, and future research will clarify the relative influence of each consideration and the combinations of factors that represent significant risk.

Finally, there is a danger of "double counting" in applying the above dynamic considerations. Sexual deviance, as a dynamic consideration, was described as useful in addition to the Static-99, for instance (by Thornton, 2000b), but not so in addition to the RRASOR (by Haynes et al., 2000). This "conflicting" finding is actually in keeping with the results from Doren and Roberts (1998) and other research described in Chapter 5 where the RRASOR was found to correlate with sexual deviance whereas the Static-99 did not show the same relationship. Dynamically assessed sexual deviance clearly relates to the sexual deviance dimension, and not specifically to the violence/antisocial dimension of sexual reoffending. If the simple presence of sexual deviance were viewed as adding risk to an actuarial result already assessing the relevant dimension (e.g., the RRASOR) in a risk assessment, one could effectively be counting the sexual deviance a second time.

A counterargument sometimes made is that plethysmographic (PPG) findings of deviance should never be discounted relative to the RRASOR because Hanson and Bussière (1998) showed a higher correlation between such deviance and recidivism than the RRASOR has shown. This argument tends to discount the findings that such deviance and the RRASOR seem to correlate and that the degree of additional variance accounted for by the deviance measure appears to be minimal and not of statistical significance. Given that recommended risk assessment procedures begin with actuarial instrumentation, adding something to those results that was already statistically incorporated represents double-counting. Indications are that the relationship between sexual arousal deviance and the RRASOR may represent such a situation.

In contrast, the addition of a finding of sexual deviance to assessments of the other dimension (e.g., the Static-99) may be proper in that the deviance represents not yet assessed, additional information compared with that already measured. On the other hand, the new information should not be viewed as directly additive to the measurements of the violent/antisocial dimensional risk, but as representative of risk stemming from "another bodily system."

The bottom line is that examiners need to remain cognizant of the very significant limitations to our current knowledge of appropriate clinical adjustments to actuarial results. Making clinical adjustments to actuarial results typically involves some untested assumptions. We at least should be aware of our assumptions when we make these adjustments.

Adjustments Based on Protective Factors

In a recent article, Rogers (2000) makes the very fine point that many risk assessment evaluators concentrate on factors related to a subject's risk to the near exclusion of factors that may protect the person from enacting a criminal offense. According to Rogers, this situation exists, at least in part, because there has been far less empirical study of protective considerations.

One of the major exceptions in this regard for sex offenders is the effect of proper sex offender treatment. Hanson et al. (2000) reported the project results from the collaborative data research committee of the Association for the Treatment of Sexual Abusers (ATSA) concerning sex offender treatment effectiveness, with rather supportive conclusions. (Using 43 studies, the average recidivism rates for treated and untreated subjects were 12% and 17%, respectively, over an average follow-up time of 46 months, the last piece of information from Andrew Harris, personal communication, August 31, 2001.) This appears to mean that treatment works for some individuals, but not for others (if the outcome of relevance is whether or not the person reoffends). Even more important, a protective effect seems to exist beyond what the actuarial (i.e., historical) information would indicate, as described above, though it is notable that virtually all of the predictive accuracy on the MnSOST–R comes from its static items (i.e., Items 1-12).

The fact is that "sex offender treatment completion" is probably another proxy variable for something more directly meaningful. After all, it seems unlikely that simply attending a number of group meetings and completing some assignments is exactly what is needed to lower a sex offender's risk. If such activities were all that was needed, all treatment programs requiring such things would show successful outcomes. This has not been true to date (e.g., Marques, 1999). "Treatment completion" also varies in what was required, sometimes meaning a lengthy involvement in intense work while at other times meaning something far less. Probably more meaningful than the simple completion of a set of requirements is (1) the degree to which the person has learned something related to his recidivism risk, and (2) his later putting that something to use. That "treatment benefit," versus simply his official completion of a program, would appear to be the underlying concept that evaluators would most wish to assess.

Maybe, evaluators should be trying to assess a subject's treatment benefit directly, and not just with a proxy variable. Unfortunately, not every reasonable, well-designed, and well-intentioned system for assessing treatment gain has been found empirically to work. Seto and Barbaree (1999) found, despite great efforts within a well-designed treatment program, that a structured rating system for clinicians' evaluations of subjects' treatment progress ranged from relatively ineffective to results *opposite* to what later recidivism rates showed to be true. The latter finding was related to the degree of psychopathy of the subjects, with the relatively more psychopathic subjects who were rated as doing well in the program actually found to have a five times higher degree of recidivism than the other subjects. (Overall, the relatively psychopathic subjects did worse as a group compared with the relatively nonpsychopathic, but the relatively psychopathic subjects rated as doing well in the program showed a much higher recidivism rate than the relatively psychopathic subjects rated by the treatment staff as doing poorly.) This seems to indicate that subjects' degrees of psychopathy needs to be assessed before an evaluator can make a meaningful interpretation of their potential benefit from treatment, with treatment staff assessments (vs. behavioral observations) of those individuals probably representing something evaluators should not place trust.

The Wong, Olver, et al. (2000) system for evaluating 20 pre- and posttreatment dynamic considerations has shown far more promise. On the other hand, that system was designed to be employed by people in a position to make both the pretreatment and posttreatment measurements. Because civil commitment evaluators are not typically in such a position (except potentially post hoc for the pretreatment variables, and then only when very complete treatment records are available), this fine system cannot easily be adopted within the civil commitment realm.

The demonstrated psychometric assessments of deviancy (in keeping with the studies by Allam, 2000; Beech et al., 1999; and Beech et al., 2001) might represent an effective method for assessing treatment benefit, but this method, too, is problematic. To use this system, one needs to have local normative data on which deviancy can be determined. If an evaluator either has access to such normative data or can first develop a normative database, then this approach holds a great deal of promise, at least in assessing the areas of attitudes and socioaffective functioning. Without such normative data, however, this approach again is not truly employable by civil commitment evaluators.

The Relapse Prevention Interview (developed by Richard Beckett, Dawn Fisher, Ruth Mann, and David Thornton, as described by Eldridge, 1998) represents the first of the two remaining structured approaches to be discussed for assessing treatment benefit. This 19-item questionnaire is for use specifically during an interview of the subject, and hence may have its utility limited by that fact. (Some civil commitment subjects do not participate in interviews.) This highly structured interview probes the subject's knowledge of his offense cycle, high-risk situations, triggering events, and ways to avoid and effectively cope with problematic situations. The interview comes with a numerical system for quantifying the answers obtained, though that additive system has reportedly not been empirically tested (David Thornton, personal communication, July 2000). Hence, this interview currently serves as a structured approach to assessing treatment benefit that has a great deal of face validity but that stands without demonstrated research support.

The Structured Risk Assessment (SRA; Thornton, 2000a, 2000b) is slightly better in regards to empirical support. There has been one direct test of segments of the instrument (which incorporates the Static-99 as its first step, but adds two steps involving dynamic considerations beyond the actuarial instrument), with support for its short-term utility (i.e., up to 3 years at risk), though this study ultimately involved quite small numbers in some of the analyses (Thornton, in press). Again, because empirical tests for the long-term validity of this assessment tool are still lacking, evaluators may prefer to think of this as a structured, potentially research-guided approach to the assessment of subjects' treatment benefit instead of the actuarial system designed. An evaluative report template for using the SRA in this fashion is offered in Appendix D.

Assessing Beyond the Actuarial Scheme

Extrapolating Beyond Actuarial Time Frames and Official Measurements

The second time when clinical adjustments should be considered, beyond those occasions supported by existing research, occurs when there is something either about the evaluation question itself or about the case that is clearly beyond what has been included in the development of the actuarial instruments. The first situation currently occurs in a vast majority of sex offender civil commitment evaluations. The type of risk being assessed by the actuarial instruments usually does not equate to the type of risk of statutory concern for commitment. The current instruments assess the likelihood for being rearrested and/or reconvicted for a new sexual offense within certain time periods. This actuarial scheme is not the same as the statutory lifetime sexual reoffense risk (as described in detail in Chapter 6). Hence, some degree of extrapolation (i.e., clinical adjustment) is typically appropriate here.

There are no uniform ways for doing this extrapolation, for the same reason that such an extrapolation is necessary. There are no data about actual lifetime sexual recidivism frequencies, only proxy measures to that effect. Recommended here is that evaluators use known approximations of base rate changes over time for those proxy measures to estimate how much change one might expect in a given case. For instance, Prentky, Lee, Knight, and Cerce (1997) developed long-term survival curves for extrafamilial child molesters and, separately, for rapists (see Table 6.1 in Chapter 6). Each type of offender was researched relative to rates for reimprisonment, reconviction, and rearrest for a new sexual offense. Those survival data go out 25 years postincarceration, though there are statistical concerns about the meaningfulness of the data toward the latter years (e.g., R. Karl Hanson, personal communication, 1998: the numbers of people still contained in the analysis in the latter years is quite small, making the results in those later years difficult to have confidence in for generalizing to other samples).

If an evaluator uses these survival data as general guidelines (as opposed to exact yardsticks) for estimating the additional degree of sexual recidivism to be expected of the type beyond what an actuarial instrument measures (e.g., reconviction), the examiner will at least have some research basis for the extrapolation to long-term, nearly lifetime recidivism risk beyond what a current actuarial instrument measures. For example, a 10-year RRASOR reconviction finding can be extrapolated to a 25-year reconviction estimate, or even a 25-year rearrest approximation, by computing the absolute amount of additional recidivism that was documented by Prentky et al. (1997) from the 10-year reconviction figure to the relevant 25-year figure. The 10-year reconviction rate (e.g., for rapists) was 16%, and the 25-year reconviction rate was estimated to be about 24%, suggesting an increase of about 8% over the years 11-25. The comparable increase for extrafamilial child molesters was 18% (41%-23%).

This method for extrapolation has two problems. First, this practice adds variability (from additional sampling error) to the original RRASOR-based risk figure, a process that statistically widens the applicable confidence interval associated with any derived percentage figure. Second, this process assumes a uniform distribution of risk exists across the different RRASOR percentages (i.e., across RRASOR scores), an assumption that may very well not be accurate.

Despite these problems, the recommendation is still made to use a procedure such as this one. The reason is because there does not seem to be anything superior at this time. I think it is better to be aware of the potential for error in one's risk estimations and to be able to describe that potential error to judges and jurors, than just to "wing it" and make a guess for which no estimation of potential error can be made.

The only other options appear to be (1) not doing this extrapolation at all, but informing the court that there is some unknown degree of more risk to be assessed beyond what the actuarial instruments describe, or (2) increasing actuarially assessed recidivism risk with a fixed amount, computed either by adding or multiplying. The extremes for this latter proposal are Karl Hanson's (1998a) addition of 5% to 10% beyond the RRASOR's 10-year reconviction figures, to David Thornton's (2000a) multiplying the actuarially derived figure by 3, including even for the Static-99's 15-year figures. The Prentky et al. figures will virtually always be somewhere in between these two extremes and thus seem both more moderate and more easily shown as research based. No matter what method for approximating lifetime reoffense risk based on current actuarial results is chosen, however, it should clearly be thought of as a current way of estimating, and not of determining such long-term risk.

Case Characteristics Beyond the Actuarial Scheme

The other occasion when an evaluator can find the information beyond what the actuarial instruments are known to assess is when there are case-specific data *both*

1. clearly beyond the type of cases previously studied for instrument applicability, and

2. for which there is good reason to believe the characteristic is relevant to the person's recidivism risk.

For instance, although an offender's number of known victims does not seem to add information to what is currently assessed in any of the previously selected actuarial instruments (this being known through actual statistical tests by the instrument developers), if one comes upon an offender with an absolutely huge number of known victims (say, 400, just to pick an arbitrary number), it might be argued that this subject is fundamentally different in an important way compared with the type of people in the actuarial instrument research samples. Knowing when such an extreme case really exists, however, is difficult. Some people find a history of 10 victims, for instance, to be extreme, but this number may be closer to average for the amount typical incarcerated offenders disclose either during their treatment or during polygraph examinations (e.g., Weinrott & Saylor, 1991). The burden is on the evaluator to be sure that the case-specific characteristic is clearly beyond the types of cases included in tested samples.

A different example of a case beyond the actuarial scheme is the subject who simply and sincerely tells the examiner that he will do the crime again whenever he has the opportunity. This type of iteration is uncommon, but awfully hard to ignore or discount. Such an iteration, of voiced intention, seems to represent a strong sign of a high degree of recidivism risk under almost all circumstances irrelevant of actuarial indications, at least where the subject is in touch with reality and is not simply self-punitive and trying to remain incarcerated.

Sexual sadism may be another example. Langevin (1990) indicates that this condition is rare even among incarcerated sex offenders (i.e., about 2%-5%), though this does not automatically mean that both prongs of the "beyond actuarial scheme" test apply to this group. Beyond rarity, there needs to be reason to believe that this attribute is related to recidivism risk in some rather unique way. It turns out that the most severe sexual sadists (i.e., those who murdered, or in particular those who murdered repetitively even as compared to those who murdered once) tend to differ from other high-risk sex offenders specifically in those characteristics typically associated with high risk. The homicidal sadists tend to be married, have higher educational backgrounds, have fewer prior criminal offenses, and have less officially recorded violence in their history (Gratzer & Bradford, 1995; Grubin, 1994; Warren, Hazelwood, & Dietz, 1996). Yet, these same sadists apparently did not stop their sexual (and homicidal) offending until incapacitated by the criminal justice system (Warren et al., 1996), suggesting a strong propensity toward sexual offending despite having what otherwise would be viewed as low-risk characteristics. The recidivism risk for sexual sadists may very well be a different nature compared with other sex offenders. Sadists as a class, therefore, based both on this characteristic and their rarity, may be beyond the actuarial scheme of any of our current instruments.

Finally, there are the people who are high both in sexual deviance and in their degree of psychopathy (as assessed on the Psychopathy Checklist–Revised [PCL–R]). Research such as Rice and Harris (1997) and Harris, Rice, Quinsey, Lalumière, Boer, and Lang (2001) suggests that those people show a far higher degree of recidivism risk compared basically with everyone else (i.e., with either just one or neither of those attributes). The degree to which these doubly afflicted people also score highly on actuarial instruments has not been tested. Actuarial findings may not be as relevant to this small group of people as (1) their identification as a member of this rather rare, doubly afflicted group, and (2) demonstrating high-risk indicators from both of the two theoretical etiological dimensions for recidivism.

Evaluator Bias

The maneuvering room under the rubric of "clinical adjustment" to actuarial findings also means there is an easy opportunity for examiner bias to enter at this place in the evaluation. There are two main ways to combat against this subconscious process.

The first is to consult with knowledgeable professionals about how clinical adjustments to actuarial results were made. One's best choice of consultant involves a person who is willing to question your underlying assumptions, and not just reflect how clever you are.

The second is to research one's own work. There is no inherent reason to believe that any of the actuarial instruments systematically under- or overestimate what they were designed to assess (e.g., 10-year sexual reconviction likelihood). Hence, any consistency by an evaluator in adjusting "up" or in adjusting "down" probably reflects the evaluator's bias (unless there is reason to believe the relevant sex offender population is atypical). This statement is *not* referring to the extrapolation to lifetime reoffending risk from time-limited reconviction rates, as that systematic increase in assessed risk is grounded in the statistical effect of differing base rates. The bias to be explored by each evaluator is to what degree one effectively discounts the actuarial results regularly in favor of either higher or lower overall assessments of risk within the same time period and measure. Consistency here across many cases, in either direction, speaks to evaluator bias and needs to be corrected.

Summary Comments

This chapter described empirical findings indicative of various kinds of clinical adjustments that potentially increase risk assessment accuracy beyond the actuarial instruments. Someday, it will likely be that most of these results will find their way into new and improved actuarial devices, such that clinical adjustments will become less and less needed.

In the meanwhile, there are two caveats to remember concerning clinical adjustments to actuarial instrument results:

1. Although an evaluator may have strong feelings about a factor's meaningfulness in a given case, there may not be support for that meaningfulness beyond actuarial results.

2. Psychological theories about what relates to risk do not tell us what empirically adds to the accuracy of the risk assessment beyond actuarial instruments.

Although there are empirical and conceptual reasons why clinical adjustments to actuarial results are needed in civil commitment evaluations, we should probably remain humble about what we truly know and do not know in this area. There are many gaps in our knowledge about what clinical adjustments are appropriate and to what degree they should be given weight beyond actuarial results. Recommended is that evaluators employ significant restraint and caution in making such adjustments, while still using them due to necessity.

Note

1. This research studied the relationship of the RRASOR, PPG results, and sexual recidivism among incarcerated sex offenders. Subjects were tested on the PPG (during treatment) before they were released from their imprisonment. After release, the RRASOR was again found statistically valid in differentiating which of the subjects sexually recidivated and which did not. When combined with PPG data, however, illuminating outcomes were found. Simply adding the information of whether or not the subjects showed deviant sexual arousal patterns in their PPG results did not change the predictive effectiveness of the RRASOR

alone. On the other hand, subjects showing PPG deviant patterns had also been told to suppress their deviant arousal after the fact of their deviance had been determined. When subjects who demonstrated an inability (or at least unwillingness) to suppress their arousal were compared with subjects who either demonstrated an ability to suppress their deviance or who did not show PPG deviance to start, a significant difference in recidivism was found even when RRASOR scores were controlled. In other words, the "inability to suppress" showed incremental predictive utility beyond the RRASOR alone.

CHAPTER 8

The Evaluation Report and Court Testimony

Helen: What were you lecturing on in India?
Patterson: Harold Pinter and the failure of communication.
Helen: How did it go?
Patterson: I don't know. They didn't seem to understand a word I said.

— Malcolm Bradbury and Christopher Bigsby,
The After Dinner Game, BBC-TV, 1975

Before any sex offender civil commitment assessment is truly done, the results must be communicated to one or more nonclinicians. The importance of performing this last task skillfully should not be underestimated. As Heilbrun, Dvoskin, Hart, and McNeil (1999) have argued, "Improvements in the accuracy of predictions . . . will not yield a comparable improvement in risk-related decision-making unless communication is effective. Improper risk communication can render a risk assessment that was otherwise well-conducted completely useless or even worse than useless, if it gives consumers the wrong impression" (p. 94).

Unfortunately, there are very few empirical studies on which an examiner can determine the best way to communicate risk assessment results. The study by Heilbrun, O'Neill, Strohman, Bowman, and Philipson (2000) is one of the first in this regard, and those researchers described their outcome more in terms of explorative and normative information than leading to specific recommendations. (Of note, "the most highly valued form of risk communication involved identifying risk factors applicable to the individual and specifying interventions to reduce risk"; p. 137.) More analytical was the research by Slovic, Monahan, and MacGregor (2000).

Those researchers found substantive *differences in perceived* risk depending on alternative ways of conceptualizing and/or communicating the *same statistical degree* of risk, a finding leading to various cautionary notes. Besides these two studies, evaluators are largely on their own in deciding how best to communicate assessment results.

Hence, most of this chapter involves descriptions of different, apparently meaningful options and guidelines for how examiners might communicate evaluation results, rather than specific empirically supported recommendations. The reader will find two main sections in this chapter: (1) the evaluation report and (2) testifying about evaluation findings.

The Evaluation Report

There are various perspectives concerning what the contents of an assessment report should be. Some clinicians take the view that a full description of evaluation findings, including a detailed account of the subject's life history, should be offered to the reader. Other examiners believe that only the most pertinent information needs to be reported, those data representing the underlying rationale for any summary opinions derived. Some evaluators attempt to achieve the professional ethical ideal involving a full explanation of all limitations to information and conclusions drawn, no matter which of the two prior options they also choose. Other people hold the view that detailed descriptions of limitations and other ethical responsibilities should wait until giving testimony because evaluation reports are rarely entered into evidence and triers of fact are only to pay attention to evidence presented in the courtroom.

None of these differing perspectives is meaningfully argued as correct or incorrect. They each involve pros and cons, depending on legal circumstances and the ability of the intended audience (i.e., judges and attorneys) to interpret the information properly (i.e., not be misled by improperly included or omitted information or by overinterpreting stated limitations). For instance, reports that contain little of the subject's history may be better than fully inclusive reports if either (1) the anticipated audience already knows the case details or (2) the report will likely be "buried" if the recommendation is not in keeping with what the hiring attorney wants (through case dismissal by a prosecutor or as a defense counsel's work product). In contrast, fully inclusive reports can be argued as allowing readers to see for themselves all of the bases for the evaluator's opinions.

Instead of arguing for one style of report writing over another, I recommend that evaluators concentrate on ensuring the clarity of their writing. The fundamental concept here is that the report needs to be written in terms the audience will plainly understand before any of the other details matter.

This means that the evaluation report needs to be written using language that is fully comprehended by legally trained personnel who are neither clinicians nor statisticians. Using concepts such as "compulsive," "psychopathy," "statistically significant," "confidence intervals," and the like, without further explanation, seems improper. Likewise, using legal language without addressing one's understanding of the term invites misinterpretation compared to the unstated intention. An evaluator's working definition of statutory terms such as "likely" should be offered, for instance, given that the court may have a very different interpretation of the law compared with the writer's.

Points to Cover in the Report

Ultimately, only one type of information needs to be in any civil commitment evaluation report (beyond a description of general evaluation procedures): information relevant to each of the clinical statutory commitment criteria. Points such as the following need to be addressed in some way:

1. The subject's mental condition

2. Whether or not that mental condition predisposes the individual to commit sexually violent offenses

3. The degree to which the person represents the relevant sexual recidivism risk (e.g., for certain types of offenses, if not placed in a secure facility)

4. The extent to which that risk is predatory in nature

Not all of these pertain to the laws in all jurisdictions, meaning there is a lesser number of points to address in some states. If a report fails to offer information relevant to one or more of these points (that are called for in the relevant state), then that report is incomplete.

The style by which an examiner addresses each of these points is open to that individual's preference. Some sample paragraphs are offered herein for addressing issues evaluators sometimes have difficulty explaining. These samples, again, are not meant to represent the only way for doing business, but rather as illustrative of how certain concepts might be communicated in keeping with the proposed national standards described in Chapter 2.

Addressing the Requisite Mental Condition

An illustrative template, found in Appendix B, serves to describe diagnoses common to commitment evaluations, along with the issue of "predisposition" for when that issue is also pertinent. Examiners can employ rather standardized paragraphs from this template, selectively deleting the paragraphs that do not pertain to a specific case while leaving those that do. Specific concepts from within any of the following paragraphs can also be "mixed and matched" to fit case details, without always needing to start from scratch.

Whereas a complete template for the diagnostic portion of the evaluation report can be found in Appendix B, the basic format is exemplified in the segment below. To see how the template fits into a complete evaluation report, an illustrative report is available in Appendix C.

Diagnostic Template Segment

Based on all of the information available to this examiner, Mr. X appears to meet criteria for the following psychiatric conditions:

Axis I: Pedophilia, sexually attracted to females, nonexclusive

Axis II: Personality Disorder, Not Otherwise Specified, with antisocial features

The first disorder listed, Pedophilia, means that the person experiences recurrent and intense fantasies, urges, and/or behavior involving sexual arousal to minor children. In Mr. X's case, this condition exists while he also shows sexual arousal to adults (this latter characteristic being the meaning of the term "nonexclusive" above). Given that this condition is so related to Mr. X's sexual offending, and given that people with this condition show a tendency toward having sexual contact with minor children, this examiner came to the opinion that this disorder predisposes Mr. X toward committing a sexually violent act as defined by State Statute # (fill in the statute under which the assessment is being done).

Addressing Actuarial Instrument Time and Legal Status Limitations

A template for writing about the actuarial risk instrument results within the context of sex offender civil commitment evaluations can be found in Appendix B. Whether or not an evaluator employs that template, there are certain topics that should make it into the report.

Simply listing scores without any interpretation is not recommended. If an evaluator wishes not to go into the explanation of what each score means, then it is suggested that a simple overall description of the results is more useful than an unexplained enumeration of scale scores. In other words, writing that "Mr. X's scores were all in the low range for recidivism risk" is probably better than an unexplained, "Mr. X scored a 2 on the RRASOR, 2 on the Static-99, and 3 on the MnSOST–R."

Also to be included in this section should be something pertaining to caveats about interpreting the actuarial scores. Issues such as their assessing reconviction or rearrest likelihood versus true reoffense rates, and the fact there is known error, should be mentioned.

Addressing Treatment Benefit Using the SRA Structure

Reexamination reports, or reports involving an assessment of any potential benefit from prior sex offender treatment, typically involve descriptions of how that portion of the assessment was conducted along with its results. Based on the summary in Chapter 7, the Structured Risk Assessment (SRA) structure is recommended here for that analysis and reporting. A template to this effect can be found in Appendix D.

That template does not use the SRA formal scoring system. The perspective not to recommend using the scoring system was in keeping with the rationale described at the end of the last chapter. In addition, modifications to Step 3 (treatment considerations) were also made based on the same perspective (i.e., there are modifications relative to the issue of the subject's degree of psychopathy not being significantly addressed in the template). The template offered in Appendix D is written as if it were part of a postcommitment reexamination report, though the SRA structure could also be applied to someone who was being evaluated precommitment.

Addressing Risk Management Considerations

Besides determining the level of risk someone represents, assessments of people already committed to a locked facility (and sometimes for people yet to be committed) also need to include a review of risk management considerations. The point here is that people who are found still to meet commitment criteria may be both legally entitled to the least restrictive environment and manageable in the community with a reasonable allocation of supervisory resources. For instance, a child molester who is not highly psychopathic, who has always shown a significantly extended grooming period (such as by developing relationships with the parents of his victims for months before he sexual assaults their children), who has not shown any history of absconding or difficulty in following supervisory rules, and who has demonstrated a desire not to recidivate (such as in his treatment participation) may be someone whose risk can be managed effectively in the community despite his high risk (determined through other considerations).

In other words, the question of whether or not someone can be managed effectively in the community is not fully addressed simply through a risk assessment as described above. One might argue that if a subject's risk is high enough, then no realistic set of risk management considerations would result in a reasonable risk for the community. On the other hand, even those cases offer more direct risk management versus risk assessment considerations that should at least be enumerated in one's report.

Risk management considerations basically involve (1) characteristics of the individual that reflect his likelihood not to abscond from supervision (or whatever the lesser restrictive environment might be); (2) characteristics of the person related to his willingness to comply with imposed rules; (3) the degree to which the supervising staff can meaningfully intervene in the person's victim-grooming process (by seeing precursors and having effective interventions to implement); (4) the person's own motivation to avoid high-risk situations, coupled with the supervising staff's ability to monitor the person's behavior in this regard; (5) the type of degree of social support system the person has, in particular people who would confront versus cover up for his high risk behaviors; and so on.

Rather than listing the myriad of considerations in this section that could be applicable to any given case, there is instead a template for writing the risk management section enumerating various categories of these issues in Appendix D. The reader is referred to that appendix for further details.

Testifying About Evaluation Findings

The final step in a sex offender civil commitment evaluation is testifying about the results during a commitment or reexamination hearing. A detailed description of how to present oneself, ask for clarification of ambiguous questions, address hypothetically posed inquiries, avoid defensive reactions and other emotional outbursts, answer "yes-no" questions with fuller explanations, and so on is beyond the scope of this book. Readers wishing to learn more about the art and skill of being an expert witness are referred to Brodsky (1991, 1999). This section addresses just those testimony issues of potential special interest to the civil commitment evaluator. Those areas are (1) standards for what qualifies as professional evidence; (2) addressing evaluator bias; (3) describing risk with frequencies, percentages, and verbal classification; (4) being accurate in differentiating relevant concepts; and (5) use of metaphors.

Standards for What Qualifies as Professional Evidence

In nonforensic clinical assessments, judgments are often made based on the general knowledge of the examiner without rigid concern for every detail. Diagnostic determinations and treatment interventions, for instance, are regularly made based on the general clinical presentation of the subject without a thorough review of the person's life history.

In the sex offender civil commitment arena, however, this mode of doing business often gets suitably punished during testimony. There appears to be one basic rule for how evaluators should determine what qualifies for inclusion during a civil commitment assessment: If you cannot point to the evidence for it, it does not exist. Examples of this rather rigid rule include the following:

1. Making a diagnosis of antisocial personality disorder only if you can delineate the before-age-15 evidence of a conduct disorder

2. Tallying any actuarial assessment only in keeping with documented (or, when acceptable under the scoring rules, subject-acknowledged) evidence

3. Scoring the Psychopathy Checklist–Revised (PCL–R) only in keeping with the test's manual

Making judgments about "what the person must have really done," about "how many victims he must really have," about "his real intention," and so forth is dangerous business in the courtroom, and it is strongly discouraged. Our role in the courtroom is to offer technical information to the trier of fact, not to make guesses about what might have happened in the past.

Addressing Evaluator Bias

Cross-examination attempting to show the evaluator to have been unduly biased in the assessment is common. Bias is a fair issue for questioning, so examiners should be fully prepared to address it. There are at least three ways to do so.

The most straightforward is to keep track of the number of civil commitment assessments one has done coupled with the proportion of times that one recommended for or against commitment. If there are different circumstances in which one does this work (e.g., pre-petition where no prior case screening occurs vs. after prior screening with probable cause already having been found), then separating out the results from each of the multiple circumstances also makes sense. One should expect to show different proportions of recommendations for and against commitment depending on the degree of prior scrutiny (both from other evaluators and the legal system) the case has already received.

The idea is that the judge or jury can be provided with your exact frequency of findings for and against commitment with concomitant information about the situations in which cases have come to you for examination, and then those people can make their own judgments about your degree of bias and in what direction. If nothing else, this approach makes it clear to the listener that you are anything but defensive about whatever bias you may have. People who do not practice in this way can be made to look more secretive, defensive, and therefore biased.

The second method for addressing questions of bias involves having consulted with one or more professional colleagues about the evaluation procedures and/or opinions. Obviously, there can be selection factors with whom one chooses to consult, but the adage that two heads are better than one can still go a long way toward validating your findings in the specific case.

The third manner for addressing bias is to be explicit about having one! The bias I have stated on many occasions, for instance, is to give the subject the benefit of any lack of clarity in data. (For example, if the records suggest but are not clear that the offender ever had a stranger victim as defined by the Static-99 or MnSOST–R, then I state that fact and give the subject the score based on no stranger victim.) This is actually a continuation of the point made above: If I cannot point to it, it does not exist. Because the baseline presumption is that a subject does not meet commitment criteria unless there exists clear enough evidence that he does, the bias described here is that a lack of clarity in evaluation data is interpreted by the author as insufficient for a commitment recommendation. I suggest that other evaluators consider if they have the same or any other bias in how they approach assessment information, and if that bias should simply be proclaimed when testifying.

Describing Risk With Frequencies, Percentages, and Verbal Classification

Is there a difference between saying, "5 out of 10" compared with "50%"? Is either of these different from saying, "middle of the possible range"? The results from research by Slovic et al. (2000) indicate there may be very important differences in the meaning given to these three phrases, despite statistical equality among them. The issue is not the statistical equality, of course, but how people interpret the words. According to the Slovic et al. findings, stating results in frequency terms (i.e., "X out of Y people") leads to the perception of higher risk than descriptions of the same statistical concept in percentage terms (i.e., "$Z\%$ of people"). This finding was rather consistent across the full range of possible percentages.

In other words, an evaluator can be equally accurate in communicating actuarial results, for instance, by using either frequency or percentage descriptions, but the audience understanding from these different types of descriptors may vary in a crucial and predictable way. How exactly the third, more general verbal narrative compares to either the frequency or percentage description has not been empirically tested. Assuming that the verbal narrative is interpreted no differently from either of the other two options may be incorrect, though exactly in what way is not known.

Based on the ethical stance that evaluators should bias their conclusions and communications toward lower versus higher risk in the face of ambiguity, the recommendation is made that communications of risk use percentage versus frequency descriptors when research findings need to be delineated, and verbal narratives everywhere else. This recommendation is based to date on only one study. Even so, there seems no reason to take the chance that using frequency statements lead to an unneeded and prejudicial bias in how judges and juries interpret what has been said.

Being Accurate in Differentiating Relevant Concepts

Various words and phrases can be used interchangeably in the courtroom quite inappropriately. The evaluator's task is to clarify these differentiations so as to avoid inaccuracies in what the triers of fact hear and various verbal "traps" during cross-examination. A couple of common concepts in need of clarification are the following:

1. The "prediction of recidivism" versus the "assessment of recidivism risk"

2. The use of the term "accuracy" to mean "right versus wrong" compared with accuracy indicating "the degree to which something is true"

As described below, these two examples are related, such that errors in one often lead to errors in the other.

Prosecutors, defense attorneys, and many evaluators use the terms "prediction" and "risk assessment" interchangeably, but are mistaken in doing so. The prediction of anything involves someone's making a statement that a certain event will or will not happen. There is no "maybe." In contrast, the assessment of risk involves a probabilistic estimate of an event's likelihood. If you make a prediction, you end up being either correct or incorrect. Your accuracy is either perfect or nonexistent. If you conduct an assessment of risk, however, the actual outcome does not determine the accuracy of the assessment. For example, if a meteorologist were to forecast that "it will rain" in a given locale, then that prediction will be either correct or incorrect. The more typical meteorological statement, however, is that there is an $X\%$ likelihood for rain today (in a given locale). If it rains, that does not make the statement right or wrong, just as would be true if it does not rain (unless the "$X\%$" equals 0% or 100%). The assessment of $X\%$ can still have been completely accurate, no matter what the actual rain outcome was later found to be. (The reader is referred to Monahan & Steadman, 1994, for further explication of these concepts.)

This differentiation is of particular importance to civil commitment evaluators because the portrayal of what they do as predictions is simply not correct and contains a dangerous implication. The concept of making a prediction inherently portrays results as simply right or wrong. No sex offender civil commitment law requires a prediction (and hence no evaluator makes a prediction) that a subject will or will not sexually recidivate, however, only an assessment of the degree to which a subject represents certain risk (and whether or not that risk is beyond the commitment threshold). Likewise, the statistics properly employed to determine the accuracy of evaluators' assessment findings differ from predictive work (e.g., confidence intervals vs. hit rates, sensitivity/specificity, and others; see Doren, 2000). Expert witnesses should not allow these two concepts to be used interchangeably.

Use of Metaphors

Metaphors can take the mystery out of professional concepts and explain things in terms understandable to the lay public. Using this communicative device while testifying is strongly recommended. Illustrative metaphors for some of the common civil commitment evaluation concepts are enumerated below:

1. "Risk factors": When one goes for a physical checkup, the doctor checks out your heart, among other things. This is done by assessing the person's heartbeat, cholesterol level, blood pressure, family history of heart problems, if the person is a smoker, and so on. These characteristics are looked at because research has shown these considerations to be related to heart problems. Each is a risk factor.

2. "Multiple pathways/dimensions to recidivism": During that same physical, the doctor checks out more than just one's heart, but also one's lungs, nervous system, and so on. Each of these can affect one's overall health. If the doctor tells me that my heart is in great shape, I will still feel very worried if the doctor also says that I have a malignant brain tumor. That is because my overall health depends on many different parts all working well.

3. "Negative correlation": This can be described as the relationship between the speed of the wind and the number of leaves still left on the trees (appreciation to David Biegen for this metaphor, personal communication, October 2000).

4. "Increase in base rates from short-term to long-term": The longer we watch frequent smokers, the more of them will die from smoking-related illnesses. The cumulative number cannot go down, and only reaches a plateau after many, many years.

5. "Short-term prediction accuracy versus long-term assessment of risk": The argument is sometimes made that we cannot even predict whether or not it is going to rain next Tuesday, so how can we possibly predict what is going to happen some years down the road? It is not accurate to compare the long-term assessment of risk with the meteorological difficulty in predicting rain. Metaphorically, this examination did not try to predict if it is going to rain next Tuesday, only assess the likelihood of it ever raining again during this person's lifetime.

By no means is this enumeration thought to be exhaustive of the possible metaphors useful in demystifying scientific concepts. Recommended is that evaluators hone their metaphoric skills as part of their civil commitment assessment training.

Summary Comments

This chapter, along with the listed appendices, described how to write an evaluation report in keeping both with the statutory requirements and the national standards. Templates for both precommitment and postcommitment assessment reports were offered with the expectation that evaluators will make their own adjustments to those templates as they see fit. Recommendations for giving testimony were also delineated. In that regard, it was recommended that evaluators become familiar with metaphoric ways of describing scientific concepts, so as to facilitate the understanding of psychological concepts by judges and juries.

CHAPTER 9

Ethical Issues

Ethics: A set of rules laid out by professionals to show the way they would like to act if it were profitable.

— Frank Dane

The above humorous quote serves as introduction to this book's final topic, ethical issues that arise during the conducting of sex offender civil commitment evaluations. With official publications concerning professional ethics standing as the general guide (e.g., American Educational Research Association et al., 1999; American Psychological Association [APA], 1992; Committee on Ethical Guidelines for Forensic Psychologists, 1991), some ethical considerations rather specific to the civil commitment evaluation arena need to be discussed. Given the more subjective nature of this topic matter compared with others described in this book, there will be little empirical basis for any conclusions or recommendations offered. Instead, certain topics and their concomitant ethical issues will be investigated, with the reader obviously left fully responsible for the ethics of any path chosen.

Seven ethical issues are delineated in the following discussion, divided into two sections: (1) procedural concerns and (2) communication concerns. This set of seven is by no means a comprehensive list of ethical issues related to sex offender civil commitment assessments, but it seems to cover some of the most pertinent issues rather uniquely confronted when doing such work. A final comment is found at the end of this chapter.

Procedural Concerns

The ethical concerns most commonly raised pertain to procedural issues surrounding evaluation interviews or the lack thereof. Four such issues are identified and explicated:

1. Assessing without an interview

2. Assessing with a court-ordered interview

3. Interview of the "incompetent" subject

4. Interviewing victims

Assessing Without an Interview

In some jurisdictions (e.g., Wisconsin), common procedure is for the evaluator to invite the inmate, respondent, or patient to participate in an interview as part of the evaluation, including to suggest to the subject that consultation with an attorney should be considered before deciding about participating in the interview. Almost no matter how the person comes to a decision (with one exception, concerning "incompetence," addressed below), the evaluator then accepts that decision. In other words, if the evaluation subject decides not to participate in an interview, no subject interview occurs within the evaluation. Likewise, only if the subject voluntarily participates (with full informed consent) in the interview does it happen.

Ethical concerns can be raised to the idea of conducting an assessment without the inclusion of the subject interview. (This concern can stem, for example, from an interpretation of Ethical Standard 7.02 in the APA's [1992] "Ethical Principles of Psychologists and Code of Conduct," though that standard uses the less than clear phrases "including personal interviews of the individual, when appropriate" and "when, despite reasonable efforts, such an examination is not feasible, psychologists clarify the impact." Psychiatrists can refer to the American Psychiatric Association's [2001] ethical standards that seem to mandate that an interview be conducted for every assessment.) The bottom-line conceptual argument appears to be that the evaluator cannot know what would have been said, and therefore cannot know what limits there were on the documented information and any conclusions drawn from that information. In its extreme, the argument is made that no conclusions can be made "to a reasonable degree of professional certainty" without interviewing the subject, such that being turned down by the subject effectively means no evaluation can be conducted (at least without a court ordering the subject's participation).

For consideration in response to this argument is that the courts are likely to be reticent to agree with the idea that a respondent can stop his commitment (i.e., stop all assessments of him) simply by refusing to be interviewed. Hence, although the above argument can be viewed as an ethical stance of potential merit, it does not appear to be one with which the courts will have much sympathy. Then again, clinicians' professional ethics do not need to be in keeping with what the judicial system might prefer.

In very strong contrast to ethical stance, however, comes the perspective that the interview actually potentially serves to interfere with effective data collection. From this viewpoint, the interview is, at best, rather irrelevant (given that sufficient historical documentation exists for certain things such as scoring the Psychopathy Checklist–Revised [PCL–R]), and at worst, the cause for decreased accuracy in our overall evaluation. Ethically, there is one piece of meta-analytic research evidence that it may be more appropriate not to conduct clinical interviews as part of assessments of risk (Grove, Zald, Lebow, Snitz, & Nelson, 2000). As those researchers concluded from their meta-analysis, "The only design variable that substantially influenced the relative efficacy of the mechanical- and clinical-prediction methods was whether the clinicians had access to a clinical interview. Alas, clinical predictions were outperformed by a substantially *greater* [emphasis added] margin when such data was [*sic*] available to the clinician" (p. 25). It would seem that evaluators' ethics should emphasize the striving for accuracy as of utmost importance. The (importantly, only single-study) indication that clinical interview information may actually lessen predictive accuracy (at least relative to purely mechanical predictive procedures, if not in more absolute terms) should therefore give us all reason to pause before assuming that evaluation interviews are always to be desired.

There is a third, less extreme ethical view, but still one that leans toward the perspective that interviews often do not matter that much specifically within the civil commitment context. This viewpoint emphasizes practical realities of civil commitment evaluations. For instance, most common diagnoses that serve as "mental abnormalities" are certain paraphilias and personality disorders. These conditions, unlike depressive and anxiety disorders, for instance, are long term in nature. Interview information will not be anywhere near as useful in determining the proper diagnoses of these conditions as will a good set of historical documents. (The one type of exception to this statement involves the handful of subjects who will tell evaluators of ongoing deviant fantasies and urges, an exception that is only in the direction of increasing the likelihood for opining that a subject meets commitment criteria.) Likewise, to the extent that actuarial instruments are used to assess subjects' recidivism risk, interview information is not relevant. Practically speaking, there are only three types of occasions where interview information might be of clear importance:

1. To obtain the subject's agreement to the accuracy of historical records

2. To obtain nondocumented information for the scoring of a PCL–R, which can often be addressed through collateral interviewing

3. Where the person has participated in some degree of sex offender treatment, and the records are not clear enough to describe the individual's potential benefit from that treatment

The first consideration is actually a one-sided argument, in that evaluators are not likely to accept a subject's denial of his recorded history to anywhere near the same degree as a subject's acknowledgment of it, a perspective that can be viewed as unfair to the subject (even if quite appropriate) unless this bias was explained in the informed consent process. The second consideration, concerning PCL–R scoring, can be addressed through collateral interviewing.

That leaves only the third consideration. Interview information can be of clear importance potentially to lower the actuarially assessed risk if the third consideration applies to a subject. If he has not gone through any treatment programming of relevance, however, there may be no real point to an interview.

An evaluator's ethical stance concerning the appropriateness of conducting an evaluation without a subject interview probably will reflect the degree to which the examiner views the interview information as important. Then again, evaluators can sidestep the issue altogether, and rely on the courts to address the issue in lieu of our doing so, as described in the next section.

Assessing With a Court-Ordered Interview

In some jurisdictions (e.g., Washington), the "standard" procedure has been for a subject to be asked if he wishes to participate in an evaluation interview, the subject declines, and a prosecutor obtains a court order (at the request of an evaluator) mandating that the subject so participate in an interview by the state's hired evaluator. Ethical concerns have been raised about this situation.

The main issue raised is that the individual is being coerced to participate in a process that is within the evaluator's purview. Of course, the whole sex offender civil commitment procedure is coerced under all but a handful of situations, but that procedure is being done to the individual through the courts, not specifically through what an evaluator does. The court-ordered interview situation may be different in that the evaluator now can realistically be seen as the enforcer (if not initiator) of a coerced process by the state against the individual. In support of that perspective, it is noteworthy that these court orders typically do not specify that the evaluator must conduct an interview, just that the commitment subject must participate in one.

The ethical basis for the concern about this "coercion" stems from an underlying theme within the "Specialty Guidelines for Forensic Psychologists" (Committee on Ethical Guidelines for Forensic Psychologists, 1991; hereafter referred to as the Forensic Guidelines). That theme is that each forensic professional should show a preference for guarding an individual's rights over society's need to protect itself.

For example, the Forensic Guidelines state:

1. in III.D., "Forensic psychologists have an obligation to understand the civil rights of parties . . . and manage their professional conduct in a manner that does not diminish or threaten those rights";

2. in IV.E.3., "After a psychologist has advised the subject of a clinical forensic evaluation of the intended uses of the evaluation and its work product, the psychologist may not use the evaluation work product for other purposes without explicit waiver to do so by the client or client's legal representative" (i.e., society's potential desire to use a work product beyond what the evaluator had advised the individual is not to be abided without specific approval);

3. in V.D., "Forensic psychologists do not provide professional forensic services to a defendant or to any party in, or in contemplation of, a legal proceeding prior to the individual's representation by counsel, except for persons judicially determined . . . to be handling their representation pro se . . . " (despite

the potential for getting more accurate information for the court during a time period more immediate to a relevant event, such as a crime for which the person might plead insanity); and

4. in VI.G.1., "Forensic psychologists . . . exercise extreme caution in preparing reports or offering testimony prior to the defendant's assertion of a mental state claim or the defendant's introduction of testimony regarding a mental condition . . . [and] avoid including statements from the defendant relating to the time period of the alleged offense" (despite the fact that society has a vested interest in learning what the defendant states happened).

If one accepts this underlying theme to the ethical standards, then using coercion to obtain an interview that is at least in part for the purpose of society's protection seems contrary to that principle.

There is a contrary ethical perspective. By accepting this type of work, the evaluator has a mandate to ensure that a complete set of information is available to the court before anything so drastic as a potentially long-term civil commitment occurs. The evaluation subject was already in a coerced process, that being involuntary commitment proceedings, such that the court order for an interview simply reflects the continuation of the same process. Ethical principles such as APA's 7.02 (1992) mentioned above can be read as suggesting that obtaining an interview is appropriate when information from an interview seems potentially relevant.

Depending on where an evaluator falls between the two extremes, evaluators may either specifically request of a prosecutor to go for such an order, or not to. Where an order already exists, the evaluator may still have competing options, as it has not typically been clear that such orders mandate the evaluator to conduct the interview.

As an aside, evaluators may wonder how they will talk in court about not having an interview. My experience is that, where a jury is involved, the evaluator may be precluded from stating anything about the respondent's declining an interview (under the concept that the information may be more prejudicial than probative). In that situation, literally nothing about this whole issue will need to be said (assuming the defense does not then raise the issue, in which a full explanation of the evaluator's thinking can be made). Being precluded from talking about this issue does not always occur in jury hearings, however, such that an evaluator needs to find out prior to testimony whether or not a court order exists against testimony concerning the respondent's declining the interview offer. If no such order exists, then the evaluator needs to be prepared to discuss the issue. To my experience, an order against such a disclosure never occurs in bench hearings, meaning that evaluators essentially always need to be prepared to discuss this topic completely.

One final word in this section: If a court order for the subject's mandated interview participation exists (through any means), evaluators should probably still fulfill their ethical duty to ensure that the subject is afforded all of the informed consent information he would typically get under more voluntary circumstances (e.g., a description of the purpose of the interview, of potential outcomes from the evaluation, that the conversation is not confidential, that a report will be written that is submitted to an attorney/court, etc.). His being coerced to participate in the interview does not suggest there should be any concomitant limitation to his being informed of everything he would have if he were participating voluntarily.

Interview of the "Incompetent" Subject

Except in Illinois and Wisconsin (where respondents are statutorily given criminal defendant rights), there may not be any legal concern about the degree to which commitment subjects are competent to give consent for an interview (i.e., competent to proceed in a legal matter). This, of course, does not necessarily mean that evaluators have no ethical issues to address under circumstances where such competence is questionable.

If, at the beginning of an interview involving "voluntary" participation, the evaluator strongly suspects that the subject clearly lacks an understanding of his legal situation, of what is happening to him, and of the potential costs (and benefits) to him for what he might say, should the evaluator proceed with the interview anyway? The Forensic Guidelines have something to say concerning this matter, under IV.E.:

> Forensic psychologists have an obligation to ensure that prospective clients are informed of their legal rights with respect to the anticipated forensic service, of the purposes of any evaluation, of the nature of procedures to be employed, of the intended uses of any product of their services, and of the party who has employed the forensic psychologist. . . . In situations where the client or party may not have the capacity to provide informed consent to services . . . the forensic psychologist provides reasonable notice to the client's legal representative of the nature of the anticipated forensic service before proceeding. If the client's legal representative objects to the evaluation, the forensic psychologist notifies the court issuing the order and responds as directed. (p. 659)

In practice, this appears to mean that the evaluator should have a conversation with the subject's attorney (or guardian, if such a person exists) before potentially proceeding. What is not addressed here is what to do if the legal representative effectively approves the interview despite the evaluator's concerns.

This has occurred once in my experience. I began the interview after spending a good deal of time trying to inform the subject of the relevant information, but after some minutes of questioning prematurely terminated the interview. It simply did not feel ethical to proceed despite the "legal authority" to do so. (The respondent demonstrated significant trouble concentrating, seemed to forget what the interview was for even just minutes after he had been told, and his answers were sometimes completely incongruous to the questions.) The whole series of events and findings were then described in the final evaluation report for the court to consider. In effect, the evaluation proceeded without an interview despite having been granted one by the subject.

The degree to which this was the proper method for handling this situation is a judgment I leave to the reader. The real point is that evaluators need to be cognizant that ethical issues of this type can arise.

Interviewing Victims

All of the aforementioned official ethical guidelines appear to be silent concerning the issue of when and how to decide which collaterally involved people to contact for an interview. For people such as parole/probation agents, treatment personnel, and so on, there are few ethical issues about contacting them beyond whether information to be shared is confidential and whether or not otherwise confidential information can nevertheless be shared with the evaluator. There is one classification of collateral interviews that regularly raises issues, however—that of victim interviews.

The ethical issue occurs within the context of an evaluator considering whether or not to contact someone who, typically years before, was the victim to one or more potentially traumatizing and humiliating sexual assaults. An evaluator does not often know the potential lasting effect of the assault on the victim, or what talking about the event(s) to a stranger (often by telephone) would do to the person. Victims can be retraumatized by reliving the experience through talking about it. On the other hand, some victims may welcome the chance to tell their stories to someone interested in every detail, and someone who can influence the potential freedoms the perpetrator will or will not have.

Putting the ethical issue succinctly, is it better to let the victims decide whether to participate or not by offering them the opportunity, or not to raise the issue with them at all given that raising it will traumatize some victims? There appear to be two regular ways in which this issue has been addressed.

The first is simply to take the stance that knowingly causing potential harm sets the limit to where information is sought. No victims are contacted despite the potentially useful information they may have. This perspective has the downside, besides potentially of not obtaining information of value, of disempowering victims who would prefer to make the choice themselves.

The second approach is to investigate if the prosecutor has already had contact with the victim. This sometimes occurs either because the prosecutor has already been exploring potential witnesses for the commitment hearing or because of statutory notification requirements. Either way, if the victim has already been contacted, then there may also be information available about whether or not the victim would wish to speak to the evaluator. If the answer comes back in the affirmative, then and only then does the evaluator make contact for an interview.

Other options certainly exist, such as using other, third parties to make initial inquiries about interview participation (e.g., a family caseworker who relates full informed consent disclosure). The real point is that this type of potential collateral contact raises ethical issues beyond virtually any other.

Communication Concerns

The remaining ethical concerns to be discussed are distinct from interviewing concerns. They instead fall under the rubric of how one communicates information to courts and attorneys.

Effectively Defining Legal Terms

Evaluators are not officially in the position of determining the legal meaning of statutory terms. At the same time, to conduct a civil commitment assessment, one needs to have some idea, even if a personal guess, about what the terms mean. Even professionals who avoid giving opinions about the ultimate commitment criteria issues have effectively interpreted the statutory terms through the clinicians' selection of what information is offered to the court. (The Forensic Guidelines, in VII.F., state that "forensic psychologists are prepared to explain the relationship between their expert testimony and the legal issues and facts of an instant case," p. 665, a standard not easily addressed if one has no idea about any such relationship.) Certainly, any ultimate opinions speak to an examiner's understanding of what the terms may mean.

One of the ethical issues that arises here relates to the fact that judges and jurors can easily be swayed by the evaluators' explicit or implicit definitions of statutory terms. This does not mean that judges and jurors will necessarily adopt evaluators' definitions, but the judgments the triers of fact make can be in response to an evaluator's definitions even when the evaluator's concepts are not adopted. In other words, evaluators probably have more influence over the legal determination of the proper interpretation of statutory terms than examiners might wish or view as appropriate.

This does not seem to fit with ethical concerns about staying within professional boundaries and the limits of our expertise. At the same time, it may be naïve to believe this process does not occur or that we can stop it from happening.

There appear to be two main ways evaluators attempt to minimize this "unwanted" influence. The first is to consult with other professionals, both legally and clinically trained, concerning the proper interpretation of statutory terms. In this way, at least the views espoused by the evaluator during testimony do not reflect simply that examiner's view on the world.

The second approach is for the evaluator explicitly to emphasize a lack of legal expertise and that the interpretation of statutory concepts was solely for the purpose of conducting the examination and may not at all reflect the proper legal interpretation. This latter approach is very much in keeping with APA Ethical Standard 1.04 (1992) and Forensic Guidelines III.B, both concerning being clear about boundaries of competence. In that sense, this approach can be viewed as very ethical. At the same time, it can be argued that simply making these statements may not significantly alter the degree to which judges and jurors are influenced by the perspectives offered.

Explaining All of the Interpretive
Caveats and Limitations to Numerical Information

The general problem with the last approach above, and to be addressed here as well, is that it is not at all clear that triers of fact comprehend well all of the caveats to interpreting information they are offered. Another place where this issue arises is in the explanations of actuarial risk assessment instrumentation results.

If one were to enumerate all of the caveats to any single research result (concerning an actuarial instrument or anything else), the list would be longer than many clinicians would even know to cite. For instance, there would be issues related to the reliability of each measure used, to the sample selection compared to the presumed population, what we actually do not know about the population (both of the latter for generalizability issues), the meaningfulness of the outcome measure (e.g., reconviction rates vs. reoffending rates), the degree to which cross-validation studies do not directly match the original work in sample selection, scoring procedures, reliability of measures, recidivism operationalization, jurisdictional practice differences, and so on.

There would also be the statistical issues to explain, such as the power of the tests, the appropriateness for the tests both for the measure's development (e.g., for prediction purposes) and for how the measure is being employed (e.g., for the assessment of risk), how statistical significance may or may not represent clinically meaningful results, and the proper interpretation of multiple statistical indices ranging from positive predictive power to receiver operator characteristics (ROCs). There is almost no limit to the degree to which limits can be described, depending on the detail to which one wishes to give attention.

This is all true of any applied science. Medical researchers have to generalize a medication's effect from groups of individuals to other individuals never tested. The design of rocket components needs to include specifications of the degree of error that is acceptable. In all cases, scientists attempt to comprehend sampling and statistical details through replications of original findings.

There is clearly some point at which explanation of limitations to interpretation becomes more confusing than helpful to judges and jurors. On the other hand, this situation should not serve as justification for ignoring obvious caveats necessary for proper interpretation of information offered, either.

Whereas finding the proper balance between these two extremes is left to the reader, the application to a couple of areas of concern specific to current civil commitment evaluation procedures can be highlighted. The foremost appears to be in explaining what the actuarial instruments measure. Offering unexplained "associated risk percentages" for a subject's scale score without further clarification seems highly inappropriate. Adding the distinction between official criminal justice outcomes (reconviction or rearrest) and reoffending, with some discussion about relative follow-up time periods, also seems necessary. Some discussions of potential error in these percentages should at least be mentioned, described in terms of "averaged over a range" or "give or take a range called a confidence interval" depending on the context. This does not mean that the judges or jurors will remember all of the caveats to interpreting the percentages. It just means that the evaluator will have appropriately described expressed limitations to the interpretation of information given to the court.

A second area pertains to psychological test results, such as from the PCL–R. Offering a subject's PCL–R score without some degree of interpretation will have no meaning to triers of fact. On the other hand, discussing the ins and outs of standard errors of measurement, interrater reliability coefficients, sampling variations, and so forth will likely lose everyone's attention and their comprehension of important information. Finding a simple way to summarize the meaning of a score without underplaying its potential error would seem to be a useful formula for presentation of PCL–R results. For instance, statements could be made such as the following: "My PCL–R score for Mr. X of 21 is interpreted as meaning it is highly likely that other trained raters would score him somewhere between 18 and 24. Since the complete range of these scores is below 25, the research-based threshold I used in determining the presence or absence of a 'high degree of psychopathy,' I feel quite confident that Mr. X should be considered as not showing that risk factor." Limitation to the evaluator's scoring is acknowledged while a clear overall interpretation is still offered.

Addressing Other Expert Witness Misstatements

The sex offender civil commitment hearing is often the setting for a "battle of experts" due to the type of testimony needed to address the commitment prongs. Within this context, there are various times when one evaluator will disagree with the findings of another. The Forensic Guidelines (in VII.B.) indicate that "when evaluating or commenting upon the professional work product or qualifications of another expert or party to a legal proceeding, forensic psychologists represent their professional disagreements with reference to a fair and accurate evaluation of the data, theories, standards, and opinions of the other expert or party" (p. 664). This guideline describes how to make comment on another evaluator's work, but not when to do so.

One perspective in this regard is that commenting on professional differences is entering into the adversarial process of the courtroom. This view suggests that engaging in such a role is beyond what the evaluator should do. As an "expert to the court" (Forensic Guidelines, p. 664), such commentary should be left to the attorneys arguing their respective sides.

The opposite viewpoint is that each evaluator has an ethical responsibility to ensure that the court has the most accurate information on which to make its judgment. Allowing inaccurate statements from other evaluators' testimony to stand unchallenged is to shirk one's responsibility in this regard.

There may not be a correct answer here about when and when not to make comments about other experts' testimony. Two concepts seem potentially useful in making this decision, though. The first is that evaluators should keep in mind that their proper role in the courtroom is not directly related to the outcome of the case. It is to give technical information to the court. If comments about another expert's testimony are beyond the issue of technical information clarification, then the comments probably should not be made. A second caveat in addressing this topic is that one's emotional reaction to aspects of other experts' testimony may not be the best guide for deciding when to make comments. A more thought-out philosophical perspective, one that carries over from case to case, is probably more reflective of a true ethical stance, rather than simply reacting to whatever you happen to be emotionally invested in at the moment.

A Final Comment

In the introduction to this book, there was discussion about different ethical stances professionals could take relative to their feelings about the sex offender civil commitment laws and clinicians' potential participation in the implementation of these laws. In a sense, this book has come full circle, both starting off with and ending with that central ethical issue. As stated in the introduction, I expect that there was little in this book that convinced anyone previously against these laws to change from that stance. Likewise, probably nothing offered in this book dissuaded someone who previously took a more participatory position concerning the implementation of these laws. This book was, of course, designed for neither purpose.

Instead, I hope that people interested in learning about the current status of the sex offender civil commitment evaluative process obtained what they sought. At least if the laws are going to exist and going to be implemented, people should have a source for relevant statutory descriptions, diagnostic guidelines, procedural recommendations, research findings, and ethical concerns. It is hoped this book has served that purpose for the reader.

Appendix A

Note from the author: The following represents a recommended segment of a civil commitment evaluation interview. Although the formal scoring system suggested by the interview's developers is herein contained, the meaningfulness of different overall scores is not yet determined through research. Hence, the suggestion is to use the questions as part of assessment interviews, but not to use the scoring system for anything beyond a shorthand method of assessing the quality of a subject's answers.

Relapse Prevention Interview

Ruth Mann, Richard Beckett,
Dawn Fisher, and David Thornton

Basic Principles of Scoring

Each response is scored from 0 to 2 according to whether the offender's response meets certain conditions. It is obviously not possible for this scoring guide to account for all possible responses. Therefore, if in doubt, please decide which of the following best describes the offender's response:

> The offender refuses to recognize risk or the need to develop coping strategies. He shows no understanding of relapse prevention concepts whatsoever.

The offender does not refuse to acknowledge risk and has some understanding of relapse prevention issues, but this is general or unsophisticated and could do with further development.

The offender has a clear and appropriate understanding of his offending behavior, risk factors, and relapse prevention concepts and has developed well-thought-out, realistic, and workable coping strategies.

Introduce these questions with the following words:

From the work that has been done with people who commit sexual offenses, it is known that they go through several stages before an offense can happen. It will be easier for you to avoid offending in the future if you are aware of these stages, and the factors that put you at risk, and you have worked out ways of controlling them. This interview is to see how good you are at doing that.

Think about the sexual offense(s) you have committed and then answer the following questions. Even if you do not believe you would be at risk of offending again, consider the factors that would be important if you were.

You may wish to allot a time limit for each answer to be produced.

1a. What feelings or moods would put you at risk of sexual offending again? Describe at least two different moods that would put you at risk.

Answer:

Q1a.	Score	Description
	0	Identified no moods.
	1	Answered the question but with reference only to his past offending or gave an answer that is not a mood (e.g., "My mother"). Identified just one distinct mood. Include cases who use different words that describe basically the same emotion (e.g., "anger, rage, frustration").
	2	Identified more than one distinct emotion.

1b. How will you cope with such feelings or moods in the future? Describe at least two ways of coping with them that you could use to reduce the risk of your reoffending.

Answer:

Q1b.	Score	Description
	0	Identified no coping strategies. Include those who discount the possibility of a mood recurring or who say "things are different now." Also score 0 for strategies that would put the offender at higher risk (e.g., "I would go for a walk along the canal").

	1	Identified only oversimplified or unconvincing strategies that are poorly thought-out, unlikely to happen, or unlikely to work (e.g., "I'll settle down and meet a nice girl"). Also only score 1 for offenders who mention only avoidance strategies (e.g., "I would keep away from children") or only escape strategies (e.g., "I would leave right away").
	2	Identified more than one strategy that is well thought-out, realistic, and workable, at least one of which should be a cognitive strategy.

2a. What thoughts, including sexual thoughts or fantasies, would put you at risk of sexual offending? Describe at least two different thoughts.

Answer:

Q2a.	Score	Description
	0	Identified no high-risk thoughts.
	1	Identified one distinct high-risk thought or gave as an answer a risk factor that is not a thought (e.g., "drunk"). Identified more than one thought but did not acknowledge the role of deviant sexual fantasy in his offending.
	2	Identified more than one distinct thought, including deviant sexual fantasy.

2b. How would you cope with such thoughts in the future? Describe at least two different ways of coping with such thoughts that you could use to reduce the risk of their leading to a sexual offense.

Answer:

Q2b	Score	Description
	0	Identified no coping strategies. Include those who discount the possibility of the thought recurring or who say that "things are different now." Also score 0 for strategies that would put the offender at higher risk ("I would go for a walk along the canal").
	1	Identified only oversimplified or unconvincing strategies that are poorly thought-out, unlikely to happen, or unlikely to work (e.g., "I'll settle down and meet a nice girl"). Also only score 1 for offenders who mention only avoidance strategies (e.g., "I would keep away from children") or only escape strategies (e.g., "I would leave right away").
	2	Identified more than one strategy that is well thought-out, realistic, and workable, at least one of which should be a cognitive strategy.

3a. What events might make you more likely to have feelings or thoughts that put you at risk of offending. Describe at least two different events.

Answer:

Q3a.	Score	Description
	0	Identified no events.
	1	Gave an answer that is a risk factor but not an event or that relates to his past behavior but not his future (e.g., "If a child is provocative—but this wouldn't affect me now"). Identified just one distinct event or type of event.
	2	Identified more than one distinct event or type of event.

3b. How would you cope with such events in the future? Describe at least two different ways of coping with each event that you could use to reduce the risk of their leading to a sexual offense.

Answer:

Q3b.	Score	Description
	0	Identified no coping strategies. Include those who discount the possibility of the event recurring or say that "things are different now." Also score 0 for strategies that would put the offender at higher risk (e.g., "I would go for a walk along the canal").
	1	Identified only oversimplified or unconvincing strategies that are poorly thought-out, unlikely to happen, or unlikely to work (e.g., "I'll settle down and meet a nice girl"). Also only score 1 for offenders who mention only avoidance strategies (e.g., "I would keep away from children") or only escape strategies (e.g., "I would leave right away").
	2	Identified more than one strategy that is well thought-out, realistic, and workable, at least one of which should be a cognitive strategy.

4a. In what situations are you most likely to offend? What situations or places should you avoid? Describe at least two situations or places.

Answer:

Q4a.	Score	Description
	0	Identified no high-risk situations.
	1	Gave an answer that is not a situation or that is not well defined (e.g., "stressful situations"). Identified just one distinct situation or type of situation (e.g., "babysitting"). (Note: Alcohol counts as a situation.)
	2	Identified more than one distinct situation or type of situation.

4b. How would you cope if you were in these situations or places in the future? Describe at least two different ways of coping that you could use to reduce the risk of each situation leading to a sexual offense.

Answer:

Q4b.	Score	Description
	0	Identified no coping strategies. Include those who discount the possibility of the event recurring or say that "things are different now." Also score 0 for strategies that would put the offender at higher risk (e.g., "I would go for a walk along the canal").
	1	Identified only oversimplified or unconvincing strategies that are poorly thought-out, unlikely to happen, or unlikely to work (e.g., "I'll settle down and meet a nice girl"). Also only score 1 for offenders who mention only avoidance strategies (e.g., "I would keep away from children") or only escape strategies (e.g., "I would leave right away").
	2	Identified more than one strategy that is well thought-out, realistic, and workable, at least one of which should be a cognitive strategy.

5a. Many offenders go to considerable effort to set up a situation in which they can offend. How did you set up your offense situation(s)? Describe at least two different methods that you have used to set up a situation in which you could offend.

Answer:

Q5a.	Score	Description
	0	Denied that the offense was set up in any way ("It just happened") or portrayed the offense as entirely opportunistic.
	1	Described one behavior that set up the offense situation.
	2	Described at least two separate behaviors that were used to set up the offense situation.

5b. What would be the warning signs that you were setting up another situation where you could offend? Describe at least two different warning signs.

Answer:

Q5b.	Score	Description
	0	Denied that offending is planned or [said] that it is unlikely to happen again.
	1	Identified only completely implausible, unrealistic, or overly inclusive warning signs (e.g., "being alone") or identified warning signs but denied the likelihood of their occurring or identified only one sign.
	2	Identified more than one warning sign.

6a. What sort of person would be most at risk from you? Describe this person in terms of looks, personality, age, attitudes, and so on.

Answer:

Q6a.	Score	Description
	0	Denied that any person is at risk or could not give any description.
	1	Gave a limited or vague description ("a woman") or a description that does not tie with his offending (e.g., offender against children claims that adults are at risk from him) or the description is reluctant and plays down risk (e.g., "Possibly women in their 20s but basically I think I am safe with anyone now").
	2	Described at least one specific personal characteristic other than age or gender and in clear detail (e.g., "6- to 8-year-old girls with blond hair and big eyes").

6b. How would you cope if on meeting someone you began to have thoughts or ideas about offending? Describe at least two different ways of coping that you could use to reduce the risk of your committing a sexual offense.

Answer:

Q6b.	Score	Description
	0	Identified no coping strategies. Include those who discount the possibility of the event recurring or say that "things are different now." Also score 0 for strategies that would put the offender at higher risk (e.g., "I would go for a walk along the canal").
	1	Identified only oversimplified or unconvincing strategies that are poorly thought-out, unlikely to happen, or unlikely to work (e.g., "I'll settle down and meet a nice girl"). Also only score 1 for offenders who mention only avoidance strategies (e.g., "I would keep away from children") or only escape strategies (e.g., "I would leave right away").
	2	Identified more than one strategy that is well thought-out, realistic, and workable, at least one of which should be a cognitive strategy.

7a. How might other people know you are at risk? Describe at least two different things they might see or observe.

Answer:

Q7a.	Score	Description
	0	Denied any future risk or listed no signs.
	1	Did not deny risk but listed no signs or completely implausible signs (e.g., "I would tell the police") or denied that others would be able to see anything—only he would know.
	2	Listed one sign or more.

7b. What could you do to obtain help if you were at risk of offending again? Describe at least two things you could do.

Answer:

Q7b.	Score	Description
	0	Had no ideas of ways to obtain help or denied any need for help.
	1	Identified an unspecified source of help only (i.e., "I'd talk to someone") or referred to people with whom he has not made contact (e.g., "I'd join a support group").
	2	Listed more than one specific source of help with which he has already established contact.

8. Who have you told fully about your past offending and enlisted to help you in preventing yourself from reoffending?

Answer:

Q8.	Score	Description
	0	Could not identify anyone to tell if worried or denied possibility of risk.
	1	Identified only one person or people with whom he has not established contact (e.g., "I would have found a group so I could tell them").
	2	Identified two or more people with whom he has established contact.

9a. Thinking about the excuses or justifications you used to give yourself permission to offend, describe at least two of them.

Answer:

Q9a.	Score	Description
	0	Identified no distortions or excuses or identified statements that are not distortions or excuses or that he does not understand as being such.
	1	Identified one or two distortions or excuses.
	2	Identified more than two distortions or excuses for offending.

9b. How would you respond to such thoughts in the future. Describe at least two things you could say to yourself or do to stop this kind of thinking leading to sexual offending.

Answer:

Q9b.	Score	Description
	0	Gave no strategy for responding to distortions or did not identify distortions.
	1	Described a vague strategy but without details about how he would put it into practice (e.g., "I'd get it out of my head"; "I'd talk to somebody") or described one sophisticated strategy only or described strategies that rely exclusively on others. Score 1 for a response of "Remind myself of the consequences" as a sole strategy.
	2	Described more than one sophisticated cognitive strategy, such as disrupting the thought, reminding himself of the consequences of offending, using an aversive visual image. And repeating a phase that will motivate him to avoid offending. Strategies are self-reliant and do not depend on others.

10a. Indicate on a scale of 0 to 10 the likelihood of you committing a sexual offense in the future (0 is not likely at all, 10 is extremely likely). What number best describes your risk?

Answer:

Q10a	Score is the number stated. In scoring the answer, it is important to make a distinction between seeing self at no risk (i.e., scoring 0) and seeing self at some risk (i.e., scoring 1-10). It is not possible to make judgments purely on the number given without taking the respondent's explanation into account. See his answer to Question 10b.

10b. Please explain why you have given yourself this rating.

Answer:

Relapse Prevention Interview Score Sheet

Question	Score	Comments
1a		
1b		
2a		
2b		
3a		
3b		
4a		
4b		
5a		
5b		
6a		
6b		
7a		
7b		
8		
9a		
9b		
10a		

Cluster	Components	Total
Recognition of risk factors	1a + 2a + 3a + 4a + 5b + 6a + 7a + 9a	
Identification of coping strategies	1b + 2b + 3b + 4b + 6b + 7b + 8 + 9b	
Acknowledgment of planning	5a	
(Self) Estimated level of risk	10a	

Appendix B

Templates for Segments of Precommitment Forms and Reports

The following templates, described in Chapters 2 and 8, are designed to assist evaluators both in obtaining informed consent and in the writing of reports. These templates include sentences and paragraphs that cover the usual multitude of findings in civil commitment assessments. Evaluators can employ these templates simply by deleting or altering the sections not applicable to a given subject, and then adding other more unique descriptions of the subject, if any.

Informed Consent Form

Date:

From: [*evaluator name, degree*]

You are being evaluated concerning a possible commitment under State Statute # [*fill in the statute under which the assessment is being done*] as a potentially [*"Sexually Violent Predator," "Sexually Violent Person," or whatever the proper legal phrase*]. The person above has been assigned [*hired*] to perform this evaluation. In doing so, he [*she*] is employed by [*the name or group for whom the evaluator works*]. He is not working specifically for you and you are not his primary client. Similarly, he is also not working against you. His responsibility is to review your case with the mission of being as objective as possible, and submit a report to [*the court, the defense attorney, the Attorney General's Office, or whomever else*] concerning whether or not you meet criteria to be committed under State Statute #.

His State Statute # assessments (1) always consist of reviewing the person's records from the department that held him previously (usually the Department of

Corrections), (2) typically involve a telephone conversation with the person's probation/parole officer, (3) may include telephone conversations with previous treatment personnel, and will, if the person agrees to participate, include (4) an interview with the person. [*If there are other procedures, such as physiological and/or psychological testing, those would also be listed here.*] It is your right to choose to participate or not with the interview, and it is recommended you speak with your attorney about this matter if you have not already done so.

The interview will take about four hours [*or whatever is true for you*] to complete, during which you will be asked many questions both of a general and very personal nature. You can choose to participate in the interview, but keep the right to refuse to answer certain types of questions if you wish. Please be aware that the interview will not be confidential (private) in that what you say will likely be repeated in [*the evaluator's report to the court and in*] future testimony if required. The interview is your opportunity to present information for yourself and to provide evidence or other argument on your behalf. Please be aware that the evaluator does not interpret your decision to participate or not to participate in the evaluation. He is aware that such decisions often reflect legal advice.

This evaluation must be conducted according to law, with or without your active participation, using the information available to the examiner. You may wish at this time to make your own information available, or you may wait until possible later court hearings to argue your position.

I, _____, as of today's date ____/____/____, have decided:

(a) _____ to participate in the interview

(b) _____ not to participate in the interview.

Witnessed by: _____ this date of ____/____/____.

Diagnostic Segment

Based on all of the information available to this examiner, Mr. X appears to meet criteria for the following psychiatric conditions:

Axis I: Pedophilia, sexually attracted to [*males, females, both males and females*], [*nonexclusive, exclusive*]

    Paraphilia, Not Otherwise Specified, Nonconsent

    Sexual Disorder Not Otherwise Specified

    Alcohol Abuse/Dependence

    Polysubstance Dependence

Axis II: Antisocial Personality Disorder

    Personality Disorder, Not Otherwise Specified, with antisocial features

    Borderline Personality Disorder, with antisocial features

The first disorder listed, Pedophilia, means that the person experiences recurrent and intense fantasies, urges, and/or behavior involving sexual arousal to minor children. In Mr. X's case, this condition exists while he also shows sexual arousal to adults (this latter characteristic being the meaning of the term "nonexclusive" above). Given that this condition is so related to Mr. X's sexual offending, and given that people with this condition show a tendency toward having sexual contact with minor children, this examiner came to the opinion that this disorder predisposes Mr. X toward committing a sexually violent act as defined by State Statute #.

The first disorder listed, Paraphilia, Not Otherwise Specified, means that the person experiences recurrent and intense fantasies, urges, and/or behavior involving sexual arousal to certain inappropriate stimuli. In Mr. X's case, his deviant sexual arousal is to nonconsenting interactions with others. Given that this condition is so related to Mr. X's sexual offending, and given that people with this condition show a tendency toward having nonconsensual sexual contact with others, this examiner came to the opinion that this disorder predisposes Mr. X toward committing a sexually violent act as defined by State Statute #.

The first disorder listed, Sexual Disorder Not Otherwise Specified (NOS), means that the person experiences a sexual disturbance that does not meet certain other criteria. In Mr. X's case, his Sexual Disorder NOS is indicated by his distress about, and the social impairment caused by, his repetitive pattern of very frequent sexual relationships involving a succession of other people who are experienced by him only as things to be used. Mr. X has described his own view of this condition various times when he has labeled himself as being a "sex addict." Given that this condition is so related to Mr. X's sexual offending and that people with this condition show a tendency toward having sexual contact with a rather indiscriminate set of people (that for the respondent includes both legal and illegal sexual contacts), this examiner came to the opinion that this disorder predisposes Mr. X toward committing a sexually violent act as defined by State Statute #.

The next condition listed, Alcohol Dependence, means that (1) Mr. X has demonstrated an ongoing lack of control of alcohol consumption to the point that it has negatively affected his life, (2) he suffers from physiological effects called tolerance and/or withdrawal (often thought of as representing an addiction), and (3) his recent nondrinking is largely due to his being incarcerated, rather than significant control of himself. Although this is a standard mental abnormality in the current psychiatric listing of disorders, this examiner came to the opinion that this disorder does not, by itself, predispose Mr. X to commit sexually violent acts as defined by State Statute #.

The other two disorders listed concerning substance abuse (marijuana and cocaine) are similar to his alcohol problem except that he does not seem to suffer the same degree of impairment or physical effects from his use of these substances. Again, this examiner came to the opinion that these disorders do not, by themselves, predispose Mr. X to commit sexually violent acts as defined by State Statute #.

While Alcohol Abuse/Dependence and Polysubstance Dependence may not by themselves predispose an individual to engage in acts of sexual violence, they often are associated with decreased behavioral self-control, decreased inhibition of socially acceptable actions, and a decreased ability to act responsibly or to take responsibility for one's actions. From Mr. X's history, these disorders clearly appear to have played such a facilitating role in his acts of sexual violence, as defined by State Statute #.

The diagnosed condition listed above for Mr. X, Antisocial Personality Disorder, implies that the person suffers from a long-term maladaptive pattern of behavior involving a disregard for and violation of the rights of others, a pattern that began by adolescence and has continued through current adult life. In Mr. X's case, his Antisocial Personality Disorder is periodically exhibited through failure to conform to social norms, aggressiveness, impulsivity, irresponsibility, and a lack of remorse. This pattern is seen as including his repetitive sexually assaultive behaviors, a pattern that is also seen as ongoing. From this perspective, this examiner came to the opinion that this mental condition predisposes Mr. X to engage in acts of sexual violence, as defined by State Statute #, and represents a mental abnormality as defined by that statute.

On the other hand, the last disorder listed above for Mr. X, Personality Disorder, Not Otherwise Specified, with antisocial features, does not appear to meet that criterion. In general, the condition called a Personality Disorder implies that the person suffers from a long-term maladaptive pattern of behavior and/or inner experience that interferes with social functioning, a pattern that began by late adolescence and has continued through current adult life. In Mr. X's case, his Personality Disorder has been exhibited through a persistent disregard for (1) rules and laws imposed on him, (2) the rights of other people, and (3) the truth. This pattern has been shown by him in some rather extreme ways, but apparently only once through sexually assaultive behavior. From this perspective, this examiner came to the opinion that this mental condition does not predispose Mr. X to engage in acts of sexual violence, as defined by State Statute #.

On the other hand, the last disorder listed above for Mr. X, Borderline Personality Disorder, with antisocial features, does appear to meet that criterion. In general, the condition called Borderline Personality Disorder implies that the person suffers from a long-term maladaptive pattern of behavior involving instability in his mood, interpersonal relationships, and self-image, a pattern that began by adolescence and has continued through current adult life. In Mr. X's case, his Borderline Personality Disorder is periodically exhibited through feelings of rage and great feelings of pain both about himself and from his interpersonal relationships. Mr. X's historical and more recent expressions of these feelings have been problematic for himself and hurtful to others, including sexual assaultiveness. From this perspective, this examiner came to the opinion that this mental condition predisposes Mr. X to engage in acts of sexual violence, as defined by State Statute #.

Actuarial Instrument Time and Legal Status Limitations Template

In this section of the risk assessment, the examiner employs knowledge gained from the professional research relevant to the assessment of sexual recidivism risk by previously convicted sex offenders. The most effective starting point in this portion of the analysis stems from screening tools that employ an actuarial method for estimating the person's degree of sexual recidivism risk. Three instruments were employed in that regard for this case: (1) the Rapid Risk Assessment for Sex Offender Recidivism (RRASOR), (2) the Static-99, and (3) the Minnesota Sex Offender Screening Tool–Revised (MnSOST–R).

A summary of this respondent's results follows. In reviewing this summary, the reader should be aware that all of these risk assessment instruments assess the likelihood for someone to be caught and legally processed (either by rearrest or reconviction) for a new sexual offense within a specified time frame. This examiner's understanding of State Statute #, however, is that the degree of risk relevant to the law does not necessarily involve the person's getting legally processed for a new sexual offense, or even caught for the new offense, but simply the redoing of such an act. Likewise, the time frame specified by these instruments in their assessments of risk is not necessarily in keeping with this examiner's understanding of the law. This examiner's understanding is that the law contains no specified time frame, meaning that the assessment herein is to look at the degree of risk the person represents over his remaining lifetime. From that perspective, this examiner believes that the risk assessment instruments potentially underestimate the degree of sexual reoffense risk represented by the respondent specifically within the context of a State Statute # evaluation.

The reader should also be aware that risk percentages listed below simply represent averaged figures. Proper interpretation of these percentages includes the consideration of a "plus or minus" estimation of possible error.

Given the caveats in the previous paragraphs, the following results are offered:

1. RRASOR: The respondent scored 5 on a scale that theoretically goes from 0 to 6 with 6 at the high end of risk, though almost no one is ever found scoring a 6 on that instrument. This means that this respondent's score represents the highest risk likelihood the instrument measures. A score of 5 on the RRASOR is associated statistically with about a 50% likelihood for being reconvicted for a new sexual offense within 5 years postincarceration, and about a 73% likelihood for being reconvicted of a new sexual offense within 10 years postrelease from incarceration.

2. Static-99: Mr. X scored a 7 on a scale that theoretically ranges from 0 to 12 with 12 at the high end of risk, though to this examiner's knowledge no one has ever been known to score 11 or 12 on that instrument. The respondent's score statistically corresponds with about a 39% likelihood for being reconvicted of a new sexual offense within 5 years postincarceration, and a 54% likelihood for being reconvicted of a new sexual offense within 16 years postrelease from incarceration. The fact that these percentages are lower than those estimated by the RRASOR should be interpreted only within the context that these percentages for the Static-99 are as high as this instrument measures.

3. MnSOST–R: The score on this instrument obtained by Mr. X was a +10, this score corresponding to what has been termed the high-risk range assessed by this scale. The score of +10 is statistically associated with a

likelihood for being rearrested for a new sexual offense within a 6-year period postincarceration of between 54% and 70%, depending on an assumption of what is called the base rate for sexual recidivism of this type. This examiner believes the risk figure of 54% (for 6-year rearrest for a new sexual offense) is clearly the more conservative and appropriate interpretation for the respondent's score, given this examiner's understanding of the proper base rate assumption.

Appendix C

Sample Precommitment Evaluation Report

The following is a sample of a precommitment evaluation report, showing the integration of both report templates in Appendix B and the various other topics that need to be addressed. Certain dates, locations, and the relevant state statute number were omitted for purposes of confidentiality of the individual.

State Statute # Evaluation

Name: T., S. B.

DOC #:   0000001

Date of Report: [*date*]

Reason for This Report

Mr. S. B. T. is a 46-year-old (DOB = date), divorced, White male who was referred for an evaluation for possible commitment under State Statute # [*fill in the statute under which the assessment is being done*] of the [*relevant state statutes*]. Probable cause for that commitment had been found on [*date*], with this new evaluation being ordered prior to the detainee's final commitment trial. This report summarizes the findings in this regard.

Evaluation Procedures

This examiner reviewed all of Mr. T.'s Department of Corrections (DOC) records made available to this examiner. These included materials describing the following types of information concerning Mr. T.: (a) demographic, (b) legal, (c) DOC placement during his years of incarceration, (d) his history under supervision, (e) family, (f) education, (g) vocational, (h) social, (i) mental status including formal diagnoses, (j) substance use, (k) sexual, (l) treatment including treatment outcome, and (m) discharge plans.

Mr. T. was asked to participate in an interview by this examiner as part of this evaluation. As part of that request, Mr. T. was informed

a. of the purpose of the interview,

b. of the potential consequences to him from the evaluation,

c. that nothing he said during the interview was confidential from the [*relevant prosecutor's office*] or the court,

d. that he had a right not to answer the examiner's questions or even participate in the interview,

e. that his decision whether or not to participate in the interview would not be interpreted in a psychological way by the examiner (i.e., declining to participate would not be interpreted as meaning he was hiding something), and

f. that the examiner would be writing a report to the [*relevant prosecutor's office*] that would likely be passed on to the court concerning Mr. T. irrelevant of the degree to which the subject participated in the interview.

Mr. T. expressed that he understood these things, and this examiner concluded that the respondent was making a knowing, voluntary, and willing acknowledgment of the above. The respondent stated he would participate in the interview and did so on [*date*] at the [*name of facility*]. This interview lasted a period of about 3.25 hours.

This examiner conducted a professional consultation simultaneously with Drs. [*names of consultants*] concerning the findings of this evaluation on [*date*]. That consultation was in person, and lasted for about 15 minutes.

Finally, this evaluator used all available information to score Mr. T. on the following inventories: (1) the Rapid Risk Assessment for Sex Offender Recidivism (RRASOR), (2) the Static-99, (3) the Minnesota Sex Offender Screening Tool–Revised (MnSOST–R), and (4) the Psychopathy Checklist–Revised (PCL–R).

Evaluation Findings

Mr. T.'s presentation during his evaluation interview was of a relaxed, low average intelligence individual who liked to brag, exaggerate, and tell stories. His demeanor throughout the interview was calm beyond what might have been expected under the circumstances. He frequently painted the picture of himself as a party wronged by the judicial system, the police, or alleged victims. Mr. T.'s comments concerning his sexual offense arrests and convictions always involved either denying the underlying behavior completely or minimizing what transpired as compared to recorded claims. Statements of other past activities were periodically beyond believable to this examiner. No signs of a disorder of thought or affect were noted. The respondent's answers to questions were always in keeping with the content of the question, albeit not always in apparent keeping with the truth.

The Issue of Mental Abnormality (as defined by State Statute #)

Based on all of the information available to this examiner, Mr. T. appears to be suffering from the following psychiatric conditions:

Axis I: Pedophilia, sexually attracted to females, nonexclusive

Paraphilia, Not Otherwise Specified (NOS), Telephone Scatologia

Axis II: Antisocial Personality Disorder with borderline features

The first disorder listed, Pedophilia, means that the person experiences recurrent and intense fantasies, urges, and/or behavior involving sexual arousal to minor children. In Mr. T.'s case, this condition exists while he also shows sexual arousal to adults (this latter factor being the meaning of the term "nonexclusive" above). Given that this condition is so related to Mr. T.'s sexual offense, and given that people with this condition show a tendency toward having sexual contact with minor children, this examiner concluded that this disorder predisposes Mr. T. toward committing a sexually violent act as defined by State Statute #.

The next disorder listed, Paraphilia, Not Otherwise Specified, means that the person experiences recurrent and intense fantasies, urges, and/or behavior involving sexual arousal to certain inappropriate stimuli. In Mr. T.'s case, his deviant sexual arousal is to making lewd telephone calls to strangers. This condition does not appear related to Mr. T.'s committing sexually violent offenses. Therefore, this examiner concluded that this disorder does not predispose Mr. T. toward committing a sexually violent act as defined by State Statute #.

The last diagnosed condition listed above for Mr. T., Antisocial Personality Disorder, implies that the person suffers from a long-term maladaptive pattern of behavior involving a disregard for and violation of the rights of others, a pattern that began in childhood and has continued through current adult life. In Mr. T.'s case, his Antisocial Personality Disorder is periodically exhibited through failure to conform to social norms, repeated lying, impulsivity, irresponsibility, and a lack of remorse. This pattern is seen as including his repetitive sexually assaultive behaviors, a pattern that is also seen as ongoing. From this perspective, this examiner concluded that this mental condition predisposes Mr. T. to engage in acts of sexual violence, as defined by State Statute #, and represents a mental abnormality as defined by that statute.

The Issue of Dangerousness (as defined by State Statute #)

To assess the potential risk Mr. T. poses for committing a sexually violent act in the future, this examiner looked at three main types of factors. The first is the set of characteristics that professional research has demonstrated to be predictive of future sexually violent acts by previously convicted sex offenders (listed below as "risk factors"). The second is the effectiveness of treatment that Mr. T. has already engaged in relative to his potential sexual violence. Such treatment has the potential to mitigate against the danger suggested by the "risk factors." Finally, this examiner considered situational or idiosyncratic concerns of potential relevance to this respondent's risk.

Risk Factors

In this section of the risk assessment, the examiner employs knowledge gained from the professional research relevant to the prediction of sexual recidivism by previously convicted sex offenders. The most effective starting point in this portion of the analysis pertains to screening tools that employ an actuarial method for estimating the person's degree of sexual recidivism risk. Three instruments were employed in that regard for this case: (a) the Rapid Risk Assessment for Sex Offender Recidivism (RRASOR), (b) the Static-99, and (c) the Minnesota Sex Offender Screening Tool–Revised (MnSOST–R).

Mr. T. was found to score highly on all three instruments. A summary of these results follows. In reviewing this summary, the reader should be aware that all of these risk assessment instruments assess the likelihood for someone to be caught and legally processed (either by rearrest or reconviction) for a new sexual offense within a specified time frame. This examiner's understanding of State Statute #, however, is that the degree of risk relevant to the law does not necessarily involve the person's getting legally processed for a new sexual offense, or even caught for the new offense, but simply the redoing of such an act. Likewise, the time frame specified by these instruments in their assessments of risk is not necessarily in keeping with this examiner's understanding of the law. This examiner's understanding in that regard is that the law contains no specified time frame, meaning that the assessment herein is to look at the degree of risk the person represents over his remaining lifetime. From that perspective, this examiner believes that the risk assessment instruments potentially underestimate the degree of recidivism risk represented by the respondent specifically within the context of a State Statute # evaluation. In interpreting the percentages in the following paragraphs, the reader should also be aware that these risk estimates also involve some degree of "plus or minus" error, a factor that this examiner took into consideration in interpreting each result listed below.

Within the context of the caveats in the previous paragraph, the following results are offered:

1. RRASOR: The respondent scored 4 on a scale that theoretically goes from 0 to 6 with 6 at the high end of risk, though almost no one is ever found scoring a 6 on that instrument. A score of 4 on the RRASOR is associated statistically with about a 37% likelihood for being reconvicted for a new sexual offense within 5 years postincarceration, and about a 49% likelihood for being reconvicted of a new sexual offense within 10 years postrelease from incarceration.

2. Static-99: Mr. T. scored at least an 8 on a scale that theoretically ranges from 0 to 12 with 12 at the high end of risk, though no one has ever been known to score 11 or 12 on that instrument. The respondent's score statistically corresponds with about a 39% likelihood for being reconvicted of a new sexual offense within 5 years postincarceration, and a 54% likelihood for being reconvicted of a new sexual offense within 16 years postrelease from incarceration.

3. MnSOST–R: The score on this instrument obtained by Mr. T. was a +15, this score corresponding to the bottom of the highest risk range assessed by this scale. The score of +15 is statistically associated with a likelihood for being rearrested for a new sexual offense within a 6-year period postincarceration of between 78% and 88%, depending on an assumption of what is called the base rate for sexual recidivism of this type. This examiner believes the risk figure of 78% (for 6-year rearrest for a new sexual offense) is clearly the more conservative interpretation for the respondent's score.

Each of the three scales indicates that Mr. T.'s risk is beyond the [*statutory words related to risk*] threshold as defined by State Statute #, as this examiner understands that legal phrase. This overall result is virtually true even before one considers the degree of underestimation of these figures compared to the lifetime reoffense risk assessment apparently mandated by State Statute #, as opposed to the time-limited reconviction and rearrest figures enumerated. If this examiner were to come to an opinion based on these findings alone, that opinion would clearly be that Mr. T. represents a high degree of sexual reoffending risk through this segment of the analysis.

The second step in this section is to look for the application of other combinations of risk factors that have been statistically associated with high recidivism risk for sex offenders. In Mr. T.'s case, three such combinations were found likely to apply to him. The one best studied is the combination of a high degree of psychopathy (as measured by the Psychopathy Checklist–Revised, or PCL–R, where the respondent was found to exceed the research threshold of 24 with a score of 31) with a deviant sexual arousal pattern (as indicated by the diagnosis of Pedophilia). The second combination involves a sex offender (1) who has had an extrafamilial child victim, (2) who has had more than two sexual encounters with children over a period spanning more than 6 months, (3) who has prior sexual offense charge(s) involving specific victims (including either physical contact and non-contact offenses), and (4) who has demonstrated behaviors representative of multiple paraphilias. This cluster has been studied in the professional literature only once, so the conclusions concerning the applicability of this study's results to Mr. T. is not viewed as strong, but more indicative. The third combination has also only been studied once, involving a multiple set of behaviors that together are categorized as "lifestyle impulsivity" in someone who has a history of a sexual assault against an adult woman.

One combination of risk factors this examiner reviewed was not found applicable to Mr. T. That combination involves the risk factor, along with others, of having sexually victimized a boy. The respondent is not known to have done such an act with a boy.

In summary, Mr. T.'s risk factors suggest a rather consistent picture of a high risk for sexual recidivism. This finding, when considered alone, indicates a substantial risk for sexual reoffense exists.

Treatment Effect

Mr. T. participated in sex offender treatment within the Department of Corrections (DOC) during an incarceration previous to his most recent. He was recorded to have completed the sex offender treatment program at [*name of facility*] in [*year*]. Unfortunately, Mr. T.'s recorded actions since that treatment strongly indicate that the treatment was insufficient to address his tendency to sexually offend, as documented in the following enumeration:

1. During his residence in the community following that incarceration, while on probation, he was arrested for grabbing an adult female stranger on the street (in full view of plainclothes police officers).

2. He was convicted of six counts of intimidation by phone call in [*later year*].

3. He was convicted of two counts of intimidation by phone call in [*later year*].

4. In [*date in later year*], a harassment order petition was filed by a 17-year-old female (when Mr. T. was 44 years old) reportedly due to his stalking her at her work site.

5. On [*date in later year*], another harassment order petition was filed by an adult female stranger reportedly due to his driving by her quite slowly many times while she was walking home. The filing followed an event on [*date*], when Mr. T. reportedly asked her if she wanted "to fuck." After she reportedly replied "go fuck yourself," he reportedly got out of his car and grabbed her shirt. She managed to free herself and run away.

6. Mr. T. pled no contest and was convicted of disturbing the peace on [*date*], apparently based in the above incident. Of note, the respondent denied during the evaluation interview that his action was a sexual assault, though he did acknowledge it was an assault and that he was on probation at the time.
   Mr. T. described his benefit from the sex offender treatment he received at [*prison facility*] with concepts such as:

1. "It helped me stay away from certain people like married women who got kids";

2. "Think about a victim you done wrong to, 'cause at the time the victims were two kids 11 and 12, think about your own kids if somebody done that to them"; and

3. "Woman out there who will give it [i.e., sex] to you. I also told them [i.e., the treatment staff] I am not looking for that [sex] now."
   In addition, he pointed out that

4. he performed work assignments while in prison where there were women around, and he never did anything wrong to any of them; and

5. he does not "beat up" on staff any more.
   On the other hand, Mr. T. also stated during his interview that

1. he had not offended in 15 years;

2. there are no feelings, mood states, thoughts, fantasies, events, or situations that could represent a risk for his reoffending sexually;

3. there were no warning signs for him to watch concerning his risk for reoffending, as he never set up situations in which to offend (presumably inferring that his offenses were completely impulsive—a particularly dangerous condition); and

4. he was virtually certain he would not sexually offend again (these comments being within the context that he had not offended in 15 years).

The respondent did not participate in sex offender treatment during more recent incarcerations. Overall, even though Mr. T. completed a sex offender treatment program during one of his incarcerations, he has shown both a behavioral pattern and a verbal description of his supposed benefit that bespeaks little benefit from that programming. In this examiner's assessment, whatever benefit Mr. T. received from that programming was clearly insufficient to reduce his risk for sexual offending significantly. This assessment is supported by the fact that Mr. T.'s degree of psychopathy (as measured on the PCL–R) is also associated with a group of people who show very little decrease in their recidivism rates even after completing typical prison sex offender treatment programming. Based on these considerations, there seems to be no reason to believe that Mr. T. has participated in enough treatment to mitigate the potential risk he represents based on the risk factors listed above.

Situational or Idiosyncratic Considerations

Mr. T. is scheduled to be released to the community without mandated community supervision if he is no longer detained under State Statute #. This is not considered by this examiner as a reason to increase the risk assessed, but as a lack of reason to lower the assessed risk.

Mr. T.'s history of sexual offenses frequently involved people with whom he had no prior relationship, though this was not invariably the case. With this fact in mind, this examiner views Mr. T.'s sexual offending as largely predatory in nature, as defined by State Statute #. His overall sexual recidivism risk, therefore, is seen as of a predatory nature.

Evaluation Conclusions and Recommendations

Mr. T. was found to suffer from three psychiatric conditions, two of which qualify as a mental abnormality as defined by State Statute #. Specifically, this examiner came to the opinion, to a reasonable degree of scientific certainty, that Mr. T.

suffers from Pedophilia, and Antisocial Personality Disorder, each of which, for Mr. T., is an acquired or congenital condition affecting his emotional or volitional capacity that predisposes him to commit sexually violent acts, as defined by State Statute #.

Based on the information summarized above, this examiner also came to the opinion, to a reasonable degree of scientific certainty, that Mr. T.'s previous treatment experience for these conditions has not adequately addressed the risk of future sexually violent offense he represents. In this examiner's opinion, to a reasonable degree of scientific certainty, each of Mr. T.'s two mental abnormalities makes him [*statutory risk threshold*] to engage in predatory acts constituting sexually violent offenses, as defined by State Statute #, if not confined in a secure facility.

Hence, it is the opinion of this examiner, again to a reasonable degree of scientific certainty, that Mr. T. should be considered a sexually violent predator as defined by State Statute #.

Appendix D

Templates for Segments of Reexamination (Postcommitment) Evaluation Report

T he following template can be used to describe an individual's treatment benefit at any stage in the commitment evaluation process, though the wording is most specific to people who have already been committed and the evaluator is doing a reexamination. As with the templates in Appendix B, it is expected that evaluators will adapt the following to each specific case.

Treatment Benefit Template

The Structured Risk Assessment (SRA) evaluative method is a research-guided multistep framework for assessing the risk presented by a sex offender. Most scales for assessing sexual reoffense risk are based on "static" (unchangeable) factors. This means that although the scales can show that someone presents a certain level of risk at a certain point in time, they don't provide a basis for individualizing treatment focus or for determining whether risk has declined through treatment. The three-step scheme of the SRA adopted here is one of the very few that provides a systematic way of going beyond static risk classification. Step 1, the Static Risk Factor Assessment, is an actuarial risk classification based on statistical research. Step 2, the Deviance Risk Factor Assessment, potentially refines the static assessment using a framework derived from research on "dynamic" (changeable) psychological and behavioral factors underlying sexual offending. In applying this dynamic psychological component of the SRA, the assessor starts from factors that are generally related to sexual offending, and then identifies those that apply to the offender being assessed both historically during his offenses and currently in his general life. In Step 3, the SRA focuses the evaluator on any change shown by the offender in his dynamic risk factors. Aspects of relevant institutional behavior and treatment performance related to the likelihood of reoffending are reviewed. Each level of assessment affects the other. The final risk assessment reflects information from all three steps. Details from each of these steps are explained below.

SRA Static Risk Factor Assessment (Step 1)

Static risk factors are those variables that do not change over time. These factors are used to assess a sex offender's initial level of risk. Included in this category are the items on the Static-99, an actuarial risk assessment instrument. Each of 10 variables is numerically rated based on specific scoring criteria, with a summary score overall being associated with a certain degree of risk. The interpretive actuarial table for the Static-99 (Step 1) places Mr. X in a group of sex offenders, who, on follow-up, showed 39% sexual reconviction at 5 years, 45% at 10 years, and 52% at 15 years. Reconviction rates are believed, in general, to represent an underestimation of true reoffense rates.

SRA Deviance Assessment (Step 2)

"Deviance" refers to the range and intensity of psychological processes that underlie an offender's sexually violent behavior. The assessment of the offender's degree of sexual deviance uses dynamic risk variables (those that can change), usually in response to intensive treatment. Four dynamic variables have been identified as essential to the determination of a sex offender's level of risk for reoffense. These variables are (1) sexual interests, (2) distorted attitudes, (3) socioaffective functioning, and (4) self-management. The SRA offers a structured grid used to code these four dynamic variables in terms of (1) whether this factor played a part in the offender's pattern of sexual offending and (2) whether this factor is a persistent and generalized feature of the offender's functioning. The outcome of this coding offers the evaluator structured information about the degree to which the patient continues to demonstrate changeable psychological and social factors that were pertinent in his historical sexual offending. In Mr. X's case, this segment of the analysis found that [#] of the four areas were of relevance to his historical sexual offending, with some degree of persistence in his general functioning.

SRA Assessment of Treatment Progress (Step 3)

The goal of sex offender treatment programs is to assist patients to modify their thinking and behavior in such ways that will lessen their degree of risk for future sexual violence. During the assessment of potential treatment benefit, evaluators study the degree to which offenders are no longer driven by their own dynamic risk variables to commit sexually violent offenses. Offenders who show apparent treatment benefit should be able to demonstrate detailed knowledge of their personal relapse prevention plan, as well as regular differences in their lifestyle.

The reader should be aware that offenders who are high risk at the time of commitment for treatment generally do not "get over" their problems and are not "cured" when they leave a secure treatment setting for a community-based program. The individual must manage his problematic behavior for many years and perhaps for the rest of his life, much in the same way as an alcoholic. In addition, research seems to indicate that certain individuals, those who show particularly high scores on the Psychopathy Checklist–Revised (PCL–R), may not substantively benefit from treatment no matter their degree of participation.

With the above in mind, the assessment was made that of Mr. X's [#] dynamic risk factor areas of relevance to his historical sexual offending, he continues to show [*few, some, or significant*] psychological and/or social problems in [#] of those areas. [*Behavioral examples can be given here.*] The evaluator interprets this finding, when coupled with the results from Steps 1 and 2 above, as indicating Mr. X [*choose one:*]

1. has made little treatment gain and still represents a high risk for sexual reoffending [*or*]

2. has made some treatment progress, but still represents a high risk because of the degree of risk he represented to start [*or*]

3. has reduced his risk through his treatment and other efforts, to the point that his risk may no longer be high

through this part of the analysis. Based on the overall findings from the SRA along with the other actuarial and PCL–R data concerning Mr. X, this evaluator came to the opinion that Mr. X does [*not*] show a substantial decrease in the degree of risk he represents.

Template for Risk Management Segment

The earlier sections of this report documented this evaluator's findings concerning the degree to which Mr. X still represents a risk for sexual reoffending. This section addresses considerations about how well his risk can be managed effectively if he were placed into the community under a reasonable and realistic degree of supervision and supervision requirements. The reason for this section is because some types of sex offenders can represent a very high degree of recidivism risk, but their risk can be effectively managed in the community with typical supervisory procedures. On the other hand, some sex offenders may not represent quite as high a degree of recidivism risk, but their specific type of risk is virtually unmanageable (i.e., involving repetitive impulsive attacks on strangers walking on the street).

For Mr. X, characteristics found to be of importance by this examiner concerning risk management considerations are the following: [*Here you should make a simple list of those considerations, with explanations only as needed. That list should include factors that are of the following types:*]

1. Historical (such as his record concerning offending or not while under community supervision in the past, his elopement/escape history that could be indicative of his willingness to remain in the state if placed in the community; his "going back" to alcohol or drug use in the past after incarceration especially if while on community supervision);

2. Generally, what we know about the problems with psychopaths (i.e., PCL–R score = 30+) in terms of how poorly they do on supervision;

3. Self-management concerns (e.g., general degree of impulsivity still showing, the intensity of his paraphiliac urges, his willingness to avoid high-risk situations vs. making excuses for placing himself at high risk such as through drinking or working for a carnival);

4. Treatment continuation versus deterioration from whatever has been gained so far through his programming (e.g., stated plan for entering treatment when he has refused treatment or hardly participated in treatment before, failure to follow through in the past, significant others who will likely undermine or promote his treatment efforts, lack of treatment options in locale to where he would go);

5. Aftercare plan (such as his plan for a residence, like living with his family where there are children either living there or likely to be visiting there; or a history of stating great plans in the past that he failed to follow through on upon prior releases from incarceration); and

6. Supervisory issues (e.g., the length of the person's overt grooming period for his offending, i.e., the likely ability for a supervising agent to intervene before an actual offense occurs; the degree to which the person's significant others will report vs. ignore or try to cover up development of his red flags or being in high-risk situations; the person's likely truthfulness in talking about sexual urges with his agent and treaters in the community).

Based on the above considerations, this examiner came to the opinion that the management of Mr. X's sexual recidivism risk in the community seems [*choose only one:*]

1. Possible with reasonable allocations of supervisory resources

2. Possible with reasonable allocation of supervisory resources as long as [*specified condition(s)*] is (are) also firmly in place

3. Not possible with an allocation of a reasonable degree of supervisory resources

References

Abel, G. G., Barlow, D. H., Blanchard, E. B., & Guild, D. (1977). The components of rapists' sexual arousal. *Archives of General Psychiatry, 34*, 894-903.

Abel, G. G., Becker, J. V., Cunningham-Rathner, J., Mittelman, M., & Rouleau, J. L. (1988). Multiple paraphilic diagnoses among sex offenders. *Bulletin of the American Academy of Psychiatry and the Law, 16*, 153-168.

Abel, G. G., Osborn, C. A., & Twigg, D. A. (1993). Sexual assault through the life span: Adult offenders with juvenile histories. In H. E. Barbaree, W. L. Marshall, & S. M. Hudson (Eds.), *The juvenile sex offender* (pp. 104-117). New York: Guilford.

Ahlmeyer, S., English, K., & Simons, D. (1998). *The impact of polygraphy on admissions of crossover offending behavior in adult sexual offenders.* Unpublished manuscript, Colorado Department of Corrections, Colorado Springs.

Allam, J. M. (2000). *Community-based treatment for child sex offenders: An evaluation.* Unpublished doctoral thesis, University of Birmingham, Birmingham, UK.

American Educational Research Association, American Psychological Association, & National Council on Measurement in Education. (1999*). Standards for educational and psychological testing.* Washington, DC: American Psychological Association.

American Psychiatric Association. (1994). *Diagnostic and statistical manual of mental disorders* (4th ed.). Washington, DC: Author.

American Psychiatric Association. (2001). *The principles of medical ethics: With annotations especially applicable to psychiatry.* Retrieved from www.psych.org/apa_members/medicalethics2001_42001.cfm

American Psychological Association. (1992, December). Ethical principles of psychologists and code of conduct. *American Psychologist, 47*(12), 1597-1611.

Atkinson, R. L., Kropp, P. R., Laws, D. R., & Hart, S. D. (1996). *Scoring manual for the Sex Offender Risk Assessment (SORA) guide.* Vancouver: British Columbia Institute Against Family Violence & the Mental Health, Law, and Policy Institute.

Barbaree, H. E. (1990). Stimulus control of sexual arousal: Its role in sexual assault. In W. L. Marshall, D. R. Laws, & H. E. Barbaree (Eds.), *Handbook of sexual assault: Issues, theories, and treatment of the offender* (pp. 115-142). New York: Plenum.

Barbaree, H. E., & Marshall, W. L. (1989). Erectile responses among heterosexual child molesters, father-daughter incest offenders, and matched non-offenders: Five distinct age preference profiles. *Canadian Journal of Behavioural Science, 21*, 70-82.

Barbaree, H. E., Marshall, W. L., & Lanthier, R. D. (1979). Deviant sexual arousal in rapists. *Behavior Research and Therapy, 14*, 215-222.

Barbaree, H. E., Seto, M. C., Langton, C., & Peacock, E. (2001). Evaluating the predictive accuracy of six risk assessment instruments for adult sex offenders. *Criminal Justice and Behavior, 28*(4), 490-521.

Barbaree, H. E., Seto, M. C., Serin, R. C., Amos, N. L., & Preston, D. L. (1994). Comparisons between sexual and nonsexual rapist subtypes: Sexual arousal to rape, offense precursors, and offense characteristics. *Criminal Justice and Behavior, 21*(1), 95-114.

Baxter, D. J., Barbaree, H. E., & Marshall, W. L. (1986). Sexual responses to consenting and forced sex in a large sample of rapists and nonrapists. *Behavior Research and Therapy, 24*, 513-520.

Becker, J. V., & Murphy, W. D. (1998). What we know and do not know about assessing and treating sex offenders. *Psychology, Public Policy, and Law, 4*(1/2), 116-137.

Beech, A., Erikson, M., Friendship, C., & Ditchfield, J. (2001). *A six year follow-up of men going through representative probation based sex offender treatment programmes.* Home Office Research Findings, Home Office Occasional Paper. London: Home Office.

Beech, A., Fisher, D., & Beckett, R. (1999). *STEP 3: An Evaluation of the Prison Sex Offender Treatment Programme.* (ISBN 1 84082 190 6) Home Office Information Publications Group, Research and Statistics Directorate, Room 201, Queen Anne's Gate, London, SW1H 9 AT, England.

Beech, A. R. (1998). A psychometric typology of child abusers. *International Journal of Offender Therapy and Comparative Criminology, 42*, 319-339.

Bélanger, N., & Earls, C. (in press). An actuarial model for the prediction of recidivism among sexual offenders. *Journal of Interpersonal Violence.*

Belfrage, H. (1998). Implementing the HCR-20 scheme for risk assessment in a forensic psychiatric hospital: Integrating research and clinical practice. *Journal of Forensic Psychiatry, 9*, 328-338.

Belfrage, H., Fransson, G., & Strand, S. (2000). Prediction of violence within the correctional system using the HCR-20 risk assessment scheme. *Journal of Forensic Psychiatry, 11*, 167-175.

Bennett, A. (1969). *Forty years on.* London: Faber.

Boer, D. P., Hart, S. D., Kropp, P. R., & Webster, C. D. (1997). *Manual for the Sexual Violence Risk-20: Professional guidelines for assessing risk of sexual violence.* Vancouver: British Columbia Institute Against Family Violence & the Mental Health, Law, and Policy Institute.

Brodsky, S. L. (1991). *Testifying in court: Guidelines and maxims for the expert witness.* Washington, DC: American Psychological Association.

Brodsky, S. L. (1999). *The expert expert witness: More maxims and guidelines for testifying in court.* Washington, DC: American Psychological Association.

Campbell, T. W. (1999). Challenging the evidentiary reliability of DSM-IV. *American Journal of Forensic Psychology, 17*(1), 47-68.

Committee on Ethical Guidelines for Forensic Psychologists. (1991). Specialty guidelines for forensic psychologists. *Law and Human Behavior, 15*(6), 655-665.

Dempster, R. (1999, September). *Prediction of sexually violent recidivism: A comparison of risk assessment instruments.* Paper presented at the 18th annual Research and Treatment Conference of the Association for the Treatment of Sexual Abusers, Lake Buena Vista, FL.

Dernevik, M. (1998). Preliminary findings on reliability and validity of the Historical-Clinical-Risk Assessment in a forensic psychiatric setting. *Psychology, Crime, and Law, 4*, 127-137.

Doren, D. M. (1998). Recidivism base rates, predictions of sex offender recidivism, and the "sexual predator" commitment laws. *Behavioral Sciences and the Law, 16*, 97-114.

Doren, D. M. (1999a, September). *A comprehensive comparison of risk assessment instruments to determine their relative value within civil commitment evaluations.* Paper presented at the 18th annual Research and Treatment Conference of the Association for the Treatment of Sexual Abusers, Lake Buena Vista, FL.

Doren, D. M. (1999b, September). *Performing and testifying about sex offender risk assessments for civil commitment purposes.* Paper presented at the 18th annual Research and Treatment Conference of the Association for the Treatment of Sexual Abusers, Lake Buena Vista, FL.

Doren, D. M. (2000, November). *Being accurate about the accuracy of the commonly used risk assessment instruments.* Paper presented at the 19th annual Research and Treatment Conference of the Association for the Treatment of Sexual Abusers, San Diego, CA.

Doren, D. M. (2001a). Analyzing the analysis: A response to Wollert (2000). *Behavioral Sciences and the Law, 19*, 185-196.

Doren, D. M. (2001b). *The relative value of the RRASOR and Static-99 in assessing sexual recidivism risk within the context of U. S. A. sex offender civil commitment statutes.* Unpublished manuscript. (Available from author).

Doren, D. M., & Roberts, C. F. (1998, October). *The proper use and interpretation of actuarial instruments in assessing recidivism risk.* Paper presented at the 17th annual Research and Treatment Conference of the Association for the Treatment of Sexual Abusers, Vancouver, British Columbia.

Douglas, K. S. (1999, July). HCR-20 violence risk assessment scheme: "International validity" in diverse settings. In D. Washington (Chair), *Violence risk assessment: Scientist-practitioner approaches in diverse settings.* Symposium presented at the International Joint Conference of the American Psychology-Law Society and the European Association of Psychology and Law, Dublin, Ireland.

Douglas, K. S., Hart, S. D., Dempster, R., & Lyon, D. R. (1999, July). *The Violence Risk Appraisal Guide (VRAG): Attempt at validation in a maximum-security forensic psychiatric sample.* Paper presented at the International Joint Conference of the American Psychology-Law Society and the European Association of Psychology and Law, Dublin, Ireland.

Douglas, K. S., Klassen, C., Ross, C. Hart, S. D., Webster, C. D., & Eaves, D. (1998, August). *Psychometric properties of HCR-20 violence risk assessment scheme in insanity acquittees.* Paper presented at the annual meeting of the American Psychological Association, San Francisco.

Douglas, K. S., Ogloff, J. R. P., Nicholls, T. L., & Grant, I. (1999). Assessing risk for violence among psychiatric patients: The HCR-20 risk assessment scheme and the Psychopathy Checklist: Screening Version. *Journal of Consulting and Clinical Psychology, 67,* 917-930.

Douglas, K. S., & Webster, C. D. (1999). The HCR-20 violence risk assessment scheme: Concurrent validity in a sample of incarcerated offenders. *Criminal Justice and Behavior, 26,* 3-19.

Dunbar, E. (1999). *A psychographic analysis of violent hate crime perpetrators: Aggressive, situational, and ideological characteristics of bias motivated offenders.* Submitted for publication, as cited in Kevin S. Douglas (1999), *HCR-20 violence risk assessment scheme: Overview and annotated bibliography.* Retrieved from www.sfu.ca

Earls, C. M., & Proulx, J. (1987). The differentiation of Francophone rapists and nonrapists using penile circumferential measures. *Criminal Justice and Behavior, 13,* 419-429.

Eccles, A., Marshall, W. L., & Barbaree, H. E. (1994). Differentiating rapists from non-offenders using the Rape Index. *Behavior Research and Therapy, 32,* 539-546.

Eldridge, H. (1998). *Therapist guide for maintaining change: Relapse prevention for adult male perpetrators.* Thousand Oaks, CA: Sage.

Epperson, D. L., Kaul, J. D., & Huot, S. J. (1995, October). *Predicting risk of recidivism for incarcerated sex offenders: Updated development on the Sex Offender Screening Tool (SOST).* Paper presented at the 14th annual Conference of the Association for the Treatment of Sexual Abusers, New Orleans, LA.

Epperson, D. L., Kaul, J. D., & Huot, S. J. (2000, November). *Cross-validation of the Minnesota Sex Offender Screening Tool–Revised (MnSOST–R).* Paper presented at the 19th annual Research and Treatment Conference of the Association for the Treatment of Sexual Abusers, San Diego, CA.

Epperson, D. L., Kaul, J. D., Huot, S. J., Hesselton, D., Alexander, W., & Goldman, R. (1999). *Minnesota Sex Offender Screening Tool–Revised (MnSOST–R): Development, performance, and recommended risk level cut scores.* Retrieved from http://www.psychology.-iastate.edu/faculty/homepage.htm

Fanning, T., Zimmel, T., Jaskulske, D., & Curran, S. (1999*). An assessment of recidivism in juvenile/young adult sex offenders.* Unpublished manuscript, Ethan Allen School, Department of Corrections, Wales, WI.

Ferguson, G. E., Eidelson, R. J., & Witt, P. H. (1999, Fall). New Jersey's sex offender risk assessment scale: Preliminary validity data. *Journal of Psychiatry and Law,* pp. 327-351.

Firestone, P., Bradford, J. M., Greenberg, D., Nunes, K. L., & Broom, I. (1999, September). *A comparison of the Sex Offender Risk Appraisal Guide (SORAG) and the Static-99.* Presentation at the 18th annual Research and Treatment Conference of the Association for the Treatment of Sexual Abusers, Lake Buena Vista, FL.

Fischer, D. (2000). *Sex offender risk assessment validation study.* Unpublished manuscript. (Available from the Arizona Department of Corrections, 1601 West Jefferson St., Phoenix, AZ 85007-3056)

Freund, K., & Watson, R. J. (1991). Assessment of the sensitivity and specificity of a phallometric test: An update of "Phallometric diagnosis of pedophilia." *Psychological Assessment, 3,* 254-260.

Freund, K., & Watson, R. J. (1992). The proportion of heterosexual and homosexual pedophiles among sex offenders against children: An exploratory study. *Journal of Sex and Marital Therapy, 18*(1), 34-43.

Garb, H. N. (1998). *Studying the clinician: Judgment research and psychological assessment.* Washington, DC: American Psychological Association.

Glover, A., Nicholson, D. E., Hemmati, T., Bernfield, G. A., & Quinsey, V. L. (in press). Comparison of predictors of general and violent recidivism among high-risk federal offenders. *Criminal Justice and Behavior.*

Gordon, A., & Packard, R. (1998). *The impact of community maintenance treatment on sex offender recidivism.* Unpublished manuscript. (Available from the senior author at Twin Rivers Corrections Center, Box 888, Monroe, WA 98272)

Grann, M., Belfrage, H., & Tengström, A. (2000). Actuarial assessment of risk for violence: Predictive validity of the VRAG and the historical part of the HCR-20. *Criminal Justice and Behavior, 27,* 97-114.

Gratzer, T., & Bradford, J. M. W. (1995). Offender and offense characteristics of sexual sadists: A comparative study. *Journal of Forensic Sciences, 40*(3), 450-455.

Groth A. N., & Birnbaum, H. J. (1979). *Men who rape: The psychology of the offender.* New York: Plenum.

Groth, A. N., Longo, R. E., & McFadin, J. B. (1982). Undetected recidivism among rapists and child molesters. *Crime & Delinquency, 28,* 450-458.

Grove, W. M., & Meehl, P. E. (1996). Comparative efficiency of informal (subjective, impressionistic) and formal (mechanical, algorithmic) prediction procedures: The clinical-statistical controversy. *Psychology, Public Policy, and Law, 2,* 293-323.

Grove, W. M., Zald, D. H., Lebow, B. S., Snitz, B. E., & Nelson, C. (2000). Clinical versus mechanical prediction: A meta-analysis. *Psychological Assessment, 12*(1), 19-30.

Grubin, D. (1994). Sexual murder. *British Journal of Psychiatry, 165,* 624-629.

Grubin, D. (1998). Sex offending against children: Understanding the risk. *Police Research Series Paper 99.* London: Home Office.

Hall, G. C. N. (1989). Sexual arousal and arousability in a sexual offender population. *Journal of Abnormal Psychology, 98,* 145-149.

Hall, G. C. N. (1995). Sexual offender recidivism revisited: A meta-analysis of recent treatment studies. *Journal of Consulting and Clinical Psychology, 69*(3), 802-809.

Hall, G. C. N., Shondrick, D. D., & Hirschman, R. (1993). The role of sexual arousal in sexually aggressive behavior: A meta-analysis. *Journal of Consulting and Clinical Psychology, 61,* 1091-1095.

Hanlon, M., Larson, S., & Zacher, S. (1999). The Minnesota SOST and sexual reoffending in North Dakota: A retrospective study. *International Journal of Offender Therapy and Comparative Criminology, 43,* 71-77.

Hanson, R. K. (1997). *The development of a brief actuarial risk scale for sexual offense recidivism.* Ottawa, Ontario: Department of the Solicitor General of Canada. Retrieved from www.sgc.gc.ca

Hanson, R. K. (1998a, April). *Predicting sex offender re-offense: Clinical application of the latest research.* Presentation sponsored by the Wisconsin Sex Offender Treatment Network, Madison, WI.

Hanson, R. K. (1998b). What do we know about sex offender risk assessment? *Psychology, Public Policy, and Law, 4*(1/2), 50-72.

Hanson, R. K., & Bussière, M. T. (1998). Predicting relapse: A meta-analysis of sexual offender recidivism studies. *Journal of Consulting and Clinical Psychology, 66*(2), 348-362.

Hanson, R. K., & Harris, A. J. R. (1997, June). Predicting sexual offender recidivism in the community: Acute risk predictors. In A. J. R. Harris (Chair), *Keeping risky men out of trouble: Ongoing research on sex offenders.* Symposium at the annual convention of the Canadian Psychological Association, Toronto.

Hanson, R. K., Harris, A. J. R., Gordon, A., Marques, J., Murphy, W., Quinsey, V. L., & Seto, M. C. (2000, November). *The effectiveness of treatment for sexual offenders: Report of the ATSA Collaborative Data Research Committee.* Paper presented at the 19th annual Research and Treatment Conference of the Association for the Treatment of Sexual Abusers, San Diego, CA.

Hanson, R. K., Steffy, R. A., & Gauthier, R. (1993). Long-term recidivism of child molesters. *Journal of Consulting and Clinical Psychology, 61,* 646-652.

Hanson, R. K., & Thornton, D. (2000). Improving risk assessments for sex offenders: A comparison of three actuarial scales. *Law and Human Behavior, 24*(1), 119-136.

Hare, R. D. (1991). *Manual for the Hare Psychopathy Checklist–Revised.* Toronto: Multi-Health Systems.

Harris, G. T., Rice, M. E., Quinsey, V. L., Chaplin, T. C., & Earls, C. (1992). Maximizing the discriminate validity of phallometric assessment data. *Psychological Assessment: A Journal of Consulting and Clinical Psychology, 4*, 502-511.

Harris, G. T., Rice, M. E., Quinsey, V. L., Lalumière, M., Boer, D., & Lang, C. (2001). *A multisite comparison of actuarial risk instruments for sex offenders.* Manuscript submitted for publication.

Hart, S. D., Cox, D., & Hare, R. D. (1995). *The Hare Psychopathy Checklist: Screening Version (PCL:SV).* Toronto: Multi-Health Systems.

Hathaway, S. R., & McKinley, J. C. (1983). *The Minnesota Multiphasic Personality Inventory manual.* New York: Psychological Corporation.

Haynes, A. K., Yates, P. M., Nicholaichuk, T., Gu, D., & Bolton, R. (2000, June). *Sexual deviancy, risk, and recidivism: The relationship between deviant arousal, the Rapid Risk Assessment for Sexual Offence Recidivism (RRASOR) and sexual recidivism.* Paper presented at the Canadian Psychological Association annual convention, Ottawa.

Heilbrun, K., Dvoskin, J., Hart, S. D., & McNeil, D. (1999). Violence risk communication: Implications for research, policy, and practice. *Health, Risk, and Society, 1*, 91-106.

Heilbrun, K., O'Neill, M. L., Strohman, L. K., Bowman, Q., & Philipson, J. (2000). Expert approaches to communicating violence risk. *Law and Human Behavior, 24*(1), 137-148.

Hilton, N. Z., Harris, G. T., & Rice, M. E. (2001). Predicting violence by serious wife assaulters. *Journal of Interpersonal Violence, 16*, 408-423.

Hilton, N. Z., & Simmons, J. L. (2001). The influence of actuarial risk assessment in clinical judgments and tribunal decisions about mentally disordered offenders in maximum security. *Law and Human Behavior, 25*(4), 393-408.

Hopper, M. (1998). *New York State Sex Offender Registry risk assessment scale.* Unpublished manuscript, New York Department of Corrections, Board of Examiners of Sex Offenders, Albany.

Hudson, S. M., Wales, D. S., Bakker, L., & Ward, T. (in press). Dynamic risk factors: The Kia Marama evaluation. *Sexual Abuse: A Journal of Research and Treatment.*

Hudson, S. M., Ward, T., & McCormack, J. C. (1999). Offense pathways in sexual offenders. *Journal of Interpersonal Violence, 14*(8), 779-798.

Hunter, J. A., Goodwin, D. W., & Becker, J. V. (1994). The relationship between phallometrically measured deviant sexual arousal and clinical considerations in juvenile sexual offenders. *Behavior Research and Therapy, 32*(5), 533-538.

Janus, E. S., & Meehl, P. E. (1997). Assessing the legal standard for predictions of dangerousness in sex offender commitment proceedings. *Psychology, Public Policy, and Law, 3*(1), 33-64.

Knight, R. A. (1998, October). *Using a new computerized developmental inventory to examine the family and early behavioral antecedents of sexual coercion.* Paper presented at the 17th annual Research and Treatment Conference of the Association for the Treatment of Sexual Abusers, Vancouver, British Columbia.

Knight, R. A. (1999, September). *Unified theory of sexual coercion.* Paper presented at the 18th annual Research and Treatment Conference of the Association for the Treatment of Sexual Abusers, Lake Buena Vista, FL.

Konicek, P. (2000). *Ten-year recidivism follow-up of 1989 sex offender releases.* Unpublished report, Ohio Department of Rehabilitation and Correction, Office of Policy, Bureau of Planning and Evaluation.

Kropp, P. R. (2000, November). *The risk for sexual violence protocol (RSVP).* Paper presented at the 19th annual Research and Treatment Conference of the Association for the Treatment of Sexual Abusers, San Diego, CA.

Kropp, P. R., Hart, S. D., Webster, C. D., & Eaves, D. (1999). *Manual for the Spousal Assault Risk Assessment Guide (Version 3).* Vancouver: British Columbia Institute on Family Violence.

Lalumière, M. L., & Quinsey, V. L. (1992). *The discriminability of rapists from non-sex offenders using phallometric measures: A meta-analysis* (Forensic/Correctional Reports No. 2). Kingston, Ontario: Queen's University.

Langevin, R. (1990). Sexual anomalies and the brain. In W. L. Marshall, D. R. Laws, & H. E. Barbaree (Eds.), *Handbook of sexual assault: Issues, theories and treatment of the offender* (pp. 103-113). New York: Plenum.

Langevin, R., Paitich, D., & Russon, A. E. (1985). Are rapists sexually anomalous, aggressive, or both? In R. Langevin (Ed.), *Erotic preference, gender identity, and aggression in men: New research studies* (pp. 130-138). Hillsdale, NJ: Lawrence Erlbaum.

Loza, W., & Dhaliwal, G. K. (1997). Psychometric evaluation of the Risk Appraisal Guide (RAG): A tool for assessing violent recidivism. *Journal of Interpersonal Violence, 12*(6), 779-793.

Marques, J. K. (1999). How to answer the question "Does sex offender treatment work?" *Journal of Interpersonal Violence, 14*(4), 437-451.

Marquis, P., Abracen, J., & Looman, J. (2001, November). *Psychopathy, treatment change, and recidivism with sexual offenders.* Presented at the 20th annual Research and Treatment Conference of the Association for the Treatment of Sexual Abusers, San Antonio, TX.

Marshall, W. L., & Barbaree, H. E. (1995). *Heterogeneity in the erectile response patterns of rapists and nonoffenders.* Unpublished manuscript, Queen's University, Kingston, Ontario.

McConaghy, N. (1999). Paraphilias. In V. B. Van Hassalt & M. Hersen (Eds.), *Handbook of psychological approaches with violent offenders: Contemporary strategies and issues.* New York: Kluwer.

McGrath, R. J., Cumming, G., Livingston, J. A., & Hoke, S. E. (2001). *The Vermont treatment program for sexual aggressors: An evaluation of a prison-based treatment program.* Manuscript submitted for publication.

Monahan, J., & Steadman, H. J. (Eds.). (1994). *Violence and mental disorder: Developments in risk assessment.* Chicago: University of Chicago Press.

Muller-Isberner, J. R., & Jockel, D. (1997, September). *The implementation of the HCR-20 in a German hospital order institution.* Paper presented at the 7th European Conference on Psychology and Law, Solna, Sweden.

Murphy, W. D., Krisak, J., Stalgaitis, S., & Anderson, K. (1984). The use of penile tumescence measures with incarcerated rapists: Further validity issues. *Archives of Sexual Behaviour, 13*, 545-554.

Nicholaichuk, T., Templeman, T. L., & Gu, D. (1999, May). *Empirically based screening for sex offender risk.* Paper presented at the Conference of the Correctional Services of Canada, Ottawa, Ontario.

Nicholaichuk, T., & Yates, P. M. (in press). Outcomes of the Clearwater Sex Offender Program. In B. Schwartz (Ed.), *The sex offender* (Vol. 4).

Nicholls, T. L., Vincent, G. M., Whittemore, K. E., & Ogloff, J. R. P. (1999, November). *Assessing risk of inpatient violence in a sample of forensic psychiatric patients: Comparing the PCL:SV, HCR-20, and VRAG.* Paper presented at the International Conference on Risk Assessment and Risk Management, Vancouver, British Columbia.

Polvi, N. (1999). *The prediction of violence in pretrial forensic patients: The relative efficacy of statistical versus clinical predictions of dangerousness.* Unpublished doctoral dissertation, Simon Fraser University, British Columbia.

Polvi, N., Webster, C. D., & Hart, S. D. (1999, November). *The prediction of violence in pretrial forensic patients: The relative efficacy of the Violence Risk Appraisal Guide (VRAG) versus clinical predictions of dangerousness.* Paper presented at the International Conference on Risk Assessment and Risk Management, Vancouver, British Columbia.

Poole, D., Liedecke, D., & Marbibi, M. (2000). *Risk assessment and recidivism in juvenile sexual offenders: A validation study of the Static 99.* Austin: Texas Youth Commission.

Poythress, N., & Hart, S. D. (1998, October). *Assessing risk for violence.* Paper presented at the Conference of the National Association of State Mental Health Program Directors (Forensic and Legal Divisions), Tampa, FL.

Prentky, R. A., & Knight, R. A. (1991). Identifying critical dimensions for discriminating among rapists. *Journal of Consulting and Clinical Psychology, 59*(5), 643-661.

Prentky, R. A., Lee, A. F. S., Knight, R. A., & Cerce, D. (1997). Recidivism rates among child molesters and rapists: A methodological analysis. *Law and Human Behavior, 21*(6), 635-659.

Quackenbush, R. (2000). *The assessment of sex offenders in Ireland and the Irish Sex Offender Risk Tool.* Unpublished manuscript, Granada Institute, Dublin, Ireland.

Quinsey, V. L., & Chaplin, T. C. (1984). Stimulus control of rapists' and non-sex offenders' sexual arousal. *Behavioral Assessment, 6*, 169-176.

Quinsey, V. L., Coleman, G., Jones, B., & Altrows, I. F. (1997). Proximal antecedents of eloping and reoffending among mentally disordered offenders. *Journal of Interpersonal Violence, 12*, 794-813.

Quinsey, V. L., Harris, G. T., Rice, M. E., & Cormier, C. A. (1998). *Violent offenders: Appraising and managing risk.* Washington, DC: American Psychological Association.

Quinsey, V. L., Lalumière, M. L., Rice, M. E., & Harris, G. T. (1995). Predicting sexual offenses. In J. C. Campbell (Ed.), *Assessing dangerousness: Violence by sexual offenders, batterers, and child abusers* (pp. 114-137). Thousand Oaks, CA: Sage.

Rice, M. E., & Harris, G. T. (1997). Cross-validation and extension of the violence risk appraisal guide for child molesters and rapists. *Law and Human Behavior, 21*(2), 231-241.

Rice, M. E., & Harris, G. T. (1999, May). *A multi-site follow-up study of sex offenders: The predictive accuracy of risk prediction instruments.* Paper presented at the third annual (University of Toronto) Forensic Psychiatry Program Research Day, Penetanguishene, Ontario.

Rice, M. E., & Harris, G. T. (in press). Men who molest their sexually immature daughters: Is a special explanation required? *Journal of Abnormal Psychology.*

Rice, M. E., Harris, G. T., & Quinsey, V. L. (1990). A follow-up of rapists assessed in a maximum-security psychiatric facility. *Journal of Interpersonal Violence, 5*(4), 435-448.

Rice, M. E., Quinsey, V. L., & Harris, G. T. (1991). Sexual recidivism among child molesters released from a maximum security psychiatric institution. *Journal of Consulting and Clinical Psychology, 59*(3), 381-386.

Roberts, C. F., Doren, D. M., & Thornton, D. (in press). Dimensions associated with assessments of sex offender recidivism risk. *Criminal Justice and Behavior.*

Rogers, R. (2000). The uncritical acceptance of risk assessment in forensic practice. *Law and Human Behavior, 24,* 595-605.

Ross, D. J., Hart, S. D., & Webster, C. D. (1998). *Facts and fates: Testing the HCR-20 against aggressive behavior in hospital and community.* Unpublished manuscript, as cited in Kevin S. Douglas (1999), *HCR-20 violence risk assessment scheme: Overview and annotated bibliography.* Retrieved from www.sfu.ca

Russell, B. (1929). *Marriage and morals.* London: Allen & Unwin.

Sachsenmaier, S. J., & Peters, J. M. (in press). Sex offender risk assessment methods and admissibility as scientific evidence. In J. M. Peters (Ed.), *Assessment and management of sex offenders: What prosecutors need to know.* Washington, DC: U.S. Department of Justice, Child Exploitation and Obscenity Section (USABooks).

Schiller, G., & Watnik, M. (2001). *A comparison of four sex offender actuarial risk assessment systems: The RRASOR, Static-99, MnSOST–R, and the CARAT–R.* Unpublished manuscript, Department of Mental Health, Sacramento, CA.

Seidman, B. T., Marshall, W. L., Hudson, S. M., & Robertson, P. J. (1994). An examination of intimacy and loneliness in sex offenders. *Journal of Interpersonal Violence, 9,* 518-534.

Seto, M. C., & Barbaree, H. E. (1999). Psychopathy, treatment behavior and sex offender recidivism. *Journal of Interpersonal Violence, 14*(12), 1235-1248.

Sjöstedt, G., & Långström, N. (2001). Actuarial assessment of sex offender recidivism risk: A cross-validation of the RRASOR and Static-99 in Sweden. *Law and Human Behavior, 25*(6), 629-645.

Sjöstedt, G., & Långström, N. (in press). Assessment of risk for criminal recidivism among rapists in Sweden: A comparison of different procedures. *Psychology, Crime, and Law.*

Slovic, P., Monahan, J., & MacGregor, D. G. (2000). Violence risk assessment and risk communication: The effects of using actual cases, providing instruction, and employing probability versus frequency formats. *Law and Human Behavior, 24*(3), 271-296.

Smiley, W. C., McHattie, L., & Mulloy, R. (1998, October). *Predicting sexual recidivism using a brief actuarial risk scale.* Paper presented at the 17th annual Research and Training Conference of the Association for the Treatment of Sexual Abusers, Vancouver, British Columbia.

Song, L., & Lieb, R. (1995). *Washington State sex offenders: Overview of recidivism studies.* Olympia: Washington State Institute of Public Policy.

Soothill, K. L., & Gibbens, T. C. N. (1978). Recidivism of sexual offenders: A re-appraisal. *British Journal of Criminology, 18,* 267-276.

Strand, S., & Belfrage, H. (1999). *Risk factors for violence in mentally disordered women measured with the HCR-20 violence risk assessment scheme.* Unpublished manuscript, as cited in Kevin S. Douglas (1999), *HCR-20 violence risk assessment scheme: Overview and annotated bibliography.* Retrieved from www.sfu.ca

Strand, S., Belfrage, H., Fransson, G., & Levander, S. (1999). Clinical and risk management factors in risk prediction of mentally disordered offenders: More important than actuarial data? *Legal and Criminological Psychology, 4*, 67-76.

Thornton, D. (2000a, June). *Continuity of care from initial commitment to release.* Presentation at Summit 2000, co-sponsored by the Sex Offender Treatment Quality Assurance Society, the Wisconsin Sex Offender Treatment Network, and the Wisconsin Resource Center, Oshkosh.

Thornton, D. (2000b, March). *Structured risk assessment.* Presentation at the Sex Offender Re-Offense Risk Prediction symposium sponsored by Sinclair Seminars, Madison, WI.

Thornton, D. (in press). Constructing and testing a framework for dynamic risk assessment. *Sexual Abuse: A Journal of Research and Treatment.*

Warren, J. I., Hazelwood, R. R., & Dietz, P. E. (1996). The sexually sadistic serial killer. *Journal of Forensic Sciences, 41*(6), 970-974.

Webster, C. D., Douglas, K. S., Eaves, D., & Hart, S. D. (1997). *HCR-20: Assessing the risk for violence (Version 2).* Vancouver: Simon Fraser University, Mental Health, Law, and Policy Institute.

Webster, C. D., Harris, G. T., Rice, M. E., Cormier, C., & Quinsey, V. L. (1994). *The violence prediction scheme: Assessing dangerousness in high risk men.* Toronto: University of Toronto, Centre of Criminology.

Weinrott, M. R., & Saylor, M. (1991). Self-report of crimes committed by sex offenders. *Journal of Interpersonal Violence, 6*, 283-300.

Wettstein, R. M. (1992). A psychiatric perspective on Washington's Sexually Violent Predators statute. *University of Puget Sound Law Review, 15*, 597-633.

Wong, K., Flahr, L., Maire, B., Wilde, S., Gu, D., & Wong, S. (2000, June). *Inter-rater reliability of the Violence Risk Scale and the Violence Risk Scale: Sex Offender version.* Poster session presented at the annual convention of the Canadian Psychological Association, Ottawa, Ontario.

Wong, S., & Gordon, A. (1999). *Violence Risk Scale (Version 2).* Unpublished manuscript, Regional Psychiatric Centre (Prairies) and University of Saskatchewan, Saskatoon.

Wong, S., Olver, M., Wilde, S., Nicholaichuk, T., & Gordon, A. (2000, June). *Violence Risk Scale and the Violence Risk Scale–Sex Offender version.* Symposium presented at the annual Convention of the Canadian Psychological Association, Ottawa, Ontario.

Zonana, H., Abel, G. G., Bradford, J., Hoge, S. K., & Metzer, J. (1999). *American Psychiatric Association task force report on sexually dangerous offenders.* Washington, DC: American Psychiatric Association.

Index

Abel, G. G., 63
Abel's Assessment of Sexual Interests
   (ASI), 46
Actuarial instruments, 109-111, 113-114
   coding rules and, 131
   error rates, 132-134, 133-134 (tables)
   instrument-dimension relationship,
      140-141
   multiple-instrument interpretation,
      140-143
   single-instrument interpretation, 139
   single vs. multiple instrument use,
      134-138
   See also Clinically adjusted actuarial
      findings; Risk assessment
      instrumentation
Allam, J. M., 165, 166
Altrows, I. F., 167
American Psychiatric Association, 31
American Psychological Association, 31
Antisocial personality disorder,
   89-90, 94
Arizona law, 2, 4, 6, 7, 9, 11, 13, 15,
   19, 23, 42
Assessment. *See* Evaluation procedures;
   Risk assessment; Risk assessment
   instrumentation
Association for the Treatment of Sexual
   Abusers (ATSA), 30-31, 172

Barbaree, H. E., 63, 80, 81, 84, 85, 172
Beech, A., 165, 167
Behavioral abnormality, 14, 23
Belfrage, H., 109
Bias, 176-177, 185, 186
Boer, D., 176
Bolton, R., 141, 167
Bowman, Q., 179
Bussière, M. T., 46, 137, 141,
   146, 150, 171

California law, 2, 4-9, 12, 13, 15, 19, 22
Case management, 8
Cerce, D., 150, 155, 159, 174
Child victimization, 11-12
   age-based interpretation, 60-61
   hebephilia/ephebophilia, 80-81
   mental disorder and, 82
   paraphiliac vs. nonparaphiliac
      offenders, 75-76
   See also Pedophilia
Civil commitment laws. *See* Sex offender
   civil commitment laws
Clinical commitment criteria, 12-13
   acquired/congenital condition, 14
   decision-making impairment, 16-17
   mental conditions, 13-19
   predatory offending, 22-23
   predisposition to crime, 18-19
   sexual violence, risk for, 19-22
   volitional/emotional capacity, 14-18
   See also Diagnostic issues; National
      evaluation standards; Risk
      assessment instrumentation
Clinical interviews, 37
   collateral interviews, 44-46
   competence to proceed and, 41-42
   contents of, 42-44
   court-ordered, 192-194
   informed consent and, 39-41, 211-212
   participation decision, 40-41
   Psychopathy Checklist-Revised and, 43
   Relapse Prevention Interview and, 43,
      201-209
   responses, recording of, 44
   timing of, 38
   victim interviews, 195
   Violence Risk Scale-Sex Offender
      and, 44
Clinically adjusted actuarial findings,
   161-162

About the Author

Dennis M. Doren, Ph.D., is Evaluation Director at the Sand Ridge Secure Treatment Center in Mauston, Wisconsin. In his Wisconsin State employment, he has assessed and treated sex offenders for the past 18 years. Since June 1994, he has been largely involved in the evaluation of sex offenders specifically for the purpose of potential civil commitments. He served as an expert witness in the first such case that went to trial in Wisconsin in the summer of 1994 and has conducted and supervised more than 300 such evaluations since then. Dr. Doren has also served as a trainer and ongoing consultant for clinicians and attorneys in most of the states with active sex offender civil commitment laws and has performed sex offender civil commitment evaluations in over half of those states. His presentations concerning sex offender assessments have been included in international and national conferences. Among other publications not specific to sex offenders, Dr. Doren has published numerous professional articles concerning the assessment of sex offenders.